Choosing Life

A Dialogue on Evangelium Vitae

Choosing Life

A Dialogue on Evangelium Vitae

EDITED BY
Kevin Wm. Wildes, S.J.
Alan C. Mitchell

GEORGETOWN UNIVERSITY PRESS / WASHINGTON, D.C.

Georgetown University Press, Washington, D.C.   20007
© 1997 by Georgetown University Press. All rights reserved.
Printed in the United States of America.
10   9   8   7   6   5   4   3   2   1   1997
THIS VOLUME IS PRINTED ON ACID-FREE OFFSET BOOKPAPER.

Library of Congress Cataloging-in-Publication Data

Choosing life   :   a dialogue on Evangelium vitae / edited by Kevin Wm.
    Wildes, Alan C. Mitchell ; foreword by Leo J. O'Donovan.
            p.   cm.
      Includes bibliographical references (p.).
      1. Catholic Church. Pope (1978– : John Paul II). Evangelium
    vitae.   2. Abortion—Religious aspects—Catholic Church.
    3. Euthanasia—Religious aspects—Catholic Church.   4. Capital
    punishment—Religious aspects—Catholic Church.   5. Catholic Church—
    Doctrines. I. Wildes, Kevin Wm. (Kevin William), 1954– .
    II. Mitchell, Alan C.
    HQ767.3.C49   1997
    241'.697—dc21
    ISBN 0-87840-646-8 (pbk)
                                                            96-47409

Contents

v

Foreword

In the *Pastoral Constitution on the Church in the Modern World* of the Second Vatican Council, the Catholic bishops of the world, assembled in Rome, introduced their document with memorable words: "The joy and hope, the grief and anguish of the women and men of our time, especially those who are poor or afflicted in any way, are the joy and hope, the grief and anguish of the followers of Christ as well. Nothing that is genuinely human fails to find an echo in their hearts. . . . Christians cherish a feeling of deep solidarity with the human race and its history." With vigor and conviction accompanied by compassion, the Council addressed the new human situation in the world, the challenges it poses for human dignity and community, and the role of the Church in facing a wide range of issues, from family life through economic development to international peace. It was charting the Church's way, as we realize now more and more, for decades to come.

Thirty years later, in March 1995, Pope John Paul II continued his effort to complete the agenda of the Council and published his eleventh encyclical, *Evangelium Vitae*. This major statement on moral issues of life and death in our time succeeded a first moral treatment, *Veritatis Splendor*, which was concerned with methodological moral issues—how to think about moral questions and the very foundations of moral thought. *Evangelium Vitae*, entitled *The Gospel of Life* in English, focuses especially on particular, practical moral issues that concern the sacredness of human life: abortion, euthanasia, capital punishment. Addressing his letter to "all men and women of good will," the Pope challenged his readers to deeper moral reflection. He urged them, as well, to assess a growing "culture of death" and in opposition to it to support a "culture of life."

Major moral and cultural themes are addressed in *Evangelium Vitae*. Because of the urgency and complexity of the questions themselves, as well as the complexity of modern, secular societies, it goes without saying that the interpretation of the encyclical's themes requires theological acumen, social and historical understanding, and empirical knowledge. To serve wider understanding and appreciation of the Pope's thought, a symposium on *Evangelium Vitae* was accordingly organized at Georgetown University in November 1995. For the scholars and Church leaders who participated, it provided an opportunity for reading, discussing, and interpreting this important document. Given the breadth of the letter's scope and address, it also seemed clear that the symposium's interpretive purpose could only be served well by involving scholars from a variety of disciplines as well as various religious perspectives.

This volume represents a further development of the symposium. In light of the discussion and exchange during the symposium itself, all its members have revised their essays to profit from mutual criticism and clarification. It is our hope that the volume will now allow many others to approach the encyclical with new awareness and insight. And so we hope to continue the discussion of the shared responsibility for human life in a threatened world to which Pope John Paul II has so eloquently summoned us. May these reflections encourage and support all our readers in their response to the ancient command: Choose life.

Leo J. O'Donovan, S.J.
Georgetown University

Acknowledgments

We are grateful to the Mary J. Donnelly Foundation, Mr. Joseph S. Kealty, and an anonymous foundation for their generous support of the conference and the production of this volume. Thanks are also due to Mary Beth Henry, Mary Elizabeth Duke, Colleen Redwood, Kelly Esseesy, and Rob Kennedy, whose hard work supported the conference and the production of the book. Special thanks are due to Tom Stahel, S.J., for his creativity, energy, and hard work initiating this project.

Introduction

KEVIN WM. WILDES, S.J.

There are profound ironies that surround the discussion of ethics today. While we live in an age of moral ambiguity in which people are often reluctant to make moral judgments, we also live in an era when many people are quite willing to make the harshest of moral judgments. It is an era of polarization and divisiveness on moral questions. Issued on March 25, 1995, it was inevitable that *Evangelium Vitae* would not only become part of many ongoing moral debates but would itself become a point of debate. In *Evangelium Vitae* Pope John Paul II articulates a moral vision for *all*. The letter speaks about crucial moral issues in our day and engages all thoughtful men and women—especially those who think about morality, ethics, and society. Because of the issues it treats, and its address to all people, *Evangelium Vitae* invites considerations, conversation, and thoughtful argument.

Just as it was inevitable that *Evangelium Vitae* should become part of many moral conversations, so it was inevitable that Catholic universities and colleges would be a natural setting for men and women who think about such ethical issues to gather and discuss the ideas and arguments articulated in the encyclical. Catholic higher education is a setting where those holding the ideas of the faith can meet, argue, embrace, and learn, as well as reject, distance, and criticize ideas of other denominations, faiths, and cultures. It is a place where believers and nonbelievers can talk, analyze, and argue about ideas. As universities, they are places of critical reflection on ideas and ongoing conversation between men and women seeking the truth in an open, honest critical discussion. In the apostolic constitution *Ex Corde Ecclesiae*, Pope John Paul II wrote of Catholic higher education, "By vocation the universitas magistrorum et scholarium is dedicated to research, to teaching and to the education of students who freely associate with their teachers in a common love of knowledge. With every other university it shares that gaudium de veritate, so precious to St. Augustine, which is that joy of searching for, discovering and communicating the truth in every field of knowledge."[1]

As a Catholic university, Georgetown has a unique place in this mission of higher education. Founded in 1789 by Archbishop John Carroll, Georgetown was founded as an academy open to all. Georgetown was envisioned as a place of learning in service for the young Church and the young Republic. Given the ecumenical roots of Georgetown and the importance of ethical questions in public life, it was most appropriate that Georgetown should host a gathering of scholars and ethicists, Catholic and non-Catholic, believers and nonbelievers, to discuss *Evangelium Vitae*. At a time when the Republic and Western society are exploring the relationship of morality, ethics, religion, and public life, it was natural that Georgetown should bring together such thinkers with *Evangelium Vitae*.

Evangelium Vitae raises different types of questions and points for discussion. These are not just questions of philosophical or theological interest. *Evangelium Vitae* raises urgent matters of the day, such as abortion, euthanasia, and capital punishment, that bear on private choices and public policy. These issues are central to the encyclical's investigation into the "culture of death" and its arguments and support for the "culture of life." The significance and richness of the encyclical's reflections on these issues, however, may be lost if *Evangelium Vitae* is not viewed in a broader context. The essays in the first part of this volume set a framework and context for the encyclical. These essays set out the underlying framework of the encyclical in the thought of John Paul II (Conley; Childress; Hollenbach). They also look at questions of methodology in how the letter thinks and argues about moral issues (Keenan; Mitchell; Boyle). Finally, they examine the encyclical in light of questions of ecclesiology; that is, a theology of the Church (Sullivan; Rausch; Orsy). For many people, Catholics and others, it is essential to understand the teaching authority of the encyclical and understand the weight it carries for members of the Catholic Christian community.

The essays in the second part of the book take up certain themes that run throughout *Evangelium Vitae* and the other essays in this book. These essays examine crucial themes that are part of the background assumptions of the encyclical. These themes about technology (Olesko; Pinkard; Lamm) and law (Kaveney; Quinn) are crucial to the way the encyclical views the specific issues of euthanasia, abortion, and capital punishment. These themes are essential for the moral arguments about specific issues discussed in the encyclical.

The essays in the third section turn to these issues: abortion (Griffin; Kopfensteiner; Alvare), experimentation (Wildes; Carlson; Walters), capital punishment (Langan; Weigel; Prejean), and euthanasia (Pellegrino; Beauchamp; O'Rourke). They illustrate the importance of the encyclical for specific moral controversies of the time, and they engage the encyclical with the different views of these issues. In so doing, they also illustrate and explore the complex nature of these issues and the teaching of the encyclical.

The essays contained in the volume do not all give a blanket endorsement to the content of the encyclical. Some readers may reject them for this or other reasons. This is as it should be. *Evangelium Vitae* invites critical discussion. All ideas, including those about ethics, need to be held up to scrutiny and discussion. And if they are sound and true, they will survive—even flourish—in honest, open discussion. This is no less true of moral ideas. Moral ideas are not like the principles of pure, theoretical knowledge. They are not like the principles of a deductive geometry, for example. Universal moral principles and knowledge must be applied to specific times, places, and circumstances. In such application, they will be the subject of discussion and argument. In an encyclical such as *Evangelium Vitae*, which addresses controversial moral issues and is addressed to "all men and women," moral principles become points of discussion and assessment. This volume is meant to promote discussion between the ideas expressed in *Evangelium Vitae* and other ideas and points of view.

To avoid any misunderstanding, it should be clear that the purpose of this volume, and the conference that shaped it, is unusual. It is neither to exegete the encyclical nor to compose a commentary on it. Rather, the purpose was to gather responses to the encyclical from all directions: Catholic, non-Catholic, believer, and nonbeliever. This is necessary so that the mind of John Paul II can meet other minds. The essays in this volume reflect these meetings and serve as a foundation for further dialogue. They reflect meaningful conversations with all men and women of goodwill, as John Paul wants it. This volume can serve the conversations of others to enable all of us to work together in the service of human life and dignity.

NOTE

1. John Paul II, *Apostolic Constitution Ex Corde Ecclesiae*, Introduction, 1, in *Catholic Universities in Church and Society*, ed. John P. Langan, S.J. (Washington: Georgetown University Press, 1993), 231.

PART 1

Foundational Discussions

Narrative, Act, Structure: John Paul II's Method of Moral Analysis

JOHN J. CONLEY, S.J.

In *Evangelium Vitae*,[1] Pope John Paul II defends the right of each human being to life, from the moment of conception until the moment of natural death. Negatively, he condemns the "culture of death," which increasingly vitiates this right. The critical discussion of the encyclical has tended to focus upon substantive questions: the criticism of capital punishment (*EV* 56) or the application of moral principles in the political arena (*EV* 71–74). In order to grasp the Pope's substantive positions, however, it is crucial to examine the distinctive method employed by the Pope in his argumentation concerning these moral issues.

METHODOLOGY

In developing his case regarding human life, the Pope employs three dominant, intertwining lines of analysis. The first might be described as "scriptural-narrative." It explores ethical questions regarding human life within the biblical context of God's response to human violence, especially within the paradigmatic account of the first murderer, Cain (*EV* 7–29). The second line of argument might be classified as "neo-scholastic." It carefully analyzes specific human acts, such as the prohibited act of directly killing an innocent human being (*EV* 52–77) and the more specific cases of this act present in the field of abortion (*EV* 58–63) and euthanasia (*EV* 64–67). This neo-scholastic analysis of the human act reflects the concern of Thomistic manualists to develop precise norms of moral action. It also reflects the Pope's concern, already explicit in *Veritatis Splendor* (*VS* 71–83),[2] to defend the traditional Thomistic analysis of the human act, especially complex acts studied under the rubric of the principle of double effect,[3] against proportionalist revision (*VS* 75). The third line of rhetoric might be characterized as one of "cultural critique." In these passages, the Pope stresses the social matrix that informs moral perception and action concerning the good of human life. In *Evangelium Vitae*, this critique is particularly severe, locating the burgeoning "culture of death" within an erroneous view of democracy (*EV* 71–77). In the passages dominated by this critique of culture, the Pope tends to analyze and denounce the ideologies of contemporary society, especially those of the affluent West, which form the often hidden background to individual acts against the good of life itself.

These interrelated strands of argument on behalf of life reflect the distinctive intellectual formation of John Paul II.[4] The use of Scripture is clearly shaped by his study of the phenomenology of Max Scheler, with its stress upon objective moral values evident to the sensitive mind.[5] The account of the human act, with its suspicion of proportionalist revision, reflects the strict Thomism of Garrigou-Lagrange, the mentor of Wojtyla during his studies at the Angelicum.[6] The fierceness of the Pope's cultural critique, often apocalyptic in tone, reflects his literary formation, bathed in the romanticism of Adam Mickiewicz.[7] It also echoes his formative struggles against the twin demons of National Socialism and Stalinist Communism. This resistance shaped Wojtyla's convictions, already present in his first plays for the Polish underground theatre,[8] concerning the fragility of a humane culture in a society driven by diabolical hatred of "burdensome" human groups.

The method of argumentation used by *Evangelium Vitae* can be clarified by placing it within the broader context of the Pope's canon. Both in method and content, *Evangelium Vitae* follows the logic of the earlier *Veritatis Splendor*, the Pope's definitive treatment of general principles of Catholic moral theology. *Evangelium Vitae* also pursues a critique of contemporary culture that echoes the posture of his earlier trilogy of social encyclicals: *Laborem Exercens* (1981),[9] *Sollicitudo Rei Socialis* (1987),[10] and *Centesimus Annus* (1991).[11] Both *Evangelium Vitae* and *Veritatis Splendor*, however, employ a biblical logic of argumentation and an apocalyptic tone that diverge sensibly from the rhetoric of the earlier social treatises.

SCRIPTURE

The entire argument of *Evangelium Vitae* is scriptural, inasmuch as each part of the encyclical copiously cites the Scriptures on behalf of the theses it defends. Each subchapter frames itself under the rubric of a scriptural quotation, drawn eclectically from both Old and New Testaments in the corpus of the argument (chaps. 2–4) and pointedly drawn only from the Book of Revelation in the concluding chapter (*EV* 102–105). The encyclical repeatedly synthesizes its various arguments under the master rubric of "the Gospel of life," manifested through the scriptural accounts of Christ himself (*EV* 29–51).

In chapter 1, the encyclical employs a more disciplined exegesis. It frames its argument in terms of an interpretation of the narrative of Cain's murder of Abel (Gn 4:2–16). The encyclical examines this paradigmatic narrative of original human violence in general (*EV* 7–9). It then examines the narrative in slow motion, by meditating upon the key moments of the God-Cain dialogue in the sequel to the first murder: God's question ("What have you done?" Gn 4:10; *EV* 10–15); Cain's question ("Am I my brother's keeper?" Gn 4:9; *EV* 18–20); Cain's postjudgment plea ("And from your face I shall be hidden," Gn 4:14; *EV* 21–24). In both the general and the particular analyses of the Cain narrative, the encyclical explores the mysterious origins of human violence before the mystery of God, simultaneously just and merciful. The exegesis discerns general lines of human action in conformity with the moral and religious values unearthed by a careful excavation of this paradigmatic account of human violence and divine judgment.

In his exegesis of the Cain narrative, the Pope employs an unusual method of analysis. It is striking how little the method owes to the predominant method of scriptural exegesis in the academy: the historical-critical.[12] Outside of a vague allusion to the "archaic" structure of the narrative (*EV* 7), the encyclical exhibits no interest in placing the narrative within the historical context of its reference or its literary genesis. Neither does it study the role of the narrative within the canonical context of the Pentateuch or the history of Israel. Its exegetical focus remains fixed upon the universal truths regarding the divine nature, human nature, and moral values that may be gleaned by a careful meditation of the narrative and its subacts.

The Pope's method of exegesis revives, in a limited way, an older type of exegesis common to medieval authors.[13] This method discerned several strands of meaning within a given scriptural text: literal (historical); spiritual; moral; allegorical (typological). The Pope provides elaborate analyses of the spiritual and moral "senses" of the Cain narrative. He details the various strands of human sinfulness manifested by the evasion of Cain: violent anger (*EV* 8), apathy (*EV* 10), false freedom (*EV* 18–20), practical atheism (*EV* 21), and materialism (*EV* 23). He simultaneously sketches the attributes of God unveiled by the narrative: perfect justice (*EV* 8–9), creativity and sovereignty over life (*EV* 10), mercy (*EV* 9). The Pope complements the "spiritual" reading of the narrative by a "moral" reading, wherein the account of Cain indicates actions to be rejected or performed by the faithful disciple of the text. The God-Cain dialogue regarding murder illumines the immorality of abortion (*EV* 13), euthanasia (*EV* 15), and genocide (*EV* 10). Conversely, God's categorical defense of human life and condemnation of murder in the narrative highlight the value of human actions that promote life, such as the establishment of crisis pregnancy centers (*EV* 26), the growth of pro-life movements (*EV* 27), and the strengthening of social assistance to the marginal (*EV* 27). By manifesting the opposed traits of divine justice and human violence, the narrative reveals the contours of those intentional actions which promote or disfigure the human person.

The Pope's spiritual-moral analysis of the Cain narrative is not a simple retrieval of a superannuated method of Catholic exegesis. This spiritual-moral reading is controlled by the Pope's formation and practice as a professional phenomenologist. In discerning the universal values and practical consequences of Cain's resort to murder, the Pope manifests the objective "essence" of the human person faced with the drive toward violence. This unveiling of the objective essence of humanity, especially the objectivity of its key moral values and attitudes, is central to the phenomenological project of Max Scheler,[14] the phenomenologist studied by the Pope in his doctoral dissertation,[15] and other Catholic participants in "Munich phenomenology," such as Dietrich von Hildenbrand.[16] Further, the Pope's movement of argument closely follows the method of phenomenological analysis, which moves from the more superficial to the more profound levels of the problematic subject of analysis. The essence of the subject is gradually unveiled through successive layers of meditation upon the multiple appearances of the subject.

The phenomenological contours of the Pope's spiritual-moral exegesis are present in the encyclical's interpretation of Cain's plight. First, Cain is immediately interpreted as the symbol of universal humanity. His violent act and twofold dialogue with God reveal the confrontation with violence common to all human beings. "The first murder is presented with singular eloquence in a page of the Book of Genesis which has unusual significance: it is a page rewritten daily, with inexorable and degrading frequency, in the book of human history" (EV 7). Cain's narrative is our own. Specific traits of Cain's plight illumine the recesses of each human person. Cain's defective moral attitudes (envy and anger) manifest the defective attitudes operative in each act of human violence, especially fratricide (EV 8). God's question, "What have you done? The voice of your brother's blood is crying from the ground" (Gn 4:10), illumines all human acts of culpable homicide (EV 10), especially the intensified acts of abortion and euthanasia in contemporary society (EV 11). Cain's cynical response, "Am I my brother's keeper?" (Gn 4:9), manifests the human apathy toward the plight of the neighbor, especially the refusal to acknowledge and defend the right to life of the neighbor (EV 18). In the Pope's reconstruction of the text, the figure of Cain reveals the general propensity toward violence that tempts the human person, as well as the more fundamental attitudes (envy and apathy) that fuel this lethal inclination.

Not only does the narrative of Cain reveal specific moral disvalues that haunt universal humanity. It indicates the moral practices by which the human person can endorse or refuse this proclivity toward violence. The encyclical sketches the lines of action closed or opened by Cain's narrative to the reader who affirms the truth of the picture of divine and human natures disclosed by the text. The fratricidal nature of Cain's crime indicates the particular evil associated with acts of abortion and euthanasia, which destroy one's own child or parent (*EV* 8). God's mercy in protecting Cain from assault by others suggests the clemency that we should exhibit in the treatment of criminals (*EV* 9), a position later echoed in the encyclical's critique of capital punishment (*EV* 56). Cain's apathy before the spilt blood of his brother illumines the disvalues of our insouciance before the death of innocents, especially in our growing tolerance of abortion and euthanasia (*EV* 10–11). Cain's nonrelational concept of freedom, with its lethal consequences, warns us of the danger to the weak if we adopt a similar libertarian posture (*EV* 23) and of the moral imperative of following the path of self-sacrificial freedom, which defends the imperiled through a legal defense of authentic rights and social policies based upon human solidarity (*EV* 26). The successful reception of the narrative of Cain is manifest in the praxis, rather than the theory, of the disciple of the Word. It is conversion to the acts of nonviolent love, the antithesis of Cain, that is the proper outcome of the narrative in the faithful reader.

The encyclical's analysis of the spiritual and moral senses of the Cain narrative reflects the phenomenological method of the Pope. The division of the narrative into discrete scenarios is not arbitrary. It permits the reader to move from a superficial to a profound grasp of the essence of humanity provoked by violence and to adopt a course of action conformed to the narrative's truths. In the first level of analysis, the exegesis dissects the surface traits of Cain. Cain's passions of envy and anger (*EV* 8) conflict with God's attributes of justice (*EV* 8) and mercy (*EV* 9). In the second layer of analysis, the encyclical studies the moral attitudes that undergird the vicious passions of Cain and, mimetically, of the reader. The text details the various phenomena of violence that fuel the surface vices (*EV* 10–12). Behind the structures of violence stands a "Promethean attitude" that simply obliterates moral values in a voluntaristic exaltation of personal power (*EV* 15). In the final level, the explicitly theological, the roots of violence emerge as practical atheism (*EV* 21), an incapacity to recognize God that reduces human relations to material exchange (*EV* 23) and that finally annihilates the moral conscience (*EV* 24). In progressively excavating the roots of the murderous act in the scriptural narrative, the exegesis follows a clear logic of movement from the surface to the depth of human violence. The argument moves from the individual (Cain) to the social (culture of death), from act (murder) to attitude (voluntarism), from the psychological (anger) to the theological (atheism).

Evangelium Vitae's phenomenological exegesis of scriptural narrative closely echoes the methods of exegesis used in *Veritatis Splendor*, its parent encyclical on fundamental moral theology. Like *Evangelium Vitae*, *Veritatis*

Splendor opens with an elaborate analysis of a scriptural narrative: the encounter between Christ and the rich young man (*VS* 6–27). Like *Evangelium Vitae*, *Veritatis Splendor* systematically discerns the moral implications of the divine-human dialogue as it employs the onion-peeling logic of analysis common to phenomenologists. The Pope's recent development of a distinctive exegesis of scriptural narrative, one that simultaneously retrieves the medieval "moral sense" and imports the techniques of phenomenology, is a clear response to Vatican II's mandate to develop a more biblically based method of moral theology.[17] The placement of the analysis of these scriptural narratives at the beginning of the argument of these encyclicals indicates the preeminence of Scripture for situating the moral dilemmas confronting the Church and the technical reflection of the Christian moralist concerning ethical principles and practical applications.

NEO-SCHOLASTIC INFLUENCES

A second strand of *Evangelium Vitae*'s argument employs a neo-scholastic method of analyzing human action. In these moments of neo-scholastic judgment, the encyclical carefully defines the prohibited act of murder in general and in particular areas of controversy. In these passages, the encyclical evinces what Avery Dulles[18] has designated as the twin traits of neo-scholastic theology: a simultaneous appeal to the power of reason to propose precise moral propositions and an appeal to the authority of the Church's magisterium, especially the papal magisterium, to fix a particular point of moral doctrine. Especially in chapter 3, the Pope repeatedly affirms such moral propositions in simultaneous appeals to philosophical argument and to ecclesiastical authority. These elaborate studies of specific prohibited actions within the particular domain of homicide clearly continue the polemic against proportionalist revision of natural law theory prominent in *Veritatis Splendor* (*VS* 75).

This neo-scholastic analysis of the human act becomes especially solemn in three passages of chapter 3 where the Pope categorically condemns particular homicidal actions. First, the Pope condemns every act of murder, defined as the direct killing of an innocent human being. "Therefore, by the authority which Christ conferred upon Peter and his Successors, and in communion with the bishops of the Catholic Church, *I confirm that the direct and voluntary killing of an innocent human being is always gravely immoral.* This doctrine, based upon that unwritten law which man, in the light of reason, finds in his own heart (cf. Rm 2:14–15), is reaffirmed by Sacred Scripture, transmitted by the Tradition of the Church and taught by the ordinary and universal Magisterium" (*EV* 57).

Several traits of the neo-scholastic, manualist method of moral theology emerge from this analysis of the act of murder. First, the passage carefully defines murder as an act of homicide with precise characteristics: "voluntary" (the will of the agent); "direct" (the nature of the act); "innocent" (the status of the victim). This careful definition of particular human acts, with the casuist's attention to subtle distinctions (direct/indirect), clearly echoes the method of neo-scholastic ethical analysis. Second, the passage appeals to both philosophical reason (the natural law accessible in principle to every human person) and to theological authorities (Scripture, tradition, magisterium) as foundations for this norm. This simultaneous appeal to reason and faith culminates a much longer argument on the witness of Scripture (*EV* 53) and tradition (*EV* 54) to the inviolability of innocent human life. Third, the argument accentuates the prerogatives of the ecclesiastical magisterium in moral matters. It emphasizes both the collegial ("in communion with the bishops of the Church") and the specifically papal ("by the authority which Christ conferred upon Peter") dimensions of this moral pedagogy concerning specific human acts. It underscores the right of the magisterium, already stated in earlier social encyclicals, to propose binding norms of moral action and not limit itself to general moral exhortation.

This neo-scholastic method of act-centered moral analysis reemerges in the encyclical's treatment of abortion and euthanasia. The Pope categorically condemns each act of direct abortion.

> Therefore, by the authority which Christ conferred upon Peter and his Successors, in communion with the bishops—who on various occasions have condemned abortion and who in the aforementioned consultation, albeit dispersed, have shown unanimous agreement concerning this doctrine—I *declare that direct abortion, that is, abortion willed as an end or as a means, always constitutes a grave moral disorder*, since it is the deliberate killing of an innocent human being. This doctrine is based upon the natural law and upon the written Word of God, as transmitted by the Church's Tradition and taught by the ordinary and universal Magisterium. (*EV* 62)

The argumentation employs both philosophical (natural law) and theological (Scripture, tradition, magisterium) authorities to justify the carefully defined moral norm. Certain traits of the norm, such as the means/end distinction, testify to the neo-scholastic influence on the analysis, especially the influence of the manualist principle of double effect.[19] While stopping short of claims of infallibility, the declaration's appeal to papal authority and to the authority of the episcopal college confers unusual solemnity upon this definitive teaching of the ordinary magisterium concerning a particular class of human acts.

The encyclical enunciates a similar position regarding the practice of active euthanasia. "In communion with the bishops of the Catholic Church, I confirm that euthanasia is a grave violation of the law of God, since it is the deliberate and morally unacceptable killing of a human person. This doctrine is based upon natural law and upon the written Word of God, is transmitted by the Church's Tradition and taught by the universal and ordinary magisterium" (*EV* 65). Previous to this definition, the Pope had carefully distinguished the act of active euthanasia from other actions, such as the refusal of heroic means of life prolongation, which are wrongly confused with this species of direct, voluntary homicide (*EV* 65). The warrant for the moral norm is again simultaneously philosophical (natural law) and theological (the trinity of Scripture, tradition, magisterium). Both papal and episcopal authority are invoked in the categorical condemnation of active euthanasia and its contemporary variants, such as assisted suicide.

The encyclical's painstaking condemnation of the act of murder and its subsets, direct abortion and active euthanasia, inscribes itself within the Pope's longstanding polemic against proportionalism. The Pope repeatedly argues that these moral norms are exceptionless, that is, no circumstance or motive or end may justify the performance of these prohibited acts of homicide. The general prohibition against the direct killing of the innocent is absolute. "The deliberate decision to deprive an innocent human being of his life is always morally evil and can never be licit either as an end in itself or as a means to a good end. . . . Before the moral norm which prohibits the direct taking of the life of an innocent human being there are no privileges or exceptions for anyone" (*EV* 57). Immediately after his solemn declaration against the evil of direct abortion, the Pope excludes any exception to this moral norm. "No circumstances, no purpose, no law whatsoever can ever make licit an act which is intrinsically illicit, since it is contrary to the Law of God" (*EV* 62). In *Evangelium Vitae*'s perspective, the carefully defined acts of murder, direct abortion, and active euthanasia are examples of the "intrinsically evil acts" that *Veritatis Splendor* analyzed. The moral norms in this area are neither ideals nor general guidelines. They categorically bar certain paths of conduct to the righteous. The Pope's careful definition of, and commentary upon, these homicidal acts meticulously close the possibility of eluding the absolute force of these moral norms through appeals to circumstance, motive, greater goods, or lesser evils. When the object of an act is the direct killing of the innocent, the decision of a properly formed conscience cannot be in doubt.

Evangelium Vitae does not confine itself to the analysis of those acts, such as murder, that merit unequivocal condemnation. It also studies certain acts related to homicide that are morally ambiguous inasmuch as they are neither intrinsically evil nor universally good. Before these complex acts, questions of circumstance, end, and proportion rightly take their place. In determining whether to employ capital punishment (an act not intrinsically evil, since it kills an aggressor rather than an innocent), the state must weigh what circumstance, if any, would justify this use of lethal means. "It is clear that, for these purposes [retribution and social defense] to be achieved, the *nature and extent of the punishment* must be carefully evaluated and decided upon, and ought not to go to the extreme of executing the offender except in cases of absolute necessity" (*EV* 56). Whether such "absolute necessity" exists in a given case requires prudential judgment. Similarly, in decisions to forego aggressive medical treatment for the dying, a weighing of goods is appropriate. In this context, the Pope explicitly uses the language of proportion. "It needs to be determined whether the means of treatment available are objectively proportionate to the prospects for improvement" (*EV* 65).

In his commentary on the encyclical, Richard McCormick[20] wryly suggests that, in such passages, the Pope employs the tools of the proportionalism he otherwise condemns. In fact, the Pope implicitly employs the criteria of the principle of double effect, as articulated by neo-scholastic manualists.[21] Faithful to the first criterion, that one may choose only acts that are morally good or indifferent, the Pope identifies certain acts as intrinsically evil and, therefore, universally excluded. He designates the direct killing of the innocent and its subvariants, direct abortion and active euthanasia, as examples of such acts. No consideration of circumstance or consequence could alter the moral character of such an act. For moralists sympathetic to a proportionalist/consequentialist revision of ethical analysis, the moral character of an act can only be determined decisively by a consideration of the circumstance, ends, and consequences that form the context of the act.[22] This difference between the Pope and his critics rests upon a different analysis of the human act, yielding opposed positions on the very existence of "intrinsically evil acts" and exceptionless norms. Once a proposed object of action manifests itself as morally neutral in a complex action producing multiple effects, the Pope then proceeds to weigh proportionate reasons and probable consequences of an act in a particular case. This prudential analysis of complex, ambiguous acts touching the good of human life presupposes, rather than contradicts, the existence of certain types of homicidal acts that are absolutely prohibited.

Evangelium Vitae's account of the human act represents a retrieval of the neo-scholastic method of moral analysis. It insists upon studying moral conduct through a precise analysis of carefully defined acts, rather than limit itself to a study of general principles or values. It resurrects the dualistic justification typical of the manualists, with its simultaneous appeals to natural law and to the fonts of revelation. In using the principle of double effect, it carefully delimits the field open to proportionalist considerations of complex moral actions. This neo-scholastic method of analysis highlights the moral character of the act itself, often obscured by the contemporary emphasis upon the motive behind the act or the consequences of the act. Rhetorically, this act-oriented method of analysis permits the Pope to isolate and condemn a particular class of acts: the direct and voluntary killing of the innocent.

CULTURAL CRITICISM

The final methodological tool employed by *Evangelium Vitae* in its analysis of human-life issues is that of cultural critique. In these passages, the Pope operates a discernment of the practical and ideological currents that dominate a particular society. The Pope's earlier social encyclicals constitute a veritable critique of culture viewed from various social matrices. *Laborem Exercens* studies the moral and spiritual currents affecting economic organization. *Sollicitudo Rei Socialis* criticizes the forces of domination in international relations. *Centesimus Annus* pays particular attention to the moral values and disvalues animating the contemporary state. In each of these encyclicals, particular moral acts (such as paying a just wage or exercising the right to religious freedom) are placed within the framework of the culture that shapes the perception, performance, and evaluation of these acts. In each of these encyclicals, the Pope criticizes cultural institutions and ideologies under the criterion of the human person (*LE* 15; *SRS* 39–40; *CA* 53–60).

Evangelium Vitae continues this personalist critique of culture through several strategies. First, it places particular moral acts within a broader framework of social influences. Second, it diagnoses the traits of the "culture of death," which legitimizes homicidal acts, and it limns the alternative "culture of life." Third, it criticizes the ideologies, especially the practical atheism, that inform this lethal culture. Finally, it develops a critique of democratic polity.

The encyclical's treatment of imputability in the area of abortion illustrates the Pope's tendency to contextualize human acts in terms of their social determinants. While the act of direct abortion is always and everywhere wrong, the responsibility of the aborted woman for the act is ambiguous. The Pope assigns possible responsibility to the consort, the family, and the medical professionals involved in a particular abortion (*EV* 59). He places particular stress upon the responsibility of larger institutions that create a social climate conducive to abortion. "Responsibility likewise falls on the legislators who have promoted and approved abortion laws. . . . A general and no less serious responsibility lies with those who have encouraged the spread of an attitude of sexual permissiveness. . . . [O]ne cannot overlook the network of complicity which reaches out to include international institutions, foundations and associations which systematically campaign for the legislation and spread of abortion" (*EV* 59). The individual act of abortion cannot be understood independently of certain cultural institutions (the state, the media, the economic structure) that strongly shape the individual's posture toward the practice. Neo-scholastic manualists have long stressed factors that can reduce the culpability of the moral agent. Typical factors are ignorance, passion, and force. [23] In the Pope's treatment of moral imputability, however, the accent is placed upon those social structures that fashion, often covertly, the individual's perceptions concerning a particular act. In such a perspective, mature moral analysis becomes a thorough unmasking and critique of the cultural institutions that modulate individual deliberation and choice.

The cultural critique operative in *Evangelium Vitae* emerges explicitly in the dialectic between the "culture of death" and the "culture of life" that the Pope discerns in contemporary society. In these passages, the growing disdain for human life, manifest in the acceptance of abortion and euthanasia, reflects a nihilism informing national and international institutions. Using the language of class struggle, the encyclical sketches the outlines of this lethal culture:

> We are confronted by an even larger reality, which can be described as a veritable *structure of sin*. The reality is characterized by the emergence of a culture which denies solidarity and in many cases takes the form of a veritable 'culture of death'. . . . It is possible to speak in a certain sense of a *war of the powerful against the weak*: a life which would require greater acceptance, love and care is considered useless, or held to be an intolerable burden, and is therefore rejected in one way or another. (*EV* 12)

The individual acts against innocent human life reflect broader, often hidden, structures of a society dominated by the interests of the powerful refusing their duties toward the weak. The result is the depersonalization of the weak as an "intolerable burden" and an ideological justification of types of homicide, such as abortion or euthanasia, that are only rationalizations of the abuse of power. In this perspective, authentic analysis of the evil of murder cannot limit itself to the critique of specific acts, such as active euthanasia. It must penetrate to a critique of the social institutions that legitimize and provoke such actions.

This cultural critique not only situates homicidal acts within a social context. It evaluates the erroneous concepts that animate these lethal structures of society. *Evangelium Vitae* diagnoses the arrogance (*EV* 13), the lack of solidarity (*EV* 57), and the misunderstanding of rights (*EV* 72) that fuel the contempt toward innocent life. Following *Veritatis Splendor* (*VS* 33–53), it devotes particular attention to the false theories of freedom that legitimize the practice of murder. Freedom is warped by its contemporary divorce from relationality and from truth. In its divorce from relationality, freedom becomes wilfulness, rather than responsibility for the other. "In view of this entrusting . . . God gives everyone freedom, a freedom which possesses an *inherently relational dimension.* This is a great gift of the Creator, placed as it is at the service of the person and of his fulfillment through the gift of self and openness to others; but when freedom is made absolute in an individualistic way, it is emptied of its original content" (*EV* 19).

When shorn of concern for the truth, freedom becomes caprice.

> Freedom negates and destroys itself, and becomes a factor leading to destruction, when it no longer recognizes and respects its *essential link with the truth.* When freedom, out of a desire to emancipate itself from all forms of tradition and authority, shuts out even the most obvious evidence of an objective and moral truth . . . then the person ends up by no longer taking as the sole and indisputable point of reference for his own choices the truth about good and evil, but only his subjective and changeable opinion, or, indeed, his selfish interest and whim. (*EV* 19)

When freedom no longer subordinates itself to the truth concerning human goods and the right derived thereof, human society quickly becomes a market (*EV* 20), where the strongest bidder overwhelms the weak. Animated by such a libertarian distortion of human freedom, contemporary society metamorphosizes into the culture of death by exchanging the objective order of human rights for the sole "right" of the powerful to act with minimal restraint.

In developing its cultural critique, *Evangelium Vitae* devotes particular attention to the distortion of democracy operative in contemporary culture. The encyclical admits certain values in democracy: "the dignity of every human person, respect for inviolable and inalienable human rights, and the adoption of the 'common good' as end" (*EV* 70). It severely criticizes, however, certain distortions of democracy that have transformed it into an ally of the culture of death. The Pope argues that democracy's increasing violations of the right to life signal the collapse of human rights as the foundation of this regime. "How can we reconcile these declarations [on behalf of human rights] with the refusal to accept those who are weak and needy, or elderly, or those who have just been conceived? These attacks go directly against respect for life and they represent a *direct threat to the entire culture of human rights.* It is a threat capable, in the end, of jeopardizing the very meaning of democratic coexistence" (*EV* 18). This corrosion of democracy stems from the substitution of individual freedom (especially the freedom of the powerful) for respect for the dignity of each human being as the telos of polity. Out of this misguided exaggeration of the autonomy of the powerful adult, the democratic regime increasingly divorces the civil law from the moral law, thus abandoning the most vulnerable members of society (such as the nascent infant and the dying patient) to lethal violence (*EV* 69–74). The very purpose of the state, the defense of the weak, collapses.

Democracy also vitiates itself by reducing its traits to one—majority rule. "In the democratic culture of our time it is commonly held that the legal system of any society should limit itself to taking account and accepting the convictions of the majority. It should therefore be based solely upon what the majority itself considers moral" (*EV* 68). In such a voluntaristic version of democracy, the link between the will and the objective order of goods/rights is sundered. The result is the destruction of the marginal under a rhetoric of "rights" that are only a mask for corporate wilfulness.

This critique of democratic culture appears to represent a growing pessimism of the Pope concerning the moral texture of the democratic regime. One need only compare this critique with the more optimistic account of democracy in *Centesimus Annus* (1991) to detect the shift.[24] Written in the flush of the fall of Communism, *Centesimus Annus* praises the moral values present in the emergent democratic regimes in Eastern Europe and Latin America. "The Church values the democratic system inasmuch as it ensures the participation of citizens in making political choices, guarantees to the governed the possibility both of electing and holding accountable those who govern them, and of replacing them through peaceful means when appropriate" (*CA* 46). This praise of electoral procedure and majority rule stands in tension with *Evangelium Vitae*'s critique of the moral dangers of majoritarianism. *Centesimus Annus* even praises the ancient bête noire of Catholic social doctrine: the free market. "On the level of individual nations and international relations, *the free market* is the most efficient responding to needs" (*CA* 34). Tellingly, *Evangelium Vitae*'s only reference to the market is a negative one, construing the market as the symbol of a society where human rights have collapsed and "everything is negotiable" for the strongest bidder. *Centesimus Annus*'s relatively positive evaluation of liberal democracy, in terms of both electoral procedure and economic organization, has yielded to the current encyclical's critique of democracy as the triumph of antisocial freedom. This theoretical critique of democracy parallels the Holy See's more critical postures at international assemblies, such as United Nations conferences in Cairo (1994)[25] and Beijing (1995),[26] where the Pope has warned the international community of the bogus expansion of "rights" that only destroy authentic rights, such as the inviolate right to life and the right of the family as the basic unit of society.

The Pope's method of cultural analysis prolongs *Gaudium et Spes*'s method of scrutinizing the signs of the times (*GS* 4) in the light of the gospel. In *Evangelium Vitae*, however, the signs emerge as markedly grimmer than they do in the Vatican II constitution. The Pope's method of cultural analysis insists that a full study of moral action only reaches its term when the act is placed within the social structures that shape the attitudes and judgments surrounding the act. Faithful to his philosophical formation, the Pope's version of this analysis is primarily a critique of dominant ideologies, such as the dissections of libertarianism, voluntarism, and materialism that figure prominently in *Veritatis Splendor* and *Evangelium Vitae*. Only through such a critique, conducted under the rubric of the human person, can the social structures behind the discrete acts of homicide emerge. In *Evangelium Vitae*, this cultural critique emerges as a pointedly political one. As opposed to certain earlier encyclicals, where the Pope tended to minimize the role of the state and exalt the cultural role of intermediate bodies (*CA* 44–52), *Evangelium Vitae* squarely analyzes the culture of death in terms of political regime. The disturbing tendency to practice and rationalize the killing of the innocent becomes intelligible only in the light of contemporary traits of liberal democracy.

LIMITATION AND CONTRIBUTION

The analytic methods employed in *Evangelium Vitae* indicate certain limits in John Paul II's moral-social discourse. First, the category of history appears to have little weight in the moral discernment. Second, the neo-scholastic norms of action, despite their precision, fail to resolve certain moral ambiguities in the fields of action they attempt to judge.

In its phenomenological study of moral values and the neo-scholastic defense of exceptionless norms, the encyclical provides little analysis of the historical development of these values and norms or of their applications. *Evangelium Vitae*'s critical treatment of capital punishment, for example, clearly diverges from the more positive treatment of such punishment typical of the Catholic magisterium earlier in the century.[27] Although the Pope does not declare capital punishment an intrinsically evil act, he treats it with patent moral skepticism. "Today, however, as a result of steady improvements in the organization of the penal system, such cases [of justifiable capital punishment] are very rare, if not practically non-existent" (*EV* 56). At the press conference accompanying the promulgation of the encyclical, Cardinal Joseph Ratzinger, the prefect of the Congregation for the Doctrine of the Faith, argued that the Pope's position on capital punishment represented a palpable "development of doctrine."[28] New editions of the Church's *Catechism* would need to be revised in light of it. The encyclical itself, however, provides scant treatment of how the Church moved from clear support for capital punishment to prudential opposition to it in the space of several decades. Similarly, the treatment of the history of Catholic doctrine concerning abortion (*EV* 61–62) capably notes the persistence of the Church's animus toward abortion through the centuries. The variations of this teaching, however, in the disputes over animation (*EV* 60) or over what kinds of abortion are in fact direct (*EV* 62), receive little analysis. The spiritualist exegesis of the Scriptures only reinforces the ahistorical cast of the methods of moral analysis.

Another problem emerges in the neo-scholastic use of exceptionless norms to guide and limit human action. As in *Veritatis Splendor* (*VS* 79–82), *Evangelium Vitae* underscores the value and absolute character of negative prohibitions (*EV* 53). In solemn and precise legal language, the Pope affirms three such exceptionless norms in the field of homicide. The general norm is: one may never voluntarily and directly kill an innocent human being (*EV* 57). Two derivative norms are: one many never practice direct abortion (*EV* 62); one may never practice active euthanasia (*EV* 65). In his commentary, the Pope carefully preempts any interpretation of these norms that would weaken their absolute character.

In practice, however, the norms are more ambiguous than their strict formulations suggest. None of these norms categorically condemns whole classes of physical acts, such as all homicide or every abortion. The norms only concern "voluntary" acts of homicide. The question of the intentions of the moral agent thus becomes relevant. The general norm only protects the "innocent," thus excluding the aggressor. The moral status of the victim becomes central. This is an especially problematic consideration in Catholic theology, where aggression can be construed as material as well as moral.[29] The norms censure only direct, rather than indirect, acts of homicide. The circumstances surrounding the act now become prominent in moral evaluation of a given homicide. Rather than excluding considerations of intention or circumstance, these nuanced norms actually highlight such considerations as crucial for moral discernment.

The application of these complex norms to particular cases further indicates their relatively porous nature. Just-war theorists, for example, have long disputed whether a particular military action does in fact constitute the direct killing of the innocent. The recent perplexity of Christian moralists concerning the ethical character of the Gulf War[30] indicates the possible moral ambiguities of homicidal acts subject to the scrutiny of precise norms. Disputes within Catholicism itself over abortion manifest the ambiguous application of such norms. The Church's hesitation over the morality of abortions performed to save the life of the mother, a hesitation that lasted well into the last century,[31] stemmed from confusion over the possible status of the nascent child in such cases as a material aggressor. The current Catholic disarray over the possible status of artificial nutrition/hydration as an "extraordinary means" of medical treatment reveals the practical difficulty in establishing clear boundaries between active euthanasia and the legitimate refusal of extraordinary means of life prolongation. While these exceptionless norms of action clearly prevent moral discernment from deteriorating into a utilitarian calculus, they resolve fewer moral quandaries than their legal rhetoric might suggest.

Despite these limitations, *Evangelium Vitae* indicates the richness of the methods of moral analysis employed by John Paul II. One of the strengths of his logic is the fusion of phenomenological and neo-scholastic approaches to moral conduct. The phenomenological versant evokes the broad attributes, values, and attitudes of the human person before the mystery of God. The neo-scholastic versant underscores the precise moral values and disvalues intrinsic to particular actions. By drawing upon both wings of his philosophical formation, the Pope intertwines poetic and legal rhetoric, general exhortation, and technical norm in the unveiling of the moral itinerary of the human person. Phenomenological analysis alone tends toward vague evocation. Neo-scholastic analysis alone tends to deteriorate into legalism. This simultaneous emphasis upon broad attitudes and specific acts provides a complementary portrait of the objective moral order, easily distorted in contemporary waves of subjectivism and relativism.

The Pope's method of analysis also indicates a double contextualization essential for contemporary Catholic moral discernment. The first is biblical; the second is cultural. The elaborate opening of *Evangelium Vitae* (*EV* 7–28), as of its predecessor *Veritatis Splendor* (*VS* 6–27), establishes scriptural narrative as the point of departure of Christian moral interrogation. The moral universe discloses itself by dialogue between God and the perplexed moral agent (Cain in *Evangelium Vitae* and the rich young man in *Veritatis Splendor*). Such narrative dialogue, which becomes mimetically the dialogue between God and every attentive disciple, provides the framework of moral discernment concerning particular acts and political applications.

The second context is the particular culture in which the Church and the individual agent must pursue their moral itinerary. While ethical interrogation rightly examines universal values and universally binding norms of action, it must attentively assess the social setting in which these values emerge and in which these acts are performed or shunned. In the Pope's perspective, this cultural analysis is not simply an enterprise of sociological description. It is itself a work of normative judgment, currently focused upon resurgent democracy in peril of divinizing self-will.

NOTES

1. John Paul II, *Evangelium Vitae* (Boston: Daughters of St. Paul, 1995). Useful symposia on the encyclical are found in *Crisis* 13 (1995): 13–23 and *First Things* 56 (1995): 32–38.

2. John Paul II, *Veritatis Splendor* (Boston: St. Paul, 1993).

3. For a presentation of the four criteria of this principle, see Richard McCormick, "Double Effect, Principle of," in *Encyclopedia of Catholicism* (San Francisco: Harper, 1995), 432.

4. On the Pope's philosophical background, see George Huntston Williams, *The Mind of John Paul II: Origins of His Thought and Action* (New York: Seabury, 1981); and Kenneth L. Schmitz, *At the Center of the Human Drama: The Philosophical Anthropology of Karol Wojtyla/John Paul II* (Washington: Catholic University of America, 1993).

5. For an analysis of Wojtyla's appropriation of Scheler's phenomenology, see Peter H. Spader, "The Primacy of the Heart: Scheler's Challenge to Phenomenology," *Philosophy Today* 29 (1985): 223–29.

6. For a study of John Paul II's Thomism, see Jude P. Dougherty, "The Thomistic Element in the Social Philosophy of John Paul II," *Proceedings of the American Catholic Philosophical Association* 60 (1986): 156–65.

7. See Tad Szulc, *Pope John Paul II* (New York: Scribner, 1995), 92–97.

8. Ibid., 109–10.

9. John Paul II, *Laborem Exercens* (Boston: St. Paul, 1981).

10. John Paul II, *Sollicitudo Rei Socialis* (Boston: St. Paul, 1987).

11. John Paul II, *Centesimus Annus* (Boston: St. Paul, 1991).

12. On the relationship between John Paul II's exegesis and historical-critical method, see Terrence Prendergast, "A Vision of Wholeness," in *The Thought of John Paul II*, ed. J. McDermott (Rome: Gregoriana, 1993), 69–72.

13. For a presentation of these methods of exegesis, see Henri de Lubac, *Exégèse médiévale: les quatre sens de l'Ecriture* (Paris: Aubier, 1959). For a contemporary defense of exegeting the spiritual and moral senses of Scripture, see Pontifical Biblical Commission, *The Interpretation of the Bible in the Church* (Boston: St. Paul, 1993), 84–88.

14. Robert Harvanek, "The Philosophical Foundations of the Thought of John Paul II," in McDermott, *Thought of Pope John Paul II*, 1–22.

15. John Nota, "Phenomenological Experience in Karol Wojtyla," in McDermott, *Thought of Pope John Paul II*, 197–204.

16. See Dietrich von Hildenbrand, *Transformation in Christ* (Baltimore: Helicon, 1948), for a phenomenological treatise on the "attitudes" essential to the Christian moral life.

17. *Optatum Totius* 16, in *Vatican Council II*, ed. Austin Flannery (Boston: St. Paul, 1975), 1: 720.

18. Avery Dulles, "Jesuits and Theology: Yesterday and Today," *Theological Studies* 52 (1991): 524–38.

19. For representative manualist presentations of the principle, see Austin Fagothey, *Right and Reason* (St. Louis: Mosby, 1959), 152–56; Martin O'Keefe, *Known from the Things That Are* (Houston: Thomistic, 1987), 51–61; Andrew Varga, *On Being Human* (New York: Paulist, 1978), 93–96.

20. Cf. Richard A. McCormick, "The Gospel of Life," *America* 172, no 15 (1995): 10–17.

21. The manualists insist that the first step is to identify the proposed object as morally good, indifferent, or evil. "Intrinsically evil" acts are excluded from any possible justification. See Fagothey, *Right and Reason*, 153–54; O'Keefe, *Known from the Things*, 53–54; Varga, *On Being Human*, 94.

22. For a critique of the proportionalist revision, see John Connery, "Morality of Consequences: A Critical Appraisal," *Theological Studies* 34 (1973): 396–414.

23. Cf. Fagothey, *Right and Reason*, 101–10.

24. For a study of this transition, see Russell Hittinger, "The Gospel of Life, A Symposium," *First Things* 56 (1995): 33–35.

25. Pope John Paul II, "Letter to President Clinton," *Origins* 23 (1994): 760.

26. Pope John Paul II, *Letter to Women* (Boston: Pauline, 1995).

27. Donald R. Campion, "Capital Punishment," in *New Catholic Encyclopedia* (New York: McGraw, 1967), 3: 79–81.

28. "On File," *Origins* 24 (1995): 690.

29. E. J. Ryan, "Aggression," in *New Catholic Encyclopedia*, 1: 202–3.

30. M. Walzer et al., *But Was It Just?* ed. David DeCosse (New York: Doubleday, 1992).

31. John Connery, *Abortion: The Development of the Roman Catholic Perspective* (Chicago: Loyola, 1977), 225–55.

Moral Rhetoric and Moral Reasoning: Some Reflections on Evangelium Vitae

JAMES F. CHILDRESS

Rather than respond directly to John Conley's excellent essay, since I find little to dispute, I will focus on two major topics in an attempt to cast light on *Evangelium Vitae*'s moral analysis from a different perspective.[1] The first topic is *Evangelium Vitae*'s logic of moral reasoning. Here I will examine *Evangelium Vitae*'s approach to moral norms in the context of some contemporary discussions. Second, *Evangelium Vitae*'s rhetoric is as important as its logic. Here I will argue that *Evangelium Vitae* is not as rhetorically coherent as it could be, particularly in its cultural analysis and critique, and that its rhetorical incoherence creates major problems, not only in interpretation but also in determining appropriate moral responses in the world.

EVANGELIUM VITAE'S MORAL NORMS AND MORAL REASONING

In an important and influential paper, Henry Richardson has distinguished three metaphors and models for connecting moral norms to concrete cases—application/deduction, balancing, and specification.[2] These three metaphors and models can illuminate the logic of moral reasoning in *Evangelium Vitae*, particularly when used in conjunction with another important distinction between two aspects or dimensions of moral norms—what we might call their scope or range of applicability, on the one hand, and their weight, strength, or stringency, on the other. The three different metaphors and models for relating norms to concrete contexts tend to emphasize one or the other of these two aspects or dimensions, even when attempting to attend to both and to relate them in various ways.

Where it might be relevant, the application/deduction framework can operate only if we assume (a) that a norm's scope and range of applicability can be firmly set, (b) that its moral weight or strength can be set a priori, and (c) that it will never come into conflict with other equally significant moral norms. The eruption of conflicts between norms in concrete cases thus creates serious perplexities that lead communities and individual agents to adjust (a) or (b) for some norms in order to dissolve or resolve their conflicts with other norms. In short, they often end up specifying or balancing conflicting moral norms.

In situations of moral conflict, both balancing and specifying norms qualify those norms in some way. In general, balancing adjusts the weight or strength of competing moral norms so that one can outweigh or override or rebut another, while specification adjusts the conditions of application by attention to range and scope. Balancing is often connected with a view of norms as prima facie binding, as W. D. Ross suggests, or as presumptively binding. They have moral weight but are not absolutely binding. However, this is only one possible view about the assignment of weights to moral norms. Arrayed from the most stringent to the least stringent, norms may be construed as (a) absolute, (b) lexically ordered (i.e., some are absolute relative to some but not to all others), (c) prima facie binding, and (d) illuminative rules of thumb. While different moral frameworks may recognize norms with different degrees of stringency or different weights, norms that are subject to balancing tend to be prima facie binding or presumptively binding with actual obligations determined by balancing in the situation rather than by some priority rules set in advance (as in a lexical ranking). Both (a) and (b) tend to be versions of application, while (d) denies prescriptivity to illuminative rules.

The main criticism of the process of balancing is its intuitive assignment of weights to conflicting norms in actual situations. Insofar as balancing is truly distinct from application, Richardson claims, "it affords no claim to rationality, for to that extent its weightings are purely intuitive, and therefore lack discursively expressible justification."[3] However, it may be possible to reduce, even if not to eliminate, the reliance on intuition by means of a modest decision procedure.

Specification presupposes a distinction between general and specific and between degrees of generality and specificity. There is, however, no hard and fast line between general and specific, since a moral species term may be a genus to some other term.[4] However general our moral norms, we interpret them in part by more specific formulations or by types of cases that we believe fall under them. Proponents of norms engage in specification in part because, as R. M. Hare notes, "any attempt to give content to a principle involves specifying the cases that are to fall under it. . . . Any principle, then, which has content goes some way down the path of specificity."[5]

Here the distinction between principles and rules, which Richardson neglects, is useful, because the latter are usually more specific than the former. Moral principles—sometimes called moral values—are frequently specified through rules that are more concrete and detailed. For example, rules that require physicians to seek voluntary informed consent before undertaking certain procedures on patients specify the requirements of the principle of respect for autonomy.

The distinction between (a) the range or scope of applicability of a norm and (b) the weight or strength of a norm helps to clarify the way specification works. Specification adjusts the circumstances of application of the relevant norm(s), its (or their) scope and range of applicability, rather than its (or their) weight or strength. As Richardson sketches this model, it "proceeds by setting out substantive qualifications that add information about the scope of applicability of the norm or the nature of the act or end enjoined or proscribed." These substantive qualifications include clauses "indicating what, where, when, why, how, by what means, by whom, or to whom, the action is to be, is not to be, or may be done or the action is to be described, or the end is to be pursued or conceived." Through such qualifications, which feature circumstances traditionally recognized by casuists, specification seeks "to rationalize away a given practical conflict"; it "yields a more coherent overall view by acceptably removing a given conflict." It is often more "flexible, realistic, fruitful, and attainable" than application/deduction, but it maintains discursive rationality, which, Richardson claims, balancing losses.[6]

The best work in ethics, according to Richardson, already involves specification, even when its practitioners fail to distinguish what they are doing from application/deduction and from balancing. However, Richardson fails to see just how widespread specification is and just how widely it is recognized as such, largely because philosophers tend not to read theologians as widely as theologians read philosophers: specification is widespread and widely recognized as such in religious ethics. Furthermore, perhaps because of his own constructive position of specification, which appeals to pragmatism and to a coherence model of wide reflective equilibrium, he fails to see that many absolutists, particularly in religious traditions, find specification not only attractive but even indispensable because it reduces conflicts between norms when their weights cannot be adjusted (because of claims of absoluteness).

A complex use of specification appears in official Roman Catholic moral theology as articulated by Pope John Paul II; it is complex because it is connected with absolutism, with application/deduction, and perhaps, or so the proportionalists argue (and *Evangelium Vitae* and *Veritatis Splendor* suggest), with balancing on some level. *Evangelium Vitae* uses the metaphor of depth to unpack the distinction between positive and negative implications of the precept "You shall not kill": "The *deepest element* of God's commandment to protect human life is the requirement to show reverence and love for every person and the life of every person" (*EV* 41, my italics). Protestant thinkers such as

John Calvin have made similar moves. While, negatively, this precept marks the "extreme limit," its deeper (positive) meaning becomes important in the tradition of interpretation.

Indeed, "as time passed, the church's tradition has always consistently taught the *absolute and unchanging value* of the commandment 'you shall not kill'" (*EV* 54, my italics), because killing a human being "in whom the image of God is present, is a particularly serious sin" and because "only God is the master of Life!" (*EV* 55). Nevertheless, difficult situations emerged—situations "in which values proposed by God's law seem to involve a genuine paradox"—and the Church had to think further, for example, about killing in self-defense, in warfare, and in capital punishment (*EV* 55). This reflection was a kind of specification, in the sense of seeking the precept's deeper meaning: "Yet from the beginning, faced with the many and often tragic cases which occur in the life of individuals and society, Christian reflection has sought *a fuller and deeper understanding* of what God's commandment prohibits and prescribes" (*EV* 55, my italics). It appears that this fuller and deeper understanding is consistent with absolute and unchanging value.

Hence, it became implausible to view the prohibition of killing in the Decalogue as absolute, unconditional, or exceptionless, in light of the sometimes conflicting fundamental values—others might say principles—behind this precept, such as the positive protection of life itself. Thus, the Church over time sought to *specify* this precept in light of those values. And this specification further determined the precept's meaning by restricting its range and scope of application in at least two ways: first, to innocent persons and, second, to direct actions (the second specification emerged later).

In short, "the commandment 'you shall not kill' has *absolute value* when it refers to the innocent person" (*EV* 57, my italics). Thus, "the direct and voluntary killing of an innocent human being is always gravely immoral" (*EV* 57). It can never be justified either as an end or as a means. Then by a process of rational deduction, and not merely by specification, the Church applies this norm to the fetus in utero, and a particular judgment against abortion, even to save a pregnant woman's life, can be rationally deduced from these premises. The specification that produces the principle or rule against directly killing an innocent person proceeds in part by considering the principles or values that underlie it, and then reflection generates a more specific rule as well as a particular judgment.

Such a combination of specification and application is consistent with an absolutist position, once the initial, unqualified norm ("Do not kill") is specified as "Do not directly kill innocent persons." Obviously the initial norm, "Do not kill," would conflict with other important norms of agape and justice that mandate the positive protection of human life. However, the specified norm can be construed as absolute, unconditional, and exceptionless.

When the potential conflict is specified away, the claim of absoluteness becomes more plausible. And once the specification occurs, then rational application/deduction also becomes more plausible.

Balancing may also play a role in this specification. *Evangelium Vitae* appears to allow balancing into the process of determining the deeper meaning of the norm, when values come into conflict. But its balancing does not go as far as some proportionalists may want to go—at least as the Vatican interprets their position. One issue concerns "a specific kind of behavior," which *Veritatis Splendor* sees expressed in various precepts, for "the object of an act . . . specifies that act morally" (*VS* 78). *Veritatis Splendor* rejects the opinion, which it attributes to the proportionalists, "that it is impossible to qualify as morally evil according to its species the deliberate choice of certain kinds of behavior or specific acts, without taking into account the intention for which the choice was made or the totality of the foreseeable consequences of that act for all persons concerned" (*VS* 82; see 79).[7]

However, despite such claims, proportionalists and traditionalists agree that certain acts are intrinsically evil—examples include murder, torture, slavery, and so forth—but they disagree about whether intentions, circumstances, and consequences went into those determinations or specifications. According to Lisa Cahill, such terms as "murder," "torture," and "slavery" "do not . . . define acts in the abstract, but acts (like intercourse or homicide) *together with the conditions or circumstances* in which they become immoral. Such acts are indeed wrong, because immoral circumstances have already been specified in the examples given. A single term like 'murder' or 'genocide' makes it clear that what might have been a justifiable 'act in itself' (homicide) was done in wrong circumstances; or a phrase like 'killing an innocent person,' which spells out exactly what circumstances of homicide are meant, results in an absolute moral norm. About this there is little disagreement."[8] In short, these moral-offense terms go beyond neutral descriptions of physical acts to include various circumstances that specify the nature of the act and the range and scope of the precept.

John Paul's discussion of killing represents a process of specification in the context of conflicting values, and it actually bears more similarity to what the proportionalists argue than the Vatican supposes. In fact, there is little disagreement about some specifications, such as the rule against murder, as distinct from disagreement about their application to particular cases; there is, however, substantial disagreement about other rules. Indeed, the substantive debate about certain rules is central, even when it is couched in methodological terms. Thus, proportionalists and others challenge such rules as the prohibition of artificial means of contraception through their methodological arguments, while the hierarchy defends such rules through its own methodological arguments. Also behind of this methodological dispute, and connected with the substantive controversy about certain rules, is a larger set of theological convictions, particularly concerning ecclesiology.[9] Another controlling conviction is also substantive: Because of the conviction that it is wrong to do (moral) evil that good might result, it is not justifiable to override one moral principle or rule by another through balancing, compromise, sacrifice, and the like.

Although philosophers such as Richardson may describe the process of specification as one of "revision" of initial normative commitments "so as to make one of them more specific," Christian theologians have difficulty describing the process of specifying the divine commandment "Do not kill" as one of *revision*, in contrast to refining or deepening our moral understanding.

Specification has been offered as a way to reduce the role of intuition in concrete decisions, but there is debate about how far it actually succeeds in this regard. Some critics charge that it falls prey to the same problems as balancing. What "motivates and guides the modification and specification of abstract principles, what compels one to lard them with qualifying clauses," John Arras asks, "if not precisely the sort of countervailing values and principles encountered by the principlist?"[10] Specification thus may be as arbitrary as intuitive balancing allegedly is, especially in the absence of controls over the interpretation of the meaning of key moral categories.

Furthermore, it is plausible to argue, as the proportionalists do, that some balancing, at least of values if not of moral norms, occurs in the very process of specification. In specifying several moral norms, we are balancing, for instance, whether saving a life is more important than verbal accuracy, or protecting the innocent is more important than killing the guilty, and so forth.

Specifying norms is often helpful for ethical guidance, especially but not exclusively in conflict situations, and it always merits a trial effort to see if a conflict can be avoided or eliminated. I am not convinced, however, that specification can serve as the exclusive or perhaps even the dominant metaphor in a model for connecting norms and concrete cases. My skepticism stems in part from my belief that moral conflict is inescapable, in the moral universe as well as between people. Hence, we will have to engage in balancing at times because we cannot specify principles fully enough to avoid or eliminate all moral conflicts. Such a perspective is clearly at odds with the one that is dominant in *Evangelium Vitae*, but this is not the place for me to argue for it.

CONTENT AND RHETORIC IN EVANGELIUM VITAE'S CULTURAL ANALYSIS AND CRITIQUE

The importance of cultural analysis/critique appears in *Evangelium Vitae's* explicit and implicit connections between such cultural analysis/critique, on the one hand, and theological meditations (based largely on Scripture) and the analysis of moral acts in relation to exceptionless negative moral norms (based largely on tradition), on the other. John Paul II has consistently argued for special connections between theology and social doctrine. For instance, the encyclical *Sollicitudo Rei Socialis* states that "the Church's social doctrine" has the aim of "guid[ing] Christian behavior. It therefore belongs to the field, not of ideology, but of theology and particularly of moral theology" (*SRS* 41).[11] This passage is referenced and partially quoted in *Veritatis Splendor* 41.

A now classic definition of culture captures its main themes in cultural anthropology and in social thought: "Culture consists of patterns, explicit and implicit, of and for behavior acquired and transmitted by symbols, constituting the distinctive achievement of human groups." Its "essential core . . . consists of traditional (i.e., historically derived and selected) ideas and especially their attached values." Cultural systems "may, on the one hand, be considered as products of action, on the other as conditioning elements of further actions."[12] A more recent definition, by sociologist James Davison Hunter, accentuates similar themes: "Culture is nothing if it is not, first and foremost, a normative order by which we comprehend ourselves, others, and the larger world and through which we order our experience. At the heart of culture is a system of norms and values. . . . But these norms and values are better understood as commanding truths so deeply embedded in our consciousness and in the habits of our lives that to question them is to question reality itself."[13] Hunter contrasts this conception with what he calls "the trivialization of culture," which reduces culture "to a product about which individuals may choose."

Culture became an important concept in contemporary Roman Catholic thought, according to Allan Figueroa Deck, S.J., as part of the Second Vatican Council's "search for terms for dialogue with the modern world."[14] It was uniquely suited "for bridging a Catholic understanding of faith and tradition rooted in Christian humanism with the changing circumstances of time and the explosion of knowledge." The concept of culture in Catholic thought, Deck argues, emerged first in the context of mission and then was "eventually assimilated into social teaching," from which it is working its way through theology itself. For John Paul II, the concept of culture clearly links two closely related and even interrelated aspects of the Church's stance toward the modern world: Its mission to evangelize the world and its mission to promote social justice. Thus, in an address in 1983 to the Pontifical Council for Culture, which he had founded a year earlier, John Paul II stated, "There are two principal and complementary aspects which correspond to the two levels on which the Church carries out its activity: that of the *evangelization of cultures* and that of the *defense of man and his cultural development.* Both tasks demand that new means for dialogue between the Church and the cultures of our time be developed."[15]

The term "culture" sometimes appears in *Evangelium Vitae* as a descriptive way, without any associated evaluation, to characterize human community and human diversity. *Evangelium Vitae* opens with "The Gospel of life is . . . to be preached . . . to the people of every age and *culture*" (*EV* 1, my italics). And later John Paul II notes that signs that point to the victory of the culture of life over the culture of death "are not lacking in our societies and *cultures*, strongly marked though they are by the '*culture of death*'" (*EV* 26, my italics). Even though *Evangelium Vitae* thus sometimes uses the term "culture" in a merely descriptive sense, most often it is accompanied by an evaluation primarily expressed in the language of "culture of death" and "culture of life."

Evangelium Vitae thus follows *Veritatis Splendor* in searching for cultural "causes" of various moral responses. Certain causes are "cultural" because they are "linked to particular ways of looking at man, society and the world" (*VS* 98). And at the heart of culture, positively understood, is the moral sense, which in turn is rooted and fulfilled in the religious sense. The moral and religious sense can be found in transcendent human dignity reflecting creation in God's image (and God's redemption).

Thus, for John Paul II, cultural analysis/critique is central. And it is conducted in light of theology and especially moral theology, in part because the Church's social doctrine is part of moral theology. Hence, the disciplinary boundaries that many emphasize—and overemphasize—are foreign to his approach.

EVANGELIUM VITAE'S CONCEPTION OF THE CULTURE OF DEATH

The main content of *Evangelium Vitae*'s cultural analysis/critique centers on what it calls "the culture of death." *Evangelium Vitae* turns to the culture of death in order to discover "what causes these attacks [against human life] and feeds them" (*EV* 10). John Paul II locates various individual acts against human life in their cultural context, stressing that the culture often mitigates the subjective responsibility of individuals, particularly through a "structure of sin," a "larger reality," which, culturally speaking, involves the denial of solidarity and represents a "culture of death" that is fostered by various "cultural, economic and political currents," particularly concerned with efficiency, and so forth (*EV* 12).

The problem is that this cultural context dulls conscience and blunts its discriminatory power. Where the culture of death is strong, it is "grave and disturbing" that "conscience itself, darkened as it were by such widespread conditioning, is finding it increasingly difficult to distinguish between good and evil in what concerns the basic value of human life" (*EV* 4). "Conscience" still points, however, to the inviolable value of life, "as is evident in the tendency to disguise certain crimes against life in its early or final stages by using innocuous medical terms" (*EV* 11).

Even though *Evangelium Vitae*'s approach is heavier and more somber than some of John Paul's other encyclicals, it still uses the images of light, shadows, and darkness along with those of voice, echo, and silence, and writing on the heart or conscience, to stress that, despite the power of the culture of death, the Gospel of life has not experienced a total eclipse in the human conscience (see, for instance, *EV* 77, 40, 80). In a traditional Roman Catholic formulation of the relation of nature and grace, *Evangelium Vitae* affirms that the Gospel of life can be known in its essential traits by reason and experience and that it "includes everything that human experience and reason tell us about the value of human life, accepting it, purifying it, exalting it and bringing it to fulfillment" (*EV* 30). Since the value of life is something that "every human being can grasp by the light of reason," the Gospel of life thus "necessarily concerns everyone" (*EV* 101).

Although John Paul II defines culture broadly, *Evangelium Vitae* pays particular attention to law's place in culture, especially as a mode of legitimation of action. To be sure, scientific and technological developments, themselves part of culture in a broad sense, provide "new forms of attacks on the dignity of the human being" (*EV* 4). But the major increases and seriousness of threats to human life, especially when it is "weak and defenseless," cannot be attributed to those developments alone (*EV* 3). What is apparently more important in *Evangelium Vitae* is another shift in culture on the level of values and norms: "A *new cultural climate* is developing and taking hold which gives crimes against life a new and—if possible—even more sinister character" (*EV* 4, my italics). In addition to "broad sectors of public opinion," part of this troubling picture is that "legislation in many countries . . . has determined not to punish these practices against life, and even to make them altogether legal [which] is both a disturbing symptom and a significant cause of grave moral decline" (*EV* 4). Law appears to be a major instrument to maintain culture, as well as a part of culture. However, against legal positivists, "a civil law authorizing abortion or euthanasia ceases by that very fact to be a true, morally binding civil law" (*EV* 72).

Behind the emergence of the culture of death is "the profound crisis of culture, which generates skepticism in relation to the very foundations of knowledge and ethics, and which makes it increasingly difficult to grasp clearly the meaning of what man is, the meaning of his rights and his duties" (*EV* 11). In addition to moral uncertainty and ethical relativism, another problem in the "cultural climate" is the failure "to perceive any meaning or value in suffering, [rather considering] suffering the epitome of evil, to be eliminated at all costs. This is especially the case in the absence of a religious outlook which could help to promote a positive understanding of the mystery of suffering" (*EV* 15). This attitude toward suffering, often coupled with a Promethean desire for control, stems in part from the "social and cultural climate" of "secularism," since the "eclipse" or loss of the sense of God and the sense of man "produces a kind of progressive darkening of the capacity to discern God's living and saving presence" (*EV* 21), as well as a failure to appreciate "the mystery of suffering" (*EV* 15). Secularism's results include practical materialism, followed by individualism, utilitarianism, and hedonism (*EV* 23).

I believe we can begin to understand *Evangelium Vitae*'s analysis of the culture of death by focusing on its use of the metaphor of warfare and related metaphors. The metaphor of warfare structures *Evangelium Vitae*'s analysis of the culture of death and, implicitly, the relation between the culture of death, on the one hand, and the culture of life, on the other, along with the Gospel of life. And as with any metaphor, we have to ask how much it illuminates and how much it distorts.

First we need to consider how John Paul II characterizes the "culture of death," which usually but not always appears in quotation marks. According to *Evangelium Vitae*, "it is possible to speak in a certain sense of a *war* of the powerful against the weak. . . . [For example, a] person who, because of illness, handicap or, more simply, just by existing, compromises the well-being or lifestyle of those who are more favored tends to be looked upon as *an enemy* to be resisted or eliminated" (*EV* 12, my italics). In the culture of death, there is an "individualistic concept of freedom, which ends up by becoming the freedom of 'the strong' against the weak who have no choice but to submit" (*EV* 19). The language of conspiracy is also central; the culture of death involves "conspiracy against life" (*EV* 12) and an "objective conspiracy against life" (*EV* 17). In addition, it targets various enemies (*EV* 12, 13, 20, 23). In such a culture, individuals are not mere strangers; instead "everyone else is considered an enemy from whom one has to defend oneself" (*EV* 20). Among the various enemies is "procreation" itself (*EV* 23).

The metaphors of warfare and enemy also undergird *Evangelium Vitae*'s effort to connect contraception and abortion. This topic is placed under "'What have you done?' (Gn. 4:10): the eclipse of the value of life." This section (*EV* 10) looks at what *causes* and *feeds* the attacks against human life, and stresses the influence of "a veritable structure of sin" marked by the culture of death. And "despite their differences of nature and moral gravity, contraception and abortion are *often* closely connected, as fruits of the same tree" (*EV* 13, my italics). Procreation is viewed as an obstacle to personal self-fulfillment, and "the life which could result from a sexual encounter thus becomes *an enemy* to be avoided at all costs, and abortion becomes the only possible decisive response to failed contraception" (*EV* 13, my italics). Then *Evangelium Vitae* goes on to stress the connection between contraception and abortion in what amounts to military technology against future life as an enemy, especially because much of the technology for contraception is in fact, according to *Evangelium Vitae*, an abortifacient.

The metaphors of war, enemy, conspiracy, and so forth, thus all play crucial roles in describing and evaluating how the culture of death opposes human life. These metaphors also shape *Evangelium Vitae*'s depiction of the relation between the culture of death and the culture of life. Even though *Evangelium Vitae* doesn't use the language of culture war(s), the idea is clearly present and is expressed in various metaphors of conflict between the two cultures. For instance, "the 'culture of death' so forcefully opposes the 'culture of life' and often seems to have the upper hand" (*EV* 87). There is a "struggle" between culture of life and culture of death (*EV* 21); it is so serious that it can be described as a "dramatic conflict" (*EV* 50), a "dramatic struggle" (*EV* 95), and an "enormous and dramatic clash between good and evil, death and life, the 'culture of death' and the 'culture of life'" (*EV* 28).

This rhetoric has serious problems. One major problem, I would suggest, is that "cultures" don't struggle with each other; instead people with certain beliefs, values, norms, and so forth, struggle with each other. Nevertheless, some of *Evangelium Vitae*'s language suggests a kind of dualistic, almost Manichaean, view of cultures and their warfare as objective reality. We are confronted by "an even *larger reality*, which can be described as a *veritable structure of sin*. This reality is characterized by the emergence of a culture" that denies solidarity and often "takes the form of a veritable 'culture of death'" (*EV* 12).

Second, cultures are rarely as monolithic as *Evangelium Vitae* suggests— even the culture of death, as it is identified, is more complex in its beliefs and values than *Evangelium Vitae* usually acknowledges. It surely has strands of support for life, but *Evangelium Vitae*'s dualistic approach, marked by oversimplification of both "cultures," fails to see or at least to address many of the complexities and ambiguities. It is difficult not to see elements of support for life in the putative culture of death and vice versa. *Evangelium Vitae*, however, often eschews ambiguous judgments in favor of firm black-and-white judgments.

The tendency to identify monolithic cultures of life and of death is, nevertheless, qualified at places by the recognition that at least some institutions and some ways of viewing the world are more complex than *Evangelium Vitae*'s simple dichotomy might suggest. And yet it is unclear what level of cultural acceptance and legitimation of such morally problematic activities as abortion and euthanasia is required before a culture becomes a "culture of death." Suppose, for instance, that a culture accepts abortion reluctantly, only under conditions of threat to maternal life and health, and perhaps rape and incest, following careful review and authorization in individual cases. Would such a culture be labeled a culture of death along with one that accepts abortion on demand? Both depart from *Evangelium Vitae*'s relevant moral norms, but not to the same degree or extent. And *Evangelium Vitae* appears to recognize this in its discussion of the problem of conscience a legislator may face in determining whether to cast the decisive vote for "a more restrictive law, aimed at limiting the number of authorized abortions, in place of a more permissive law already passed or ready to be voted on" (*EV* 73). In such a case, an elected official with a well-recognized "absolute personal opposition to procured abortion" could vote for the more restrictive law as a way to limit the evil aspects of abortion legislation where it cannot be banned altogether. This would not be "illicit cooperation with an unjust law" (*EV* 74).

Third, we need to ask about the strength and power of the culture of death. Although John Paul II sometimes suggests that a democracy expressing the culture of death will simply "self-destruct," *Evangelium Vitae* also calls people to take vigorous action against the culture of death because it appears to be quite strong and threatening. Indeed, *Evangelium Vitae*'s language is at places almost apocalyptic, for the threat is real, because of the "enormous disparity between the *powerful* resources available to the forces promoting the 'culture of death' and the means at the disposal of those working for a 'culture of life and love.' But we know that we can rely on the help of God, for whom nothing is impossible. (cf. Mt. 19:26)" (*EV* 100, my italics). Yet any particular society or culture may indeed be somewhat ambiguous; signs that point to the "victory" of the "culture of life" are "not lacking in our societies and cultures, strongly marked though they are by the 'culture of death'" (*EV* 26).

THE STANCE OF THE CHURCH TOWARD THE WORLD

Decades ago, in a classic work, H. R. Niebuhr identified several types of conception of the relation between Christ and culture within Christian thought and practice: (1) Christ *against* culture—the sectarian definition of the Church over against the world, which can move in the direction of withdrawal (e.g., the Mennonites) or in the direction of violent confrontation (e.g., Thomas Muntzer); (2) Christ *of* culture—the identification of Christ with a particular culture (e.g., Leo XIII or the Social Gospel); (3) Christ *above* culture—affirming the best in culture, then adding Christ to it (e.g., Thomas Aquinas); (4) Christ and culture *in dualism*, perhaps through a distinction between the inner life and outer life (e.g., Martin Luther); (5) Christ *transforming* culture (e.g., Augustine).[16]

Now there are problems with this typology (or any such typology) as well as with the placement of particular historical figures and groups, but, if it is not taken too literally, it can help us consider *Evangelium Vitae*'s stance toward the world. *Evangelium Vitae*'s dominant rhetoric is Christ *against* culture, because of the strength of the culture of death. The Gospel of life, which is not itself biblical language and which is based on reason and experience as well as revelation, stands against the (powerful) culture of death. The conflict between the two cultures of life and death is a form of warfare, and the Gospel of life joins in this warfare. But in doing so it obviously affirms the culture of life, wherever it appears. Nevertheless, when *Evangelium Vitae* proposes concrete actions for Christians and others, it combines two approaches that may not fit well with the reality of culture as *Evangelium Vitae* depicts it.

On the one hand, we find the withdrawal version of Christ against culture, not the violent confrontation version that might seem to fit with the metaphors of warfare, conspiracy, and enemy. Hence, *Evangelium Vitae* discusses at length problems of cooperation, collaboration, and complicity in evil, especially because the structure of evil involves a network of complicity. On the other hand, we find the transformationist perspective. Both responses appear to be at odds with *Evangelium Vitae*'s primary analysis/critique, which focuses on the culture of death's warfare against the weak and vulnerable. *Withdrawal* may protect personal and ecclesiastical integrity in various ways, but it would appear to be relatively ineffective, in light of the putative power of the culture of death, while *transformation* appears to presuppose that there is more to the culture of death than *Evangelium Vitae*'s analysis acknowledges. Otherwise, it could not be transformed but only destroyed. In its transformationist mode, *Evangelium Vitae* supposes, in ways not fully developed, that it is possible to reverse the "large reality" of the culture of death as a "structure of sin" through various individual and communal acts of withdrawal and affirmation. It would be possible to interpret the transformationist themes in *Evangelium Vitae* as involving the transformation of culture in its descriptive sense by shifting the balance, within any culture, away from the "culture of death" in favor of the "culture of life." In part the Church should endeavor to offer "this world of ours new signs of hope and work to ensure that justice and solidarity will increase and that a new culture of life will be affirmed for the building of an authentic civilization of truth and love" (*EV* 7). *Evangelium Vitae* also notes the importance of "everyday heroism," which is "made up of gestures of sharing, big or small, which build up an authentic culture of life" (*EV* 86, cf. *EV* 95)—these include motherhood, organ donation, and the like. With the renewal of the Gospel of life within Christian communities, it is possible to hope for a "cultural change" (*EV* 98), indeed a "cultural transformation" (*EV* 96), and even a "new culture of human life" (*EV* 98), despite the disparity of resources between the culture of death and the culture of life.

It may be illuminating to relate *Evangelium Vitae* to the current debates about "culture war" or "culture wars" in the United States, in part to further probe its rhetoric and logic and in part to probe the rhetoric and logic of its reception in the United States, since what is going on in a particular culture will in part shape the reception of any encyclical. In his book *Culture Wars: The Struggle to Define America*, James Davison Hunter attempts to make "sense of the battles over the family, art, education, law, and politics."[17] According to his analysis, "America is in the midst of a culture war" over "our most fundamental and cherished assumptions about how to order our lives" and about "who we are as Americans." The conflict is about "the power to define reality," that is, to interpret society's collective myths and symbols. Rather than being reduced to particular struggles, it is in fact "a fundamental struggle over the 'first principles' of how we will order our life together. Through these seemingly disparate issues we find ourselves, in other words, in a struggle to define ourselves as Americans and what kind of society we want to build and sustain."

Without doubt Americans are always tempted to throw the term "war" around carelessly, in debates about the "war" on AIDS, on cancer, on drugs, and so forth. Neoconservatives in the United States appropriated the phrase "culture war" or "cultural war" from the German term *Kulturkampf*, which referred to Bismarck's campaign against the Roman Catholic Church in Germany. While using the term "war" descriptively, that is, to describe what is happening in our society at this time, Hunter sometimes questions its normative use, that is, its use as a guide to our action, other than to downplay the war and to concentrate on how the conflict is waged. However, as Peter Steinfels notes, Hunter's description makes it difficult—perhaps even morally irresponsible—not to take sides. For if the metaphor of war expresses what is "the inevitably dominant reality" and "if the stakes are so high, the competing moral visions so non-negotiable and rational moral discussion so unlikely, then isn't the responsible thing to choose sides and plunge in?" By describing reality, Steinfels continues, Hunter "wants to correct it, not perpetuate it. But can he do this without questioning the adequacy of the military metaphor itself? When culture becomes the continuation of war by other means (to paraphrase Clausewitz), something is seriously wrong."[18] In short, the metaphor of war appears to serve as an "evaluative description," which both characterizes and evaluates at the same time. However, there are other evaluative descriptions.

I am not convinced that the metaphor of warfare helps us understand all that clearly what is going on in our cultural conflicts or that it helpfully guides our actions in these conflicts. Not all efforts to define society are conflicts, and not all conflicts are best understood as warfare. Even when they are properly understood as warfare, it is important to ask whether the moral constraints, from the just-war tradition, are operative, or whether a crusade or holy war has been declared, with a real threat to a democratic society's fundamental commitments to ordered liberty.

A similar direction of reflection has already emerged from our examination of *Evangelium Vitae*, particularly the rhetoric of its cultural analysis/critique, and it is supported by *Evangelium Vitae*'s reception and interpretation in the United States. On March 31, 1995, in its coverage of *Evangelium Vitae*, the *New York Times* had a major front-page article by Celestine Bohlen entitled "Pope Offers 'Gospel of Life' vs. 'Culture of Death,'" and it devoted a full page (A12) to excerpts from the encyclical under the headline "Pope's Letter: A 'Sinister' World Has Led to 'Crimes against Life.'" This interpretation matched *Evangelium Vitae*'s dominant rhetoric.

I have suggested, however, there is a disjuncture in *Evangelium Vitae*'s rhetoric. War is used both descriptively and normatively. There is, rhetorically speaking, a call to arms. And yet on the level of specific recommendations the analysis is more nuanced than on the level of culture, where *Evangelium Vitae* appears to warrant a crusade or holy war, perhaps stripped of the restraints that mark the conduct of a just war.[19]

In short, the rhetoric of *Evangelium Vitae*'s cultural analysis/critique appears to oversimplify the culture of death by making it a monolithic reality in order to illuminate our situation and to motivate action on behalf of life. But the recommended actions may not match reality as depicted. A major war is going on, according to *Evangelium Vitae*, but the recommended responses fit other kinds of social conflict that stop far short of warfare. We all have, I believe, a serious moral responsibility in the use of the metaphor of warfare descriptively and prescriptively, because this metaphor, like other metaphors, has social consequences. It is performative. To change my own analytical metaphor, *Evangelium Vitae*'s diagnosis, prognosis, and therapy are not fully coherent with each other, in view of the virulence of the "culture of death."

NOTES

1. *Evangelium Vitae*, English text, *Origins* 24, no. 42 (April 6, 1995): 689–727.

2. Henry S. Richardson, "Specifying Norms as a Way to Resolve Concrete Ethical Problems," *Philosophy and Public Affairs* 19 (1990): 279–320.

3. Ibid.

4. See Paul Ramsey, "The Case of the Curious Exception," in *Norm and Context in Christian Ethics*, ed. Gene H. Outka and Paul Ramsey (New York: Charles Scribner's Sons, 1968), 67–135.

5. R. M. Hare, "Principles," in *Essays in Ethical Theory* (Oxford: Clarendon Press, 1989), 49–65.

6. Richardson, "Specifying Norms," 296, 302, 283, and passim.

7. *Veritatis Splendor*, English edition, *Origins* 23, no. 18 (October 14, 1993): 297–334.

8. Lisa Sowle Cahill, "Accent on the Masculine," in *Considering "Veritatis Splendor*," ed. John Wilkins (Cleveland: Pilgrim Press, 1994), 57–58.

9. Richard A. McCormick, S.J., "Some Early Reactions to *Veritatis Splendor*," *Theological Studies* 55 (1994): 481–506.

10. John Arras, "Principles and Particularity: The Role of Cases in Bioethics," *Indiana Law Journal* 69 (1994): 983–1014.

11. *Sollicitudo Rei Socialis* 41, in *Catholic Social Thought: The Documentary Heritage*, ed. David J. O'Brien and Thomas A. Shannon (Maryknoll, N.Y.: Orbis Books, 1992), 393–436.

12. A. L. Kroeber and Clyde Kluckhon, *Culture: A Critical Review of Concepts and Definitions* (New York: Vintage, 1952), 66.

13. James Davison Hunter, *Before the Shooting Starts: Searching for Democracy in America's Culture Wars* (New York: Free Press, 1994), 200. See also Hunter's *Culture Wars: The Struggle to Define America* (New York: Basic Books, 1991).

14. Allan Figueroa Deck, S.J., "Culture," in *The New Dictionary of Catholic Social Thought*, ed. Judith A. Dwyer and Elizabeth L. Montgomery (Collegeville, Minn.: Liturgical Press/Michael Glazier, 1994), 257.

15. Quoted ibid., 261. See also H. Carrier, "Understanding Culture: The Ultimate Challenge of the World-Church," in *The Church and Culture since Vatican II*, ed. J. Gremillion (Notre Dame, In.: University of Notre Dame Press, 1985); and H. Carrier, "The Contribution of the Council to Culture," in *Vatican II: Assessment and Perspectives*, ed. R. Latourelle (New York: Paulist, 1989).

16. H. Richard Niebuhr, *Christ and Culture* (New York: Harper & Row, 1951).

17. Hunter, *Culture Wars*.

18. Peter Steinfels, "Beliefs: Metaphors Are Flying . . . ," *New York Times*, December 12, 1991, 10.

19. Quite interestingly, despite *Evangelium Vitae*'s discussion of the Gospel of life and its use of the military metaphor, it pays little attention to the question of warfare.

The Gospel of Life and the Culture of *Death:* A RESPONSE TO JOHN CONLEY

DAVID HOLLENBACH, S.J.

The most provocative theme in John Paul II's *Evangelium Vitae* is its portrayal of a dramatic conflict between a "culture of life" and a "culture of death." As John Conley has pointed out, the Pope's reading of the forces operating on the cultural level in the world today sets the context for the encyclical's specifically religious and moral agenda. Both John Paul's presentation of a biblical/theological narrative concerning the meaning of human life and his neo-scholastic understanding of the norms governing respect for human life are important in themselves. But *Evangelium Vitae*'s distinctiveness among recent papal writings lies in its picture of an agonic cultural struggle between forces of life and death today. Conley has pointed to the "fierceness of the Pope's cultural critique, often apocalyptic in tone." For example, the entire chapter that serves as a conclusion to the encyclical is constructed as a meditation on selected texts from the Book of Revelation, invoking the end-time clash between the satanic beast of death and the life that is Christ's gift.

The phrase "culture of death" appears twelve times in the encyclical. It is clearly central to the message the Pope intends to convey. In these remarks I want to situate this phrase in the overall argument of the encyclical, suggest a contribution the cultural analysis upon which it rests can make in the United States today, and conclude by noting some unresolved problems. In this way, some light may be shed on how the Pope frames the more concrete moral issues of abortion, euthanasia, capital punishment, poverty, and war.

HUMAN RIGHTS AND THE CULTURE OF DEATH

Central to the Pope's description of this "culture of death" is his description of the way many people understand human rights today, particularly those rights that guarantee fundamental freedoms. John Paul II states several times that the threat to human life takes a particularly ominous form today. These threats involve "attacks which present new characteristics with respect to the past and which raise questions of extraordinary seriousness" (*EV* 11).[1] This newness is chiefly a separation of the understanding of human rights from commitment to objective values, particularly the value of solidarity with the weak, the suffering, and the poor. This separation is rooted in our culture's elevation of the freedom of individual choice to the level of the highest, even the only, value. In the United States this philosophy is called libertarian; in Europe it goes by the name of liberalism. De facto, it grants greater freedom of action to those who already possess greater power, and subjects the weak and the powerless to severe threats to their dignity and even their lives. *Evangelium Vitae* focuses on abortion and euthanasia as key symptoms of this threat, but all that the encyclical says about inadequate response to global poverty, war, and the plight of refugees is traced to this philosophy as well. Abortion and euthanasia are particularly symptomatic, however, because of the way that individual freedom of choice is related to an understanding of civil law in the debates about these issues. Abortion and euthanasia are not new phenomena today, but the call for "legal recognition" or "legal approval" is new. Thus the "sign of the times" that so alarms the Pope is the fact that these forms of life taking are increasingly not regarded as crimes but as *"legitimate expressions of individual freedom, to be acknowledged and protected as actual rights"* (*EV* 18; emphasis in original).

At the root of the encyclical's discussion of abortion and euthanasia, therefore, is its alarm over a libertarian/liberal understanding of the meaning of human rights. The Pope is firmly committed to human rights as norms for the formation of policy and law both in the internal life of nation-states and on the international level. In his recent speech at the United Nations, for example, he called the U.N.'s Universal Declaration of Human Rights "one of the highest expressions of the human conscience of our time." At the U.N. he also celebrated the fact that the "universal longing for freedom is one of the truly distinguishing marks of our time" and called the quest for freedom "one of the great dynamics of human history."[2] *Evangelium Vitae*, however, argues that the quest for rights and freedoms is marred by internal contradictions today. The great historical achievement that has brought the importance of these rights and freedoms to the fore is in danger of negating itself because of these contradictions.

A frame of mind engendered by the experience of pluralism is at the root of the problem the Pope sees in some contemporary understandings of human rights. The diversity of moral and religious worldviews suggests that judgment of their truth or falsity is unattainable. One must avoid imposing a moral belief on those who do not already accept its validity. Thus, the freedom to choose one's own understanding of how to live becomes the central or even the only value on which social agreement can be expected. The Pope sees this as an ethical relativism. It is at the heart of the cultural tendencies that so alarm him. On the political and social level, respect for individual freedom becomes the sole moral criterion for judging public policy and legislation. In practice, however, absolute respect for the moral opinions of every single citizen would give a lone dissenter veto power over every legislative proposal. Thus, the best that can be achieved under conditions of pluralism is respect for the opinion of the majority, whatever this opinion may be. What begins as tolerance ends as simple majority rule. Minorities, especially those whose physical weakness, social marginalization, or economic poverty gives them little public influence, become radically vulnerable to the power of the strong (*EV* 68–70). John Paul does not hesitate to call this kind of politics totalitarian.[3] Relativism on the level of culture thus leads to the political denial of the human rights of the weak, including the right to life of the unborn through abortion and of those at the end of their lives through euthanasia. The critique, however, extends much wider than this, touching the inadequate acknowledgment of the rights of the poor, of victims of war, and of migrants and refugees, to mention only a few examples. The "culture of death" is the Pope's name for the value system that "tolerates" violation of the human life and dignity of the weak whenever their protection demands limitations on the freedom of the strong.

Evangelium Vitae, therefore, opposes theories of democracy based on libertarian and individualistic presuppositions and proposes an alternative understanding of democracy. The Pope would agree with John Courtney Murray's assertion that the democratic experiment rests on the existence of a public philosophy willing to affirm with Jefferson that "there are truths, and we hold them."[4] Among these truths is the affirmation that the human person possesses a dignity that is sacred (*res sacra homo*) and that all those conditions necessary to the realization of human dignity are due persons as human rights.[5] These rights include freedom of conscience and religious liberty, to be sure. But they also include a wide array of other rights, such as the rights to life, to at least minimal levels of nutrition, to adequate health care, to political participation and participation in economic life, and to the juridical protection of all these rights through due process of law and adequately designed public policies.[6]

In other words, the Pope is proposing a theory of human rights based upon truth claims about the human good. He rejects the notion that human rights can be secured or that democracy can be stable without agreement about basic elements of a good human life. The Pope's statements in *Evangelium Vitae* that human freedom has an "essential link with the truth" must be understood in this light.[7] Political democracy depends on the presence of a certain level of cultural consensus about the human good. Skepticism about whether we can know what is genuinely good, even when this is accompanied by tolerance of diverse visions of the good life, is not enough to sustain the democratic experiment. A culture of "pure tolerance" becomes a culture in self-contradiction. It has no standards to which it can appeal to protect the weak against the strong. This, the Pope argues, is evident in the appeal to tolerance to legitimate permissive abortion and euthanasia laws. It is also evident in appeals to individual freedom in the marketplace without regard to the impact of the market on the poor. John Paul II thus advances an ethic similar to Cardinal Joseph Bernardin's consistent ethic of life, which seeks to defend human life across an array of issues, from abortion, to the provision of health care, to overcoming poverty in developing nations, to warfare, to capital punishment, to euthanasia.[8] But the distinctiveness of the Pope's quest of such a consistent ethic is his strong insistence that skepticism and tolerance are insufficient to sustain such an ethic, even in presently democratic nations. Without richer virtues than tolerance, these democracies risk destroying themselves (*EV* 20). Indeed, in the Pope's analysis, such self-destruction has already begun in such societies. Legalized abortion and efforts to liberalize legal restrictions on euthanasia are signs of this, in the Pope's analysis.

RELEVANCE IN THE UNITED STATES TODAY

I think that this diagnosis of the moral challenges facing the public life in countries such as the United States contains large elements of truth. For example, American liberal theorists, ranging from Bruce Ackerman, to John Rawls, to Richard Rorty, each in a different way, regard tolerance as the highest social virtue, largely because they have abandoned hope of achieving agreement on values other than individual freedom. Indeed, their political theories are designed to avoid introducing stronger claims about the human good into public discourse. John Rawls, for example, has advocated a form of democracy built on what he calls "the method of avoidance." This method demands that "we try, so far as we can, neither to assert nor to deny any religious, philosophical or moral views, or their associated philosophical accounts of truth and the status of values." Avoidance of such basic questions is necessary in politics, Rawls thinks, if we are to have a chance of achieving consensus. "We apply the principle of toleration to philosophy itself" when debating the basic political and economic institutions that will structure social life.[9] Nor is this disengagement from questions of truth present only in sophisticated political and moral theory. More important, it is widespread in both the educated public and in popular culture. It is evident in what Albert Borgmann has called the "sullenness" of the postmodern mentality. In this mentality the stress on individual autonomy "is usually the flourish of moral retreat, the refusal to discuss, explain, and justify a decision."[10] Thus, if tolerance is pushed to the limit as the highest or only value in the public sphere, it can serve as a screen for sullen disengagement. Such disengagement will not sustain democracy but destroy it.

The Pope's response to this disengaged mood of hypertolerance is first of all to lay out his full vision of the human good in all of its theological depth. *Evangelium Vitae* is unique among modern papal encyclicals for the range and depth of its biblical and theological reflection on the fundamental concerns it addresses. Several commentators have noted the meditative quality of the encyclical and its extensive use of biblical quotations. This suggests that the extensive presentation of a biblical theology of the meaning, value, and destiny of human life is a secondary or adjunct concern to the Pope's real interest— precisely stated moral norms concerning the taking of human life as they apply to the concrete issues of abortion and euthanasia. Conley is considerably more accurate in pointing to the centrality of this narrative theology in the argument of the encyclical. As I read it, *Evangelium Vitae* is suggesting that the sullen disengagement of our present culture can be overcome only by the presentation of a much larger vision of the human good than any moral principle can supply. Further, the Pope is quite unabashed in claiming that the sacredness of human life is rooted in God's love for every human being, a love made manifest in the redemptive death and resurrection of Jesus Christ. Though the Pope holds firm to traditional Catholic convictions about the role of reason and natural law in ethics, he is also claiming that the truth about the value of human life is finally and fully appreciated only in the light of Christian revelation. Indeed in a culture where "reasonableness" is far too often equated with skeptical tolerance and sullen disengagement from the question of truth itself, the encyclical's presentation of its rich religious vision is intended as a direct challenge to such an understanding of reason. Catholic natural law thinking has always been understood as a commitment to reason informed by faith. *Evangelium Vitae* stresses the crucial role revelation must play in shaping a vision within which rationality takes form. This is the type of ethic that H. Richard Niebuhr called "Christ transforming culture"—the encyclical's theological vision aims not just to motivate adherence to moral principles otherwise known from reason but to challenge and transform what present-day culture regards as reasonable.[11]

UNRESOLVED ISSUES

It is here that several issues left unresolved in the encyclical must be addressed. The Pope's aim is to challenge *cultural* presuppositions that he sees operative today. At the same time, his critique of culture focuses on the *legal* manifestations of the cultural presuppositions to which he objects. The unresolved problem can be put this way: does culture shape law, or does law shape culture? It is doubtless true that the relation between culture and law is a two-way street; the values embedded in the *mentalité* of a people will set the direction and limits for what they think law can accomplish. At the same time, the juridical norms that are operative in a society play an important role in educating its people about what that society regards as valuable. There is a significant practical difference, however, between an understanding of the law-culture relation that stresses the former aspect of this relation and one that stresses the latter aspect. In the former, law expresses the will of the people; there can be no legitimate legislation that does not reflect some significant degree of consensus on the values held by the people. In the latter view, law has an educative role. It can take the lead in forming the values of the culture and the people. *Evangelium Vitae* clearly holds the latter view.[12]

This, however, raises questions that are inadequately addressed in the Pope's discussions of the right to freedom of conscience, including religious freedom. His writings on the topic contain a significant ambiguity. On the one hand, the conviction that relativism threatens the very foundation of human rights and democracy had led the Pope to argue that genuine freedom is achieved only through adherence to certain fundamental truths about the human condition. For example, *Evangelium Vitae* states that "freedom negates and destroys itself, and becomes a factor leading to the destruction of others, when it no longer recognizes and respects *its essential link with the truth*" (*EV* 19; emphasis in original). In an earlier encyclical, *Centesimus Annus,* he wrote that "obedience to the truth about God and man is the first condition of freedom" (*CA* 41).[13] From a theological and ethical point of view, this makes an important point. The full good of the human person, including the fullness of freedom, is a goal human beings must attain rather than a condition they possess spontaneously or automatically. Both St. Paul's understanding of Christian freedom and humanistic understandings of freedom as the goal of authentic human development recognize that genuine freedom is something persons must strive to attain, that they can fail to do so, and that knowledge of the true conditions of human flourishing is crucial in this process. This line of thinking was evident when the Pope wrote in *Centesimus Annus* that "freedom attains its full development only by accepting the truth" (*CA* 48). It was also at the basis of the philosophy of human rights he recently sketched before the U.N. General Assembly, where he declared that "freedom has an inner 'logic' which distinguishes it and ennobles it: freedom is ordered to the truth, and it is fulfilled in man's quest for truth and in man's living in the truth."[14]

It is one thing, however, to affirm that all human endeavors in the domain of culture should enable freedom to advance toward its fulfillment in knowing and living the truth; it is quite another thing to maintain that political freedom and freedom under the law can be restricted to those who already hold this truth. The theology and political theory that would deny civil freedom to those who do not accept the church's understanding of the truth was rejected by the Second Vatican Council. The Council's *Declaration on Religious Freedom* definitively rejected earlier Catholic teaching that "error has no rights" in the civil and political spheres. According to the Council, the right to freedom of religious belief as a human and civil right is based on the intrinsic dignity of the person, not on the truth or falsity of the religious convictions held. In a letter to the 1980 Madrid Conference on Security and Cooperation in Europe, John Paul II reaffirmed this conciliar teaching: "This concrete liberty has its foundation in man's very nature, the characteristic of which is to be free, and it continues to exist—as stated in the Second Vatican Council's declaration—'even in those who do not live up to their obligation of seeking the truth and adhering to it.'"[15] Thus, the linkage between civil freedom and adherence to truth as a political/juridical question is quite different from the fulfillment of freedom through attainment of a full vision of the human good on the level of culture.

The encyclical *Evangelium Vitae* does not distinguish these two matters with sufficient care. A generous reading would suggest that such a distinction could be drawn forth from what it says. But I am not sure this would be faithful to the actual text.[16] In any case, the unresolved practical issue remains. Ought one to challenge the skepticism and moral relativism that the Pope has rightly identified in our culture by seeking first to change the law in the hope changed laws will have an educational impact on the culture? Or, on the other hand, should one first seek to influence the culture through philosophical and religious argument, with the hope of building a new consensus that will eventually be reflected in new laws and public policies? Persons of different ideological orientations will answer this question differently depending on the area of policy that is the focus of attention. For example, some who applaud Martin Luther King's efforts to challenge the deep-seated racism of American culture by seeking civil-rights legislation support an educational view of the law on matters of race. Some of these same people would object to an educative use of law on matters such as abortion. And there are surely those who would support the opposite positions on both of these issues.

My own judgment on this question is that the appeal to law, whether the matter be race or abortion, must generally follow the cultural consensus rather than lead or form it. This does not at all mean that I accept the skepticism and sullen tolerance that has such a strong grip on the public philosophy and culture of the United States today. With the Pope, I think this cultural *mentalité* is deadly. It does mean I hope that the route of education and persuasion is more likely to improve the moral quality of our culture than is a premature reach for law, which remains coercive even when it intends to be educative. The wariness of so many Americans today is, I think, only likely to be intensified when the arm of the state enters the scene on matters about which they experience uncertainty. Whether such hope will be realized remains very much an open question. John Paul II seems to have staked the effectiveness of his recent speeches and homilies in the United States on a wager that this hope is not unreasonable. During his recent visit he dropped his references to "the culture of death" and repeatedly appealed to the better angels of American culture. I think he was well advised in doing so.

NOTES

1. *Evangelium Vitae*, English text, *Origins* 24, no. 42 (April 6, 1995): 689–727.

2. John Paul II, "Address to the U.N. General Assembly," October 10, 1995, no. 2. Text in *Origins* 25, no. 18 (October 19, 1995).

3. *EV* 20. Here the Pope, perhaps without knowing it, echoes John Courtney Murray's critique of theories of democracy that eschewed all truth claims. See, for example, John Courtney Murray, "The Church and Totalitarian Democracy," *Theological Studies* 13 (1952): 525–63. Murray borrowed the phrase from J. L. Talmon, *The Rise of Totalitarian Democracy* (Boston: Beacon Press, 1952). Murray, however, was at pains to distinguish this form of democracy from that stemming from the American founding, though some of his later work expressed serious doubts whether American public philosophy in the 1950s remained true to its own best insights. To the degree that Murray's fears have been realized in the United States today, the Pope's critique hits home in this country. I think, therefore, that the question of whether the encyclical's description of the "culture of death" applies to the United States depends on how democracy is in fact understood in the political culture of this country today. Recent discussions of this question are not encouraging.

4. John Courtney Murray, *We Hold These Truths: Catholic Reflections on the American Proposition* (New York: Sheed and Ward, 1960), pp. viii–ix.

5. See ibid., chap. 3.

6. I have outlined an interpretation of this alternative view of democracy and human rights in R. Bruce Douglass and David Hollenbach, eds., *Catholicism and Liberalism: Contributions to American Public Philosophy* (Cambridge/New York: Cambridge University Press, 1994), chap. 5 and "Afterword."

7. *EV* 19. I have discussed the way the relation of freedom and truth is understood by John Paul II and Vatican II more fully in "Freedom and Truth: Religious Liberty as Immunity and Empowerment," in *John Courtney Murray and The Growth of Tradition*, ed. J. Leon Hooper and Todd Whitmore (Kansas City, Mo.: Sheed and Ward, 1996).

8. See Joseph Cardinal Bernardin et al., *Consistent Ethic of Life*, ed. Thomas G. Fuechtmann (Kansas City, Mo.: Sheed and Ward, 1988).

9. John Rawls, "The Idea of an Overlapping Consensus," *Oxford Journal of Legal Studies* 7 (1987): 12–13. Rawls has somewhat modified his statement of this approach in *Political Liberalism* (New York: Columbia University Press, 1993), esp. lectures 4 and 6. My concern that Rawls's position remains inadequate despite the recent refinements has been briefly treated in "Public Reason/Private Religion? A Response to Paul J. Weithman," *Journal of Religious Ethics* 22, no. 1 (spring 1994): 39–46.

10. Albert Borgmann, *Crossing the Postmodern Divide* (Chicago: University of Chicago Press, 1992), 10.

11. Thus, I agree with Leslie Griffin's essay in this volume on the centrality of theology in the Pope's argument. At the same time, I think natural law plays a larger role in *Evangelium Vitae* than Griffin does. The divergence between these two readings is rooted in how the relation between faith and reason is to be interpreted.

12. M. Cathleen Kaveny's contribution to this volume develops this point. Kaveny's gradualist understanding of the educative function of law is analogous to the point I am making by distinguishing the influence of culture on law from the influence of law on culture.

13. *Centesimus Annus*, no. 41. English text, *Origins* 21 (May 16, 1991).

14. John Paul II, "Address to the U.N. General Assembly," no. 12.

15. John Paul II, "Freedom of Conscience and of Religion," letter on the eve of the Madrid Conference on European Security and Cooperation, September 1, 1980, no. 2. French original in *Acta Apostolicae Sedis* 72, no. 9 (December 29, 1980): 1252–60, at 1254. (The internal quotation is from *DH* 2.) This document is available electronically in English on the "Christus Rex" World Wide Web site: http://www.christusrex.org/. I have not been able to locate the English version in print.

16. Leslie Griffin's essay in this volume presents a plausible interpretation, revealing the ambiguity of *Evangelium Vitae* on this point.

The Moral Argumentation of Evangelium Vitae

JAMES F. KEENAN, S.J.

My task is to examine the foundational moral-theological arguments within *Evangelium Vitae*. First I acknowledge four methodological questions that have been widely discussed since its promulgation. Then I present the standard "traditional" position for the preservation of life. I also note how the distinction between direct and indirect killing emerged from this position. I then turn to the "sanctity of life" argument in the new encyclical, where I contend that despite its being overlooked[1] this is a major step forward in the moral debate about preserving life. I conclude with five questions regarding the origins of the sanctity of life in Scripture; the issues of vitalism and speciesism; the need to teach a more positive theology; and the distinctions between direct and indirect killing, innocent and guilty.

METHODOLOGICAL ISSUES

The four methodological issues that have been the major focus of recent critical reflection on the encyclical are the text's presentation, its use of Scripture, its search for dialogue, and its application. The presentation of the argument suffers. More than any of the Pope's ten other encyclicals, this one is a call to contemporary culture as it is. If only because he wants a serious hearing, the Pope should use language the way contemporary culture understands it. His gender-exclusive presentation dismisses a major cultural claim. His decision is all the more striking given his evident appreciation of language.[2] Moreover, the encyclical should have been briefer and more focused and coherent. "The characteristic meditative style" is confusing.[3] This is particularly important because, I think, this document is more than an analysis and exhortation.[4] As Bruno Schüller has shown, if an encyclical is exhortatory, then we have to look elsewhere for explanations to justify the assertions found in an encyclical.[5] But the Pope clearly is interested in putting forward new argumentation.[6] That significant commentators on the Pope have overlooked this newness highlights my point. In a word, the encyclical lacks discipline: its language should

46

be inclusive; its length should be cut; and its arguments should be more clearly presented.

Second, the use of Scripture is somewhat problematic. Certainly the Pope's turn to the Scriptures as an ample source of moral enlightenment is to be applauded. In this way he refreshingly imitates early Church leaders who plumbed the Scriptures to understand better how we are to proceed morally on the way of the Lord. Thus at the beginning we find the exposition on Cain (as we did the meditation on the rich young man in *Veritatis Splendor*), which introduces us to questions of life and death. Throughout, the Pope leads us with a variety of phrases and pericopes that are illuminating for his Gospel of life. But when in the middle of the text the Pope leaves his homiletic course and pursues doctrinal teaching, the use of Scripture should be more exact. Particularly in part 3, if he wants to demonstrate the importance of the fifth commandment as it is presented in the Scriptures, then he must convey it as it actually is understood. Again the issue of discipline is apparent; it is one matter to use the Scriptures in a homiletic, exhortatory sense; it is another to use the Scriptures as a source of specific moral teaching. The latter use requires more specific exegesis.[7]

This insistence on specific exegesis is important because the Pope (as Leslie Griffin notes in her essay) relies more on theological than on natural law argumentation.[8] Thus, using Scripture texts to support his own arguments, the Pope implicitly invokes an authority that has a greater claim on our consciences. Those selected texts, then, enjoy their authority not to the extent that they are congruent with the Pope's theology but to the extent that they are presented as faithful to the actual intent of revelation.

Third, any engagement of contemporary culture is frustrated by the encyclical's repeated attacks on it. The editors of *Commonweal* complain that the Pope unnecessarily characterizes a culture of "conflict and moral pluralism—and, yes, grave sin" as a "culture of death."[9] The Pope's stance toward moral debates and moral pluralism upholds, Jean Porter contends, a view that only the Church can determine the right. But this view fails to acknowledge adequately that its determination is itself no more than an act of judgment. She writes, "Even more than *Veritatis Splendor*, the more recent encyclical leaves no room for any acknowledgment that moral reasoning involves an ineliminable element of judgment. Correlatively, it goes further than *Veritatis Splendor* in the direction of taking the moral debates in modern society as evidences of moral corruption."[10] Porter is not alone. John O'Neill, a Marxist atheist who argues for the legitimacy of the concept of "intrinsic evil," criticizes this authoritarianism. "A central virtue of moral realism is that it is a condition for accepting that one's own views can be mistaken. . . . Hence combined with the virtue of intellectual humility, it allows space for being corrected. Correction, however, requires openness to public dissent." Writing specifically of *Veritatis Splendor*, O'Neill's words seem, in light of Porter's assessment, equally applicable to *Evangelium Vitae*: "The strong social authoritarianism of the papal document undermines the conditions for the correction of belief. Hence it undermines the grounds for claims on others to defer to its putative epistemological authority. The document defines its epistemological authority in a way that is incompatible with one necessary condition of any proper instance of it, that is, reasoned dialogue."[11]

Finally, these criticisms aside, the encyclical enjoyed a fairly good reception on the local level. Journalists and other nontheological commentators found the text to be naming something about contemporary culture that bears acknowledgment, that is, an insufficient regard for human life. But few asked whether the encyclical was accurate in its depiction of local cultures. One exception was Patrick Vespieren, who gave the encyclical a French reading. He argued that the culture of death was more glaring in the United States, where autonomy reigns, but that France, by ignoring her own practices, for example, euthanasia, has a very fragile protection of life.[12] Similarly, John Berry examined the medical culture in light of the encyclical.[13]

"TRADITIONAL" POSITION FOR THE PRESERVATION OF LIFE

In 1908, Thomas Slater wrote the first English-language manual of moral theology. There, treating the fifth commandment, he turned in true manualist[14] fashion first to suicide and declared, "The reason why suicide is unlawful is because we have not the free disposal of our own lives. God is the author of life and death, and He has reserved the ownership of human life to Himself."[15] The ownership-of-life issue was raised again in considering "mutilation" of self: "As we have not the ownership of life, so neither are we the owners of our limbs."[16] Slater's stance was repeated throughout modern times. For instance, at the beginning of his presentation on the fifth commandment, Henry Davis wrote forty years later about the duty to preserve life, "By Natural law, man enjoys the use not the dominion of his life. He neither gave it nor may he take it away. God only is the author of life."[17]

In *Casti Connubii* Pope Pius XI declared, "The life of each is equally sacred and no one has the power, not even the public authority to destroy it."[18] Commenting on this encyclical, the Australian moralist Augustine Regan added, "His successor Pius XII made many pronouncements and statements during his long pontificate. . . . He reiterates as a constant refrain that man is not the author, and consequently is never the master, of human life, which is entrusted to him as its administrator. Therefore, it is always wrong for him to dispose of it as though he were its owner. In particular it can never be justified to attack directly the life of any innocent human being."[19]

In more contemporary teachings the same argument is found. In the *Declaration on Euthanasia*, we read that suicide, like murder, "is to be considered a rejection of God's sovereignty and loving plan."[20] Gerald Coleman sums up the tradition well: "Human persons, then, have only a right to the use of human life, not to dominion over human life. What makes killing forbidden is that it usurps a divine prerogative and violates divine rights."[21]

Many of the above authors added two basic distinctions. First, only the direct taking of human life usurped God's authority; some indirect instances (indirect abortion, dangerous pain relief, etc.) were clearly considered permitted. Moreover, since there were sanctioned instances of self-defense and, in the history of capital punishment, sanctioned instances of execution, the prohibition protected *innocent* human life. To directly take innocent human life was to violate God's prerogative and rights.

The position was very disturbing. First, it suggested an incredible view of God that leaves to God, among other tasks, the work of killing. Aware that we may look on God as Lord of life with some discomfort, Pope John Paul II notes in *Evangelium Vitae*, "God does not exercise this power in an arbitrary and threatening way, but rather as part of his care and loving concern for his creatures. If it is true that human life is in the hands of God, it is no less true that these are loving hands, like those of a mother who accepts, nurtures and takes care of her child" (*EV* 39).[22]

More important, the position functioned as nothing more than a divine injunction;[23] that is, it provided no reasoned argumentation against the direct killing of the innocent. It was simply a declared prohibition. A look at Aquinas's treatment of killing illustrates how the injunction worked. In his famous question in the *Summa* on murder, Aquinas asked whether suicide is lawful. He answered negatively, giving three responses: it is against both natural inclinations and the common good, and "life is God's gift to man, and is subject to His power, Who kills and makes to live. Hence whoever takes his own life, sins against God" (*ST* II–II, 64, 5c; see *ST* I–II 73, 9, ad 2). On this last point he asked whether Samson sinned in causing his own death. Instead of invoking the principle of double effect,[24] he quoted Augustine, who argued that Samson was excused because the Holy Ghost "had secretly commanded him to do this." Aquinas even added that certain holy women, "who at the time of persecution took their own lives, and who are commemorated by the Church" were so addressed by the Holy Spirit (*ST* II–II, 64, 5, ad 4).

Later, in the question on killing the innocent, Aquinas did not raise divine dominion as an argument, but when he inquired into the licitness of

Abraham's intention to kill his son, he answered, "God is Lord of death and life, for by His decree both the sinful and the righteous die. Hence he who at God's command kills an innocent man does not sin, as neither does God whose behest he executes" (*ST* 64, 6, ad 1). Generally, Aquinas did not appeal to divine-law language to validate his moral argument, and indeed, in the section on killing it only appeared in the suicide argument. But when the divine injunction was used, he was forced to invoke specific divine contrary commands to substantiate those cases from the Scriptures that were seemingly contradictions to the general injunction.

Though Aquinas used divine-injunction language rarely, it became over the past few centuries the singular teaching position concerning the direct killing of the innocent.[25] This language is problematic on three fronts. First, secular society sees no compelling force in such language. Second, in Roman Catholic ethics the abdication of reasoned argument for such voluntaristic argumentation marks a significant shift in a longstanding tradition. Indeed, in *Evangelium Vitae* (e.g., *EV* 19, 20), John Paul II makes an important attack on the fundamentally arbitrary nature of voluntarism wherever it is endorsed. Third, were anomalies accepted, pertinent questions must still be asked regarding how we can have access to the mind—or, better, the explicit will—of God. For instance, when the American bishops' drafts of the pastoral on women declared that the restriction of priestly ordination to men is expressive of the will of the Lord, they left the reader with questions regarding hermeneutics, epistemology, moral reasoning, anthropology, and the doctrine of God.[26] Such assertions only theomorphize a voluntaristic argument. In theological circles, they are "conversation stoppers": they require obedience of the will *and* a cessation of reasoned reflection.[27]

The effects of grounding the prohibition against killing in divine-injunction language are especially problematic. Years ago, Gerald Hughes noted that if the Church were to meet the rising interests in death-dealing practices such as euthanasia, then the decision to stand against that tide needed to be based on reasoned and not voluntaristic grounds.[28] Moreover, Bruno Schüller argued that the "traditional" opposition to direct killing was nothing more than reiterating what needed to be proven: why God's will is against it.[29] In answer to these charges, Benedict Ashley agreed on the need to turn to other arguments to "bolster this *argument from God's dominion.*" Ashley also seemed to suggest that Aquinas was right to know that the argument from God's dominion should not stand alone, and that his insight should never have been abandoned. Thus, Ashley returned to the natural-inclinations argument.[30]

The voluntarism of the "God's dominion" or "divine prerogatives" position had particular effect on exceptions to any direct attack on human life. For this reason we see the manualists making an uncanny turn to the Scriptures to find passages legitimating the use of force by the state. Thus Davis wrote, "God has given to the State the right to life and death, as He has given to every man the right of self-defense against unjust aggression. This moral power of the State has been universally acknowledged in Christian tradition. It is explicitly declared in Scripture to have existed in the Jewish State (Exod. 22, 18sqq.); it was recognized in the Roman polity by St. Paul (Rom. 13,4)."[31] Slater[32] argued likewise before him, and the greatest innovator of moral theology in the twentieth century, Fritz Tillmann, wrote on the importance of Rom 13:4 and commented, "The sword is the symbol of the punitive power which the Creator has placed in the hands of legitimate authority. To the state He has confided . . . the punishment of evil-doers who harm peace and order. Hence, when it punishes, the authority does not arrogate to itself a right that belongs to God, but it exercises the power that God has confided to it."[33] Like Aquinas, those who invoked God's dominion needed to find the expressed will of God to further interpret the divine injunction against killing. Thus Davis wrote, "It is never permitted to kill oneself intentionally, without either explicit divine inspiration to do so, or—probably—the sanction of the State in the case of a just death penalty."[34]

In this context, the distinction between direct and indirect killing arose. Moralists needed to find what was permitted. Here the issue was not to find the right but, rather, the permitted, for the permitted in terms of killing was considered the exception to the general prohibition "The innocent and the just person thou shalt not put to death" (Ex 23:7).[35] In this legalistic context, the moralists looked for what the law would permit and found that where a killing could be described as indirect, proportionate reasoning could be invoked. Thus, the dividing line between the prohibited and the permitted was found on the description of the physical action of killing. Intentionality was not at stake here. Rather, free of reasoned argument, moral distinction was based on simple physical description. An indirect abortion to save a mother's life was morally permitted; a direct abortion—for the same proportionate reason and with the same intentionality—was morally prohibited. The key term for permitting the death of the innocent was that the action must be "indirect".[36] Indirect killing became a moral loophole against the divine injunction, as Schüller and others have correctly argued.[37]

We should not underestimate the voluntaristic context here. The "traditional" distinction between direct and indirect killing is not founded primarily on some reasoned ground for excluding all instances of direct killing. Rather, the distinction is founded on advancing the indirect as permissible. Moral theologians "received" both a divine injunction and, subsequently, some papal teaching. In that context, they refused to violate the divine prerogatives but sought legalistic solutions to particular moral dilemmas. Thus, about ectopic pregnancy Davis wrote, "In regard to the positive decrees of the Holy Office forbidding every direct interference with the life of the fetus, it is sufficient to state that theologians commonly hold—with negligible exceptions—that what is forbidden is *direct* interference with the fetus or embryo."[38] The distinction between direct and indirect was basically a legalistic creation articulated out of a voluntaristic context to provide some permissible grounds for killing. When the new argumentation for preserving life arises, the grounds for distinguishing the two physical actions change.

NEW MORAL ARGUMENTATION FOR THE PRESERVATION OF HUMAN LIFE

Pope John Paul II has provided other argumentation for the preservation of life besides that of divine prerogative or divine dominion. Early, in "Celebrate Life," he quoted from his address in Poland, "The Church defends the right to life, not only in regard to the majesty of the Creator, who is the first giver of this life, but also in respect of the essential good of the human person."[39] The essential good of the person has emerged more clearly as the years of his pontificate advance. Often it appears in language regarding the sanctity of life.

Surprisingly, "sanctity of life" is a rather new expression. For instance, in the fifteen-volume collection of the *New Catholic Encyclopedia*, it had no entry.[40] It appeared as a modest afterthought in the later supplement.[41] It is not found in relatively new theological dictionaries from the United States, England, or Germany: the *New Dictionary of Theology*,[42] *The Oxford Dictionary of the Christian Church*,[43] and the *Theological Dictionary*.[44] It did not appear in the German *Concise Dictionary of Christian Ethics*;[45] in Palazzini's Italian *Dictionary of Moral Theology* there was only "Life, Respect for: see Murder, Suicide."[46] Only the Anglican John MacQuarrie ran entries in the two dictionaries he edited: *A Dictionary of Christian Ethics*[47] and *The Westminster Dictionary of Christian Ethics*.[48]

The phrase first appeared in papal writings in the encyclical *Mater and Magistra* (MM 194): "All must regard the life of man as sacred, since from its inception, it requires the action of God the Creator. Those who depart from this plan of God not only offend His divine majesty and dishonor themselves and the human race, but they also weaken the inner fibre of the commonwealth."[49] This phrase became key in *Humanae Vitae* (HV 13). There Pope Paul VI used it to affirm the limited dominion that the human has over human life and human generativity. Thus, in its early use in papal encyclicals the phrase only emphasized divine prerogative.

Pope John Paul II's contribution, then, is not that he introduced the sanctity-of-life concept. What he did was to give it new meaning in the context of magisterial teaching.[50] In its original form, "sanctity of life" functioned as a euphemism for God's dominion: "Closely related to the principles of sanctity and sovereignty is the divine law prohibiting killing as found in the fifth commandment."[51] Thus, in the *Humanae Vitae* text, life is sacred because its owner, God, willed it so; like other objects that God owned and sanctified (the marital bond, the temple), life could not be violated.[52] The sacredness rested not necessarily in anything intrinsic to the marital bond, the temple, or life but, rather, singularly in the claim of God, who is definitively extrinsic to bonds, temples, and human lives. Their sacral quality rested simply in the fact that they were divine possessions. Aquinas underlined this positivistic nature of "sanctity." In distinguishing one meaning of "sanctity" as purity, he wrote of the other, "It denotes firmness, wherefore in older times the term *sancta* was applied to such things as were upheld by law and were not to be violated. Hence a thing is said to be sacred when it is ratified by law" (*ST* II–II, 81, 8c).

In Pope John Paul II's writings, the sanctity-of-life argument takes center stage. In 1987, in his apostolic exhortation *Christifideles Laici*, the Pope spoke at length about the inviolable right to life (*CL* 38). He remarked, "The inviolability of the person, which is a reflection of the absolute inviolability of God, finds its primary and fundamental expression in the inviolability of human life"[53] Nowhere did the Pope refer to God's dominion or prerogatives. Rather the argument was simply that we are in God's image; as God's person is inviolable, so is God's image.

In *Donum Vitae*, the Congregation for the Doctrine of the Faith developed the passage from *Mater et Magistra*: "From the moment of conception, the life of every human being is to be respected in an absolute way because man is the only creature on earth that God has 'wished for himself' and the spiritual soul of each man is 'immediately created by God'; his whole image bears the image of the Creator. Human life is sacred because from its beginning it involves the 'creative action of God' and it remains forever in a special relationship with the Creator, who is its sole end. God alone is Lord of life from its beginning until its end: no one can in any circumstance, claim for himself the right directly to destroy an innocent human being" (*DV* 5). The latter section, which expanded the Lord-of-life position, is repeated later in *Evangelium Vitae* 53 and becomes the singular text in the *Catechism* (no. 2258) to interpret the fifth commandment. The entire paragraph is the most extensive statement on both the sanctity of life and God as Lord of life prior to *Evangelium Vitae*. In it we see some of the key elements that later appear in the encyclical: that human life is singular, in God's image, uniquely created by God for a special relationship that is, in turn, the human's destiny; and that as source and end of human life, God is Lord of life. While not at all abandoning the Lord-of-life argument, the author of this paragraph gives it newer meaning by not emphasizing God's dominion or prerogatives but by highlighting the uniqueness of human life.

In the encyclical a certain tension between these two interests develops. On the one hand, human life has something intrinsic to it that makes it in itself inviolable; on the other hand, that which it has derives from God the Creator, who is Lord of life. Thus, a new argument for preserving life, the intrinsic worth of the human, is used to bolster the Lord-of-life argument and as a result, the Lord of life becomes less a declaration of God's sovereignty and prerogatives and more a description of the Creator. In *Evangelium Vitae* 53, these two play in tandem: "God proclaims that he is absolute Lord of the life of man, who is formed in his image and likeness (cf. GN. 1:26–28). Human life is thus given a sacred and inviolable character, which reflects the inviolability of God." Here clearly human life has *in se* an inviolable character.

Moreover, while the Lord-of-life argument recurs repeatedly, it is always asserted in relationship to God's investment into human life: "Man's life comes from God; it is his gift, his image and imprint, a sharing in his breath of life. God therefore is the sole Lord of this life: Man cannot do with it as he wills" (*EV* 39); "In the depths of his conscience, man is always reminded of the inviolability of life—his own life and that of others—as something that does not belong to him, because it is the property and gift of God the Creator and Father" (*EV* 40); "To kill a human being, in whom the image of God is present, is a particularly serious sin. Only God is the master of life!" (*EV* 55).

Still, the inviolability of life is never extrinsic to human nature, as it was in the "traditional" position. Thus, "life is indelibly marked by a truth of its own" (*EV* 48). The "Vatican Summary" highlights this: "The light of revelation, which reaches its fulness in Jesus Christ, confirms and completes all that human reason can grasp concerning the value of human life. Precious and fragile, full of promises and threatened by suffering and death, man's life bears within itself that seed of immortal life planted by the Creator in the human heart. . . . At this point we come to the decisive question, Why is life a good? Why is it always a good? The answer is simple and clear: because it is a gift from the Creator, who breathed into man the divine breath, thus making the human person the image of God."[54] The act by which God created the human is that which invests each human life with its inviolable character that now lies within the human, the image of God. The human is not to be killed, therefore, because of what the human is. This image of God is hardly extrinsic. Speaking of the Yahwist account of Creation, the Pope writes that we have within us that divine breath which draws us naturally to God (*EV* 35).

Of course, for John Paul II all of this must be understood by locating not only the source of this initiative in God but the end as well. "The plan of life given to the first Adam finds at last its fulfillment in Christ" (*EV* 35). By

Christ's blood (*EV* 9, 25) we are both strengthened and given the ground of hope that God's plan will be victorious. Indeed, in that piercing by which Christ gives up his spirit, he gives us his spirit; by his death he gives us life: "It is the very life of God which is now shared with man" (*EV* 51). Eternal life, the life that we are destined for, is "a sharing in the life of God himself" (*EV* 52), "the life of God himself and at the same time the life of the children of God" (*EV* 38). Thus, though "this supernatural calling highlights the relative character of each individual's earthly life," our earthly lives "remain a sacred reality" (*EV* 2). Because of its origin and destiny, human life remains from its very beginning until its end sacred. For this reason, "the life which the Son of God came to give to human beings cannot be reduced to mere existence in time" (*EV* 37; see 34). Thus, the life that God bestows on us, through Creation, Redemption, and the Promise, "is a drive toward fulness of life; it is the seed of an existence which transcends the very limits of time" (*EV* 34).

Throughout the text, in particular in the second section, we see greatly expanded the grounds for the inviolable character of human life. This is not simply the invoking of a sanctity-of-life position, for, as we saw earlier, all that language did was emphasize God's dominion. But in John Paul II's personalist writings something terribly distinctive about human life emerges, and all people are invited to see within human life an indelible mark of its sacredness. The Pope breathes life into the concept of sanctity of life. For the first time since the manualist era, we have reasoned argumentation that places the God's-dominion position into the context of Creation and leaves us looking at the human as having *in se* the dignity to claim inviolability.

CRITICAL QUESTIONS

Despite this groundwork five questions of considerable importance arise. First, I confess a certain confusion: I do not understand what the scriptural roots for the sanctity-of-life argument are. Does the "life" that we have as a sharing in the divine life come from God's act of Creation (and even here the Pope seems to mean both the act of creating humanity and the act by which an individual human life begins) or from Redemption? Though clearly the Pope refers more frequently to the Creation, nonetheless often (*EV* 9, 25, 34, 38, 51, 52) he argues that our participation in divine life is caused by the Redemption. Cardinal Ratzinger, for instance, insists that the Pope's anthropology is fundamentally theological and, in particular, soteriological.[55] But Antonio Autiero argues that the sanctity of life is rooted in the *imago Dei*.[56]

The issue is somewhat important for how we understand the importance of our corporeity. For instance, Elio Sgreccia insists that *Donum Vitae* places inestimable value of the person immediately in its origins and argues that the only way to understand why there is such a strong connection between the value of life and the value of procreation is the value of human corporeity.[57] A strong emphasis on corporeity results from an anthropology rooted in creation and *imago Dei* language. In *Evangelium Vitae*, however, certain scriptural texts, in particular the Johanninones, highlight the singularity of human life in terms not of our corporeity but of our being redeemed by Christ. Thus, while one might (perhaps) refer to creational texts to substantiate the teachings of an encyclical, as do *Donum Vitae* or the similar paragraphs (42–44) in *Evangelium Vitae*, it is hard to see how Johannine literature suggests God's immediate participation in procreative activity. The variety of theologies that appear in the Sacred Scriptures should not be used as a collective foundation for specific practices that regard the body and reproduction.

Second, in 1987 the conservative commentator William Buckley offered these words of advice to the pontiff: "Every age has its heresies, and the one to watch in the nuclear age is that which ends by venerating life at the expense of all other values."[58] The advice is surprisingly different from the Pope's own concerns, for the Pope has vested "life" with more intrinsic theological authority than ever. But what does he mean by "life"? The term is fluid. More to the point, at times he borders on vitalism, the doctrine that life is the highest good. True, we read, "Certainly the life of the body in its earthly state is not an absolute good for the believer" (*EV* 47). Yet throughout the text human life is accorded near sacramental status. Again, the scriptural texts are important here. Johannine literature as well as Wisdom literature do not use "life" in the same ways as the Pentateuch does. The latter writing could arguably support claims for protecting and preserving human dignity from the moment of conception, but the former do not. In the encyclical, because of a variety of scriptural texts invoked, "life" has sometimes a sacramental, a Hebraic, a christological, an eschatological, and even sometimes a very physical meaning. But those many meanings cannot be suddenly conflated, for "life" in these very different instances is nothing more than a homonym.[59] While clearly, undeniably, physical human life has never been so dignified as by this pope, that is not the intention of *all* the different Scriptural writers who use the word "life" and whose texts are used in this encyclical.

Even the very title, *The Gospel of Life*, has an odd ring to it, as Josef Fuchs notes.[60] If this Gospel is about life in a christological sense, then the title is perfectly appropriate. But the encyclical is about the inviolability of human life, and therein a high degree of moralism creeps into the understanding of the Gospel. And the Gospel becomes an instrument for morality. While the basic attempt to invest physical human life with this indelible mark is important, can anyone credibly argue that John's Gospel is a source for that claim? While

I think a scriptural case could be made for the inviolability of human life, the texts would be definitively fewer and only of particular traditions.

Third, we need to be attentive to the argument of speciesism.[61] In particular, at a time when we recognize that other mammals enjoy rational functions analogous to our own, we must ask how we can expand certain assertions that argue that "the life which God gives man is quite different from the life of all other living creatures" (*EV* 34). The exclusively anthropocentric creational theology apparent in the encyclical needs rethinking.

Fourth, this anthropocentrism appears, I think, because the purpose of the encyclical is clearly to offer theologically reasoned arguments against the killing of human beings. Creational theology (as well as the other scripturally based theologies) are marshaled to that end. But such a negative purpose truncates the theological expression that one normally associates with creational theology. In particular, it fails to recognize the particular positive responsibilities that we all share for one another and with and for all other creatures.

Finally, if the context for understanding the inviolability of life changes or at least develops significantly, do we not need to reexamine what the distinction between direct and indirect killing means? Both McCormick and Fuchs note that the philosophical meaning of the word "direct" is presently subject to a variety of interpretations.[62] But I ask, since the distinction originated from an extrinsic, voluntaristic context, does it not need reconsideration in its present context? Earlier the distinction simply meant that we had *no right* to directly take innocent human life. Does our understanding of what is morally required change when we insist within reasoned discourse that human life is *in se* sacred? Moreover, if we understand life in a creational theology that imparts to us certain responsibilities, then may we not be obliged to act where previously we were prohibited from acting? For instance, if one life is doomed inescapably to death and another is as well unless the first person is killed, can we still stand by and not act? Or are we now required to *rescue*? Can we allow a second sacred life to die when it is salvageable? The Pope has changed and developed the meaning of several key concepts and provided new argumentation for preserving life. In like manner, the changes must prompt a reexamination of the distinction between the physical acts of direct and indirect killing.[63]

Likewise the concept "innocent" needs scrutiny. Clearly, in rare times of threat or rescue we may need to kill, but the term "innocent," which belonged to the manualistic prohibited/permitted legalism, is not helpful. It infers that we are at times permitted to kill not only the aggressor but also the prisoner, not only the one who threatens but also the one who is no longer a threat. The dividing line between innocent and guilty means that we are permitted to kill on punitive grounds. Now that the sacredness of life is intrinsic to created human life, it is hard to see how we can limit the claim of preserving life only to those we deem innocent.[64] Is there reasoned argumentation that would permit us to violate this sanctity on punitive grounds, that is, beyond actual threat and rescue?

CONCLUSION

There are two important trends in moral theology today. The first was ratified by *Optatam Totius 16*, which declared that moral theology must be nurtured by the Scriptures. The second is a return to early Christian interest in the human body.[65] These two interests are tied together in *Evangelium Vitae*, which tries to preserve life by advancing new argumentation. In so doing, the Pope provides the grounds to revisit the questions of killing and preserving life in the context of theologically reasoned, and not voluntaristic or legalistic, discourse. The advance is of particular moment.

NOTES

1. Curiously, the most helpful American commentator on John Paul II, Avery Dulles, makes no reference to this in his survey of the eight major themes in this pontificate, "The Prophetic Humanism of John Paul II," *America* 169, no. 12 (October 23, 1993): 6–11. See his "John Paul II and the New Evangelization," *America* 166, no. 3 (February 1, 1992): 52–59, 69–72. Likewise, J. Bryan Hehir's position is that "neither the vision (chapter 2) nor the moral argument (chapter 3) breaks new ground," "(Get a [Culture of] Life," *Commonweal* 122, no. 10 [May 19, 1995]: 8–9, at 9).

2. On a similar note, see Lisa Sowle Cahill's remarks in her comments on *Veritatis Splendor* in "Accent on the Masculine," in *Understanding "Veritatis Splendor,"* ed. John Wilkins (London: SPCK, 1994), 52–60.

3. Richard McCormick describes the style in this way in "The Gospel of Life," *America* 172, no. 15 (April 29, 1995): 10–17, at 10.

4. See Avery Dulles's remark that "the obligatory force of a pastoral analysis and exhortation of this type is difficult to pin down" ("The Gospel of Life," *First Things* 56 [1995]: 32–33, at 32). Clearly, Dulles is only referring to its doctrinal import, but neither he nor Hehir seem to acknowledge that the Pope is proposing new argumentation.

5. Bruno Schüller, "Paranesis and Moral Argument in *Donum Vitae*," in *The Gift of Life: Catholic Scholars Respond to Vatican the Instruction*, ed. Edmund Pellegrino et al. (Washington: Georgetown University Press, 1990), 81–98.

6. Sergio Bastianel argues how distinctively this pontiff tries to find reasonable, comprehensible, and communicable arguments for moral conduct in "L'enciclica sulla morale: *Veritatis Splendor*," *Civilta Cattolica* 144 (1993): 209–19, esp. 210–11.

7. See Lisa Sowle Cahill's essays, which occasionally reflect on, among other things, the Pope's use of Scripture: *Is Catholic Ethics Biblical? The Example of Sex and Gender*, Warren Lecture Series in Catholic Studies No. 20 (Tulsa: University of Tulsa Press, 1992); *Between the Sexes: Foundations for a Christian Ethics of Sexuality* (Philadelphia: Fortress, 1985), 15–82; "Scripture and Ethics," in *Essays in Ethics*, ed. Lisa Sowle Cahill and James Childress (Pilgrim Press, 1996).

8. Leslie C. Griffin, "*Evangelium Vitae*: Abortion," this volume.

9. "Culture of Death?" *Commonweal* 122, no. 8 (April 21, 1995): 3–4, at 4.

10. Jean Porter, "Moral Reasoning, Authority, and Community in *Veritatis Splendor*," in *The Annual of the Society of Christian Ethics*, ed. Harlan Beckley (Washington: Georgetown University Press, 1995), 201–19, at 216. Related to these problems is also that of depicting others' viewpoints; see Joseph A. Selling and Jan Jans, eds., *The Splendor of Accuracy: An Examination of the Arguments Made by Veritatis Splendor* (Grand Rapids: Eerdmans, 1994).

11. John O'Neill, "Intrinsic Evil, Truth, and Authority," *Religious Studies* 31 (1995): 209–19, at 219. Russell Hittinger offers a much different position in "The Gospel of Life," *First Things* 56 (1995): 33–35.

12. Patrick Vespieren, "Pour une lecture française de l'encyclique *Evangelium Vitae*," *Etudes* (1995): 809–12. McCormick, "The Gospel of Life," echoes Vesperien's concern about the exalted American notion of autonomy.

13. John Berry, "The Gospel of Life and the Medical Profession," *Catholic Medical Quarterly* 46, no. 1 (1995): 5–13.

14. See John Conley's wonderful description of this neo-scholastic method in his essay in this collection.

15. Thomas Slater, *A Manual of Moral Theology* (New York: Benziger Brothers, 1908),1: 302.

16. Ibid., 303.

17. Henry Davis, *Moral and Pastoral Theology* (London: Sheed and Ward, 1945), 2:141.

18. Pius XI, *Encyclical Letter on Christian Marriage* (Boston: St. Paul Editions, 1930), 32.

19. Augustine Regan, *Thou Shalt Not Kill* (Dublin: Mercier Press, 1977), 29.

20. Sacred Congregation for the Doctrine of the Faith, *Declaration on Euthanasia*, in *Vatican Council II: More Postconciliar Documents*, ed. Austin Flannery (Northport, New York: Costello, 1982), 510–17, at 512.

21. Gerald Coleman, "Assisted Suicide: An Ethical Perspective," in *Euthanasia*, ed. Robert Baird and Stuart Rosenbaum (Buffalo: Prometheus Books, 1989), 103–9, at 108.

22. See also "Annunciare 'Con Coraggiosa Fedelta' il 'Vangelo della vita,'" *La Civilta Cattolica* 146 (1995): 107–17, at 111.

23. On divine command, see P. Helm, ed., *Divine Commands and Morality* (Oxford: Oxford University Press, 1981).

24. A principle he did not establish. See Josef Ghoos, "L'acte à double effet, étude de théologie positive," *Ephemerides Theologicae Lovanienses* 27 (1951): 30–52.

Ghoos attacks Mangan, who tried to make the argument. Joseph Mangan, "An Historical Analysis of the Principle of Double Effect," *Theological Studies* 10 (1949): 41–61.

25. I have the suspicion that Suarez, de Vitoria, and Cardinal de Lugo may have
developed the prohibition against killing as singularly based on the violation of divine
dominion. The sixteenth- and seventeenth-century theologians developed considerable
arguments for the divine, positive law. See John Mahoney, *The Making of Moral Theology* (Oxford: Clarendon Press, 1987), 224–58; John Treloar, "Moral Virtue and the
Demise of Prudence in the Thought of Francis Suarez," *American Catholic Philosophical
Quarterly* 65 (1991): 387–405. See also Benedict Ashley's comments, "Dominion or
Stewardship? Theological Reflections," in *Birth, Suffering, and Death*, ed. Kevin Wildes
(Dordrecht: Kluwer Academic Publishers, 1992), 85–106, esp. 95, 101.

26. See Josef Fuchs, "Our Image of God and the Morality of Innerworldly
Behavior" and "Christian Faith and the Disposing of Human Life," in *Christian Morality: The Word Becomes Flesh* (Dublin: Gill and Macmillan, 1987): 28–49; 62–82.

27. See Schüller, "Paranesis and Moral Argument in *Donum Vitae*."

28. Gerald Hughes, "Killing and Letting Die," *Month* 236 (February 1975): 42–
45; James Keenan, "Töten oder Sterbenlassen," *Stimmen der Zeit* 201 (1983): 825–37.

29. Bruno Schüller, "The Double Effect in Catholic Thought," in *Doing Evil to
Achieve God*, ed. Richard McCormick and Paul Ramsey (Chicago: Loyola University
Press, 1978), 165–92.

30. See Ashley, "Dominion or Stewardship?"

31. Davis, *Moral and Pastoral Theology* 2:151.

32. Slater, *Manual of Moral Theology*, 1:305ff.

33. Fritz Tillmann, *The Master Calls: A Handbook of Christian Living*, trans.
Gregory Roettger (Baltimore: Helicon Press, 1960), 337.

34. Davis, *Moral and Pastoral Theology*, 2:142.

35. See Slater, *Manual of Moral Theology*, 1:311.

36. Ibid., 311–14.

37. This is basically part of Schüller's broader argument in "Direct Killing/Indi-
rect Killing," in *Readings in Moral Theology*, ed. Charles Curran and Richard McCormick (New York: Paulist Press, 1979), 1:138–57; see also his "The Double Effect."
Perhaps the most thorough study of direct and indirect killing appears in the superb
work by Lucius Ugorji, *The Principle of Double Effect* (New York: Peter Lang, 1985).
Interestingly, Richard McCormick tried to find rational grounds for preserving the distinction in "Ambiguity in Moral Choice," in *Doing Evil to Achieve Good*, 7–53, esp. 30–
50.

38. Davis, *Moral and Pastoral Theology*, 2:171–82, at 180; see his series of indirect cases of killing, 143–46.

39. John Paul II, "Celebrate Life," *The Pope Speaks* 24, no.4 (1979): 371–74, at
372.

40. *New Catholic Encyclopedia* (New York: McGraw-Hill, 1967).

41. *New Catholic Encyclopedia: Supplement, 1967–1978* (New York: McGraw-
Hill, 1978) 16: 400–401.

42. *New Dictionary of Theology*, ed. J. Komonchack (Wilmington: Michael Glazier, 1987).

43. *The Oxford Dictionary of the Christian Church*, ed. F. Cross (Oxford: Oxford University Press, 1974).

44. *Theological Dictionary*, ed. K. Rahner and H. Vorgrimler (New York: Herder and Herder, 1965).

45. *The Concise Dictionary of Christian Ethics*, ed. Bernhard Stoeckle (New York: Seabury, 1979).

46. *Dictionary of Moral Theology*, ed. P. Palazzini (Westminster, Md.: Newman Press, 1962).

47. *A Dictionary of Christian Ethics*, ed. John MacQuarrie (London: SCM Press, 1967).

48. *The Westminster Dictionary of Christian Ethics*, ed. J. Childress and J. Mac-Quarrie (Philadelphia: Westminster Press, 1967).

49. John XXIII, *Mater et Magistra*, in *Gospel of Peace and Justice*, ed. Joseph Gremillion (Maryknoll: Orbis, 1976), 143–201, at 184–85.

50. Here I must note the incredible failure to acknowledge any contribution from Joseph Cardinal Bernardin. See his *Consistent Ethic of Life* (New York: Sheed and Ward, 1988). One wonders why, if Gueric of Igny could be cited in the encyclical, the concept's most articulate spokesperson was not.

51. Richard Gula, *Euthanasia* (New York: Paulist Press, 1994), 26.

52. See my "Sanctity of Life and Its Role in Contemporary Biomedical Discussion," in *Sanctity of Life and Menschenwurde: Ethical Conflicts in Modern Medicine*, ed. Kurt Bayertz (Boston: Kluwer Academic Publishers, 1996) 1–18. Also Joseph Boyle, "Sanctity of Life and Suicide: Tensions and Developments within Common Morality," in *Suicide and Euthanasia*, ed. Baruch Brody (Boston: Kluwer Academic Publishers, 1989), 221–50.

53. *Christifideles Laici*, English Text, *Origins* 18, no. 35 (1989):561, 563–89, at 579.

54. "The Vatican's Summary of *Evangelium Vitae*," *Origins* 24, no. 42 (1995): 728–30, at 729.

55. Joseph Cardinal Ratzinger, "God in John Paul II's *Crossing the Threshold of Hope*," *Communio* 22 (1995): 107–12.

56. Antonio Autiero, "Dignity, Solidarity, and the Sanctity of Human Life," in *Birth, Suffering, and Death*, ed. Kevin Wildes (Boston: Kluwer Academic Publishers, 1992), 79–83.

57. Elio Sgreccia, "Moral Theology and Artificial Procreation in Light of *Donum Vitae*," in Pellegrino et. al., *Gift of Life*, 115–36, esp. 119–20, 125.

58. William Buckley, "If I Had Five Minutes with the Pope . . . ," *America* 157, no. 6 (1987): 127.

59. On "homonym," Bruno Schüller, *Wholly Human* (Washington: Georgetown University Press, 1986).

60. Josef Fuchs, "Das 'Evangelium vom Leben' und die 'Kultur des Todes,'" *Stimmen der Zeit* 213, no. 120 (1995): 579–92.

61. See Helga Kuhse, *The Sanctity-of-Life Doctrine in Medicine* (Oxford: Clarendon Press, 1987); Helga Kuhse and Peter Singer, "Resolving Arguments about the Sanctity of Life," *Journal of Medical Ethics* 14 (1988): 198–99. That they support the

infanticide of certain handicapped infants is distinguishable from their claim that other species ought to be protected.

62. McCormick, "The Gospel of Life," 16; Josef Fuchs, "Das 'Evangelium vom Leben.'"

63. Servais Pinckaers suggests that the Pope is offering us in his recent teachings a theology that definitely requires a rethinking of the Decalogue ("The Use of Scripture and the Renewal of Moral Theology: The *Catechism* and *Veritatis Splendor*," *Thomist* 59 [1995]: 1–19).

64. See the extraordinarily eloquent testimony of Sister Helen Prejean, *Dead Man Walking* (New York: Random House, 1993).

65. For a bibliographical survey see James Keenan, "Christian Perspectives on the Human Body," *Theological Studies* 55 (1994): 330–46.

The Use of Scripture in Evangelium Vitae:

A RESPONSE TO JAMES KEENAN

ALAN C. MITCHELL

Professor Keenan notes, early in his paper, a dilemma in the use of Scripture in *Evangelium Vitae*. On the one hand, there is a welcome attempt to ground the encyclical's teaching in Scripture. On the other hand, the use of Scripture itself is problematic. Especially in part 3 is there need for a more precise exegesis of texts, where one would draw the distinction Keenan makes between the hortatory and the instructional applications of the Bible. Yet another complication arises in trying to evaluate the role of the appeal to scripture in *Evangelium Vitae*. Keenan rightly questions whether this appeal is intended perhaps to invest the encyclical's argument with greater authority than it merits.

In the section entitled "Critical Questions," Keenan revisits the problematic use of Scripture in this encyclical. He expresses confusion over the scriptural roots of the Pope's "sanctity of life" argument: whether they derive from the biblical teaching on Creation or that on Redemption. Still unclear is how the Pope's understanding of the word "life" itself relates to the ways the Bible understands the word. This lack of clarity raises a question about the extent to which the biblical view of life has been adjusted to fit the Pope's intention of dignifying human physical life in ways that might not have concerned the biblical authors he cites.

As an exegete, I applaud the Pope's attempt to base the letter's teaching in the scriptural tradition. Pope Leo XIII, in *Providentissimus Deus*, referred to Scripture as the soul of theology,[1] a role ratified by *Dei Verbum* 24. The number of biblical citations in *Evangelium Vitae* bulks large; my count finds 390 in the text alone. When you add in the section headings, the footnotes, and the "Vatican Summary," the number rises to 451. On the basis of this count, I would say Scripture has a vital role to play in *Evangelium Vitae*, but like Keenan, I too am confused by some of the ways Scripture is used in the letter, and in general I agree with Keenan that its use is problematic. This is most often the case where Scripture is used in an unsophisticated manner.

The problem, of course, is larger than the encyclical or its theme. The Pontifical Biblical Commission observed in its recent document *The Interpretation of the Bible in the Church* (3.D.3) that the relationship of exegesis to moral theology is not a simple one. First, biblical texts do not often distinguish universal moral principles from particular prescriptions and legal ordinances. Second, there is moral development within the Bible itself. So, not all biblical citations can be treated as equal in what they might yield as useful for moral theology today. When one factors in the very problematic question of the relationship between the Testaments, the matter is considerably more complicated. Third, and perhaps more germane to *Evangelium Vitae*, sometimes no biblical text explicitly addresses the moral problem under consideration. The Pope himself acknowledges this problem in *Evangelium Vitae* 61: "The texts of Sacred Scripture never address the question of deliberate abortion and so do not directly and specifically condemn it." Likewise, there are no scriptural citations in sections 11–15 of the encyclical, where the Pope describes the "eclipse" of the value of life in the contemporary world, or in sections 59–60 and 62–63, where he addresses the question of abortion itself. One notes fewer biblical citations in the sections dealing with the relationship between civil and moral law in democratic culture (*EV* 69–75) than in other parts of the encyclical.

Therefore, regarding these contemporary problems that emerge from the culture of death, the Pope seems to follow more the principle we find in Augustine: "Not because scripture says it, but because scripture does not contradict it" (*De Trinitate* 7.4.8).[2] Even if it is the case that Scripture does not contradict the arguments the Pope makes for the inviolability of life, how much better if the biblical citations employed clarified the argument and did not impede the reader's ability to grasp it. Rahner once exhorted the guild of systematic theologians thus: "Your exegesis in dogmatic theology must be convincing also to the specialist in exegesis."[3] True, the encyclical is not intended for exegetes alone. Rather, it hopes for a broad reception among all peoples regardless of their religious background or persuasion. Today Catholics and non-Catholics alike are familiar with trends in biblical interpretation and the problems that accompany it. This seems to make it even more important that the results of careful exegesis be reflected in the Church's teaching documents, lest the value of the teaching be placed in jeopardy by a less than careful use of biblical citations to undergird its arguments.

In *Evangelium Vitae*, Scripture is used in two ways. First, in the section headings scriptural citations announce themes that attempt to tie the various parts of the encyclical's arguments together. The pattern is to cite a brief text from Scripture and then to assign a theme to it. Second, Scripture is used to ground the moral arguments themselves. In both instances a unitary view of Scripture is assumed, at times, without regard to the variety of traditions represented in the Bible. The weight of the various texts quoted seems to be equal throughout *Evangelium Vitae*. The melding of distinct genres and differing authorial viewpoints as well as the ease with which the scriptural citations are placed in the letter suggest a clarity of meaning in the Bible on the divine origins of life, its value and inviolability, and its eschatological goal.

There are places in the encyclical where the use of Scripture works especially well. For example, the use of the story of Cain and Abel helps to give a quasi-narrative structure to the encyclical's first part. This arrangement helps the reader to grasp the essential steps of the Pope's argument in this section of the encyclical. There are other places, however, where it is not clear why a certain text has been selected to highlight the argument. Consequently, in these instances the use of Scripture seems only to ground the argument in a general way, and sometimes it renders the argument obscure. Thus the use of Scripture in *Evangelium Vitae* is mixed. At times it fits, and at other times it seems not to. In my opinion, the Pope's purposes would have been better served if he had omitted some of the more obscure references to Scripture and, instead, had relied more on the tradition of the Church to establish the authority he seeks for certain points. This is particularly true of those instances where the teaching of Scripture itself is not clear. Space does not permit a comprehensive treatment of the problem here, so I can give only a few examples of what I mean.

Regarding the use of the word "life" itself, many references are drawn from Johannine literature. John's Gospel is cited 55 times, the second most cited biblical book in the encyclical after Genesis, which is cited 63 times; 1 John is cited 21 times. Many of the encyclical's combined 76 references to the Johannine literature invoke the word "life." Often in this literature "life" refers to eternal life (*aiōnios zōē*), meaning the life of God as communicated through Jesus.[4] Sometimes the Pope places references to the Johannine literature in contexts where the meaning of "life" is referred to eternity, and the citations seem to work well (*EV* 1, 29, 37). In the second part of the encyclical, entitled "I Came That They May Have Life," however, there seems to be a move in the argument that is almost as enigmatic as John's Gospel itself. In *Evangelium Vitae* 29 the Pope, referring to the Johannine context of life writes, "Through the words, the actions and the very person of Jesus, man is given the possibility of 'knowing' the complete truth concerning the value of human life. From this 'source' he receives in particular the capacity to 'accomplish' this truth perfectly (cf. Jn 3:21), that is to accept and fulfill completely the responsibility of loving and serving, of defending and promoting human life." This understanding of the relationship of the revelation of Jesus to perfect accomplishment of the truth of that revelation in everyday life seems problematic. Jesus, in John, points the way to God and to eternal life (Jn 12:44–50) and in this way reveals the ultimate value and end of human life.[5] Less clear is how exactly the truth of eternal life informs our choices in everyday life.[6] For John, love is paramount. But he does not seem to specify the exercise of that love in more than a general way. While the conclusion the Pope makes here is consistent with the command to love in John, the specificity to which he concludes seems not to be so developed in John's thought.

It is not always clear to me how the citations in the section headings express the corresponding themes they are assigned. For example, in *Evangelium Vitae* 31 the relationship of the text of Ex 15:2, "The Lord is my strength and my song, and he has become my salvation," to the theme that "life is always a good" is obscure. In origin, that verse comes from a victory song attributed to Moses. In form it is a thanksgiving song, placed in the narrative after the crossing of the sea. In context it is a celebration of redemption and not a proclamation of life as a good. It seems as if the Pope himself understands this problem as he tries to reason through the section: "Thus in coming to know the value of its own existence as a people, Israel also grows in its perception of the meaning and value of life itself. This reflection is developed more specifically in the wisdom literature on the basis of daily experience of the precariousness of life and awareness of the threats which assail it" (*Evangelium Vitae* 31). Perhaps in light of the Pope's own observation, the truth of life's value could have been grasped better with the citation from Job 2:4, "All that people have they will give to save their lives," than with Ex 15:2. But that having been said, one has to recognize that if the wisdom literature expresses the value of life as a good, it also relativizes it. Sirach 29:24 speaks of how miserable the life of a wanderer is, and in 30:17 teaches that death is better than a life of misery. Later in 40:28 we read that it is better to die than to be a beggar.

Problematic, too, are the scriptural references in the sections dealing with the dignity of life in the womb. Psalm 139:13 is cited in the heading of *Evangelium Vitae* 44, "'For you formed my inmost being' (Ps 139:13): the dignity of the unborn child." In the section following, other references to life in the womb are included, such as Jer 1:5, "Before I formed you in the womb I knew you, and before you were born I consecrated you." There follows a citation from Job 10:8–12, who refers to the creative work on his behalf in his mother's womb. Given the theme of this section, the Pope understands these references to support the argument that in ancient Israel's religious and cultural life there was universal agreement on the dignity of the fetus: "Although there are no direct and explicit [biblical] calls to protect human life at its very beginning, specifically life not yet born, and life nearing its end, this can easily be explained by the fact that the mere possibility of harming, attacking or denying life in these circumstances is completely foreign to the religious and cultural way of thinking of the people of God" (*Evangelium Vitae* 44). By citing texts in that section, the Pope is right to call attention to a motif used in some of the Psalms, wisdom literature, and prophetic writings. Sometimes this motif is applied to the formation of Israel herself, as in Is 44:2, "Thus says the

Lord who made you, who formed you in the womb and will help you." It is indeed curious that this text is not cited in the encyclical. The motif is also a stock element of the prophetic call, as in Jer 1:5. In these instances, it points to the special relationship between Israel and God or between Israel and the prophet, whom God has destined to that role from the moment of conception. Implicitly, one could argue that such care and tending speak to the value of unborn life, and I don't dispute that. When one looks at Ex 21:22–25, however, the question of the value of that life from the point of conception could be seen in a different light.

> "When people who are fighting injure a pregnant woman so that there is a miscarriage, and yet no further harm follows, the one responsible shall be fined what the woman's husband demands, paying as much as the judges determine. If any harm follows, then you shall give life for life, eye for eye, tooth for tooth, hand for hand, foot for foot, burn for burn, wound for wound, stripe for stripe (NRSV)."

This legal text addresses the case of a pregnant woman who is injured when others around her are fighting and, as a result, suffers a miscarriage. If the woman is not further injured, the penalty stipulated is a fine. If, however, the woman suffers additional injury, then the *lex talionis* is to be applied. In this case the penalty imposed for the miscarriage is different from that imposed for further injury to the mother. When this text is translated into Greek in the Septuagint, it is further qualified by a distinction between the status of the fetus's development. In third-century Alexandria the fine is to be imposed if the fetus is not yet fully formed, and the *lex talionis* in the case of a fully formed fetus. There is no reference here to injury done the mother. As Connery points out, the fully formed fetus had greater valuation in the Septuagint than in the Masoretic text, indicating that there was some development in Jewish thought on the status of the fetus as human in the biblical period.[7] These texts show ambiguity about the value of fetal life from the very moment of conception, despite the other witnesses that extol the wonders of God's creative love by use of this metaphor.

On the relation of civil law to moral law in *Evangelium Vitae* 68, the Pope cites Acts 5:29, "We must obey God rather than men." What is interesting here is that the original situation of this text does not address a conflict between civil law and moral law. The setting is the second trial of the Apostles before the Sanhedrin, who had forbidden them to teach in the name of Jesus (Acts 4:18). Peter's response echoes the one he gave in the first trial, and he argues for their right to continue their preaching.[8] The problem with the way the encyclical uses this text is that it presupposes a modern distinction between the secular and the religious in the spheres of the Sanhedrin's authority.[9] Rather, these spheres were integrated, and if an analogy for modern distinction between church and state is appropriate here, it should probably be located in the relationship between the Sanhedrin and the Roman imperial government. Thus, the text supports the right of religious dissent in an intrareligious dispute and not the right to except themselves from the secular law. Therefore, it strikes me as a little odd that this text should be used in support of the distinction between civil and moral law. The principle of obeying a higher authority may be a part of the Church's received moral tradition, but the situation described in Acts 5:29 seems not to support that in the way the Pope intends it to.

One last example comes from the use of 1 Jn 1:4 in *Evangelium Vitae* 101: "'We are writing this that our joy may be complete' (1 Jn 1:4): The Gospel of life is for the whole of human society." In this first Johannine letter the immediate audience is Christians who have been divided by factionalism.[10] The author writes this to bind these Christians more closely to himself. The joy referred to there is an eschatological benefit received on becoming a believer and entering the Johannine community. The completion of that joy is the growth of a gift received earlier—a growth achieved through *koinōnia* with God, Christ, and other Johannine Christians. In the New Testament, *koinōnia* refers to the sharing among Christians. It seems only to be possible among Christians with one another. In this section, the Pope develops the argument that the Gospel of life is not for believers alone: it is for everyone. But on the basis of what I just said about joy and *koinōnia* in 1 Jn 1:3–4, it is difficult to see how the Gospel of life can be shared with nonbelievers. I do not doubt that, were it to take place, it would be good and a milestone in the relationship between the Church and nonbelievers. Given the demands of fellowship in the New Testament, however, I wonder how possible it is.

In sum, the use of Scripture in *Evangelium Vitae* is uneven: sometimes it works to enhance the argument, and sometimes it does not. Although many scriptural references are included in the document, their function is not always clear to me, and at times, they seem to impede the easy flow of the argument. As can be the problem with proof-texting, citations are at times taken out of context and are made to fit arguments in less than precise ways. The approach the Pope takes is synchronic rather than diachronic, and there is always the danger of rendering Scripture ahistorical in synchronic methods of interpretation.[11] I don't want to say that there is no room for a synchronic approach to Scripture, for surely there is. Catholic biblical scholarship in the last fifty years, however, has largely followed diachronic methods of interpretation. Since the encyclical hopes for a positive reception from a broad audience made up of Catholics and non-Catholics, Christians and non-Christians, indeed believers and nonbelievers, a more historically and contextually based exegesis of scriptural texts may have helped to render the encyclical's important arguments more accessible to the broad constituency it addresses.

NOTES

1. Leo XIII, *Providentissimus Deus*, found in *Acta Sanctae Sedis* 26 (1893–94): 269–92; *Enchiridion Biblicum*, 4th ed. (Naples: M. D'Auria, 1961), no. 114. Cf. Joseph A. Fitzmyer, S.J., *The Biblical Commission's Document "The Interpretation of the Bible in the Church": Text and Commentary*, Sources bibliques 18 (Rome: Editrice Pontificio Istituto Biblico, 1995), 158.

2. Cf. Joseph A. Fitzmyer, S.J., *Scripture, the Soul of Theology* (New York/Mahwah, N.J.: Paulist Press, 1994), 80.

3. Karl Rahner, "Exegesis and Dogmatic Theology," in *Theological Investigations* (Baltimore: Helicon; New York: Crossroad, 1966) 5:77; cf. Fitzmyer, *Scripture, the Soul of Theology*, 83.

4. John's Gospel uses two nouns for the word "life," *zōē* (33 times) and *psychē* (9 times), reserving the latter for physical earthly life. In the Johannine letters *zōē* occurs 11 times and *psychē* twice. On the meaning of "life" in John, see Raymond E. Brown, *The Gospel according to John I–XII*, Anchor Bible 29 (Garden City, N.Y.: Doubleday, 1966), 505–8; Rudolf Schnackenburg, *The Gospel according to St. John*, vol. 2, *Commentary on Chapters 5–12* (New York: Crossroad, 1982), 352–61.

5. Schnackenburg, 419–25.

6. According to Schnackenburg (*Commentary on Chapters 5–12*, 361), "the Johannine idea of life has no direct connection with life in society or the future of the human race." Cf. ibid., 259–70, 352–60.

7. For a full discussion of this textual phenomenon, see John Connery, S.J., *Abortion: The Development of the Roman Catholic Perspective* (Chicago: Loyola University Press, 1977), 8–17.

8. See Luke Timothy Johnson, *The Acts of the Apostles*, Sacra Pagina 5 (Collegeville, Minn.: Liturgical Press, 1992), 94–104.

9. See Anthony J. Saldarini, "Sanhedrin," in *The Anchor Bible Dictionary*, ed. David Noel Freedman (New York, London, Toronto, Sidney, Auckland: Doubleday, 1992), 5: 975–80.

10. I depend here on the interpretation of the prologue of 1 John given by Raymond E. Brown, *The Epistles of John: A New Translation with Introduction and Commentary*, Anchor Bible 30 (Garden City, N.Y.: Doubleday, 1982), 151–88.

11. On the distinction between diachronic and synchronic methodologies, see Fitzmyer, *The Biblical Commission's Document*, 19–20. Some might suggest that in taking a synchronic approach, the Pope is following recent developments in biblical interpretation, which favor this methodology. Upon examination, however, it seems that the Pope does not employ these contemporary forms of biblical interpretation either. It is difficult to locate the method of interpretation used in *Evangelium Vitae*. For a brief

introduction to contemporary methods of biblical interpetation, see Fitzmyer, *The Biblical Commission's Document*, 26–101; Steven L. McKenzie and Stephen R. Haynes, eds., *To Each Its Own Meaning: An Introduction to Biblical Criticisms and Their Application* (Louisville, Ky.: Westminster/John Knox, 1993). For an evaluation of some of the problems of synchronic methodologies, see Fitzmyer, *Scripture, the Soul of Theology*, 39–53.

Sanctity of Life and Its Implications:
REFLECTIONS ON JAMES KEENAN'S ESSAY

JOSEPH BOYLE

Since sanctity of life is plainly a key idea in this encyclical and in James Keenan's essay about it, I will focus in these comments on how, in Keenan's view, Pope John Paul has developed this important idea and on Keenan's views about the implications of these developments. I assume, as I believe Keenan does, that "sanctity of life" is the name of a moral argument; it does not refer simply to the inviolability of human life or to its value but to the grounding of that inviolability in some property, or relationship, or value that a human life must have.

Keenan's thesis is that John Paul has used the language of the sanctity of life to formulate a new basis for Catholic teaching on the ethics of killing, including abortion, suicide, and euthanasia. The relatively recent language of sanctity of life originally developed, at least within the Catholic tradition, within the normative framework that emphasized the divine dominion over human life. In this view, killing is wrong because God, not humans, is the Lord of life, and life's sanctity is found in this extrinsic relationship to its Lord. This divine dominion over human life is, according to Keenan, the basic ground for rejecting killing within the manualist tradition and within magisterial teaching during most of this century. With John Paul, however, sanctity of life is developed into an idea in which the grounds for the inviolability of human life are not extrinsic but intrinsic to it.

The intrinsic basis for the inviolability of human life is indicated in several ways in this encyclical and in prior magisterial teaching influenced by John Paul's development. It seems to me that there are at least three distinct affirmations here: each human life is immediately created by God; humans are created in God's image; humans are created for a special relationship with God (I think it would be more precise to say that humans are created in order that each uniquely instantiate a special kind of relationship to God, but the Pope and Keenan are not explicit on this). As Keenan indicates, each of these interconnected affirmations makes reference to God. Moreover, independently and together they provide a reason why a special form of divine dominion over human life is normatively appropriate. So, these affirmations seem to bolster the rationale for the traditional Catholic norms on killing.

Still, at least two of these affirmations plainly indicate properties of human beings: to say of something that it images something else presupposes that we know something about what is imaged but the predication is about the image, not what it images; and a creature's destiny is its destiny, even if it would not have that destiny except for its Creator's plans and action. Keenan suggests that even the special creation of each person tells us of something intrinsic to the person: "The act by which God created the human is that which invests each human life with its inviolable character that now lies within the human, the image of God."

Sanctity of life, then, at least as developed by John Paul, becomes a basis for the inviolability of human life that is found in what human beings are, not in extrinsic relationships, such as that of divine dominion. Quite the opposite, divine dominion over human life, as a moral consideration, is now grounded in the intrinsic character of human life. Human life would not have this character had God not created it as he does and for the purposes he has, but this feature is located within what God created human beings to be and to become.

This account of John Paul's teaching seems to me correct and important to the extent it underlines the inherent dignity of human beings.

Keenan wonders how this idea is verified in Scripture. Sanctity of life is developed in *Evangelium Vitae* from a variety of scriptural sources that appear to be talking about different aspects of human life and even about different meanings of the term "life." But if part of the story about the inherent dignity of humans and their bodily lives emerges in the creation accounts and the image-of-God statements and if a further part emerges in what John and Paul say about the destiny each person has because of Jesus' redemptive activity and God's response to it, perhaps the full story needs to depend on all of what Scripture teaches and all of what the Church believes about these matters, even if some parts of Scripture support some but not all aspects of the complex idea the Pope has developed as sanctity of life.

Still, there does seem to be a real problem about the roots of the sanctity-of-life idea in revelation. For the transcendent greatness of God and the fundamental importance of keeping his law seem to swamp altogether any ideas about the inviolability of the lives of those who run afoul of either. The implications for the ethics of killing abound in the Old Testament. A plain reading of many passages in the Old Testament has seemed to many Catholics, both theologians and others, to teach that divinely authorized killing is morally permissible and perhaps in some cases mandatory. These scriptural accounts occur often enough and their message has seemed plain enough that the Church's greatest theologians, for example, Aquinas, had very complex and seemingly ad hoc stories to tell about the ethics of killing. The Old Testament passages and the theological accounts are hard to square with a modern, humanistic, and Kantian story about the intrinsic dignity of human life— namely, the kind of story the Pope wants to tell and Keenan recounts. Nobody would suppose that Abraham, Moses, Joshua, or King David held developed sanctity-of-life views or that the authors of the scriptural accounts about them meant to affirm any such idea.

Still, many of us late-twentieth-century Christians are convinced that the scriptural passages that caused the Catholic theology of the ethics of killing to become so complex and unsatisfying do not really represent God's revelation. I suspect that Keenan and I agree on this. Something like the Pope's developed idea of sanctity of life seems correct to many of us: "Only he or she can rightly kill who is authorized to kill" seems not only incomplete but somehow wrong, offensive to human dignity.

But if the problem with the roots of a developed sanctity-of-life concept lies in a plain reading of scriptural texts, the divine-dominion ethics of killing likely goes deeper in the tradition than the manualists and the limits of their approach to moral theology. Aquinas, for example, although no manualist and surely not a voluntarist in normative theory, articulates an ethics of killing that I would characterize as an ethics of authorization: no one may kill intentionally unless one is authorized to do the killing in question. The final authority, presumably, is God, the Creator and Lord of life, and, of course, authority is understood nonvoluntaristically as service to the common good by those in certain social roles. Most of the authorized are authorized by their role and by the requirements of carrying it out; some few are directly authorized by divine inspiration.[1]

I think Aquinas gives hints of a view of killing based on the inherent dignity of human persons, for example, in what he says about suicide being contrary to the love people should have for their own selves, in the objection to capital punishment that killing is always according to itself wrong because of the charity we should have for all human beings, and in his premise in the discussion of killing the innocent that even in the case of sinners we should love the nature that God created.[2] But these hints are all but swamped by considerations concerning who is authorized and who is not authorized to kill. Keenan has noted the special dispensations to handle the troublesome Scripture passages, but I think the authorization idea runs through the entire question. Capital punishment is justified by reference to the common good, and so only those officials with responsibility for the common good may rightly punish criminals. The innocent they may not punish, as their authority is limited by service to the common good, which cannot be served by killing the innocent. And those other than the authorized may not intentionally kill, even if they act for the common good; indeed, those other than public officials may use lethal force in self-defense only if the attacker's death is *praeter intentionem*. Presumably, they lack authorization to kill intentionally.

If, as I believe, there is a tension between the sanctity-of-life elements and the ethics-of-authorization elements in Aquinas's story, I would like to see them settled in favor of the former.[3] But part of my reason for talking about Aquinas here is to suggest the extent of the problem John Paul's development takes on and to suggest that one can hold the divine-dominion view of the ethics of killing with little or no commitment to a voluntaristic normative theory.

Presumably, if one holds for a divine-dominion view on killing and is not a voluntarist, then one must also hold what Benedict Ashley appears to believe: that there must be some very special reason why God has such a special and immediate concern over the disposition of human life. Sanctity-of-life considerations come to mind and seem to do this work in the encyclical. But if divine dominion is a subordinate element in a view dominated by sanctity-of-life concerns, then one cannot have reasoning like St. Thomas's—reasoning in which the authorization to kill overrides the inherent dignity of the person. So, I cannot see how anything like St. Thomas's argument for capital punishment can be sustained if one takes the Pope's strong sanctity-of-life position as one's framework, even though the encyclical seems to allow it as an extreme form of social self-defense (*EV* 56). More generally, I agree with Keenan about the use of the concept of innocence within the tradition as a basis for limiting the scope of the prohibition against killing. Whatever motivated this limitation, it does not make much sense if the inherent value of human beings is the most basic reason for prohibiting the killing of humans; it is being human, not being guilty or innocent, that counts.[4]

But Keenan sees another implication of the encyclical's developed sanctity-of-life view that I think is questionable. He does not think the direct/indirect distinction can be maintained in the new conceptual terrain defined by the encyclical. Keenan thinks that this distinction originated in the voluntaristic context of the manualist tradition and at least needs rethinking in the new context determined by John Paul's development.

I agree with Keenan that this distinction can mean various things. The language is plainly causal and behavioristic. But one plausible interpretation is that it marks the distinction between what is brought about intentionally and what is brought about as a side effect but not intentionally. Thus understood, the direct/indirect distinction marks the intended/merely permitted (or merely accepted) distinction, which is not a behavioral or causal difference but a difference in willing. Perhaps there are two distinctions here, and perhaps, as I think more likely, the direct/indirect distinction is a muddled way of getting at the intended/accepted distinction. Whichever it is, the incompatibility of the behavioristic distinction between direct and indirect causality with the Pope's sanctity-of-life position does not imply that the volitional distinction between intended and accepted outcomes will not provide for a very similar, double-effect-style casuistry within a sanctity-of-life framework.

The moral significance of this volitional difference goes deep into the Christian view of things. God causes all that is but does not intend evil. He permits or accepts it; he does not choose or intend it. Aquinas makes use of the distinction to draw an important moral boundary in his discussion of killing in self-defense: a private person may not intentionally kill an assailant, but may cause death if it is *praeter intentionem* and if other conditions are met.

But Aquinas never says much about why this difference should be such an important moral dividing line. Here he simply announces that moral acts receive their species according to what is intended and not by virtue of what is *praeter intentionem* since that is accidental.[5] Not much of a proof—and not, as it stands, either sound or easy to square with the rest of Aquinas's story about action. For example, what are we to say when an action is wrong in the first instance because of an expected side effect? Here the side effect is not intended but morally decisive—hardly accidental. As far as I can discover, the tradition does not do better than St. Thomas in vindicating the moral significance of this distinction. But this inadequacy does not seem to me to be evidence that the moral use of the volitional distinction is simply a function of the manualist tradition and its voluntarism.

In Aquinas the distinction does not function as a loophole and does not seem to depend on the ethics of authorization, which justifies the applicable norms. Surely, the distinction can be used or abused as a loophole, but this is true of many concepts and principles in ethics. Our tradition has much conceptual space for loopholes; why did it pick this one? Perhaps because this difference appears so deeply embedded in the common moral discourse and legal thought that was shaped by Christian moral conceptions. Given this, it is not surprising that people have given it a place of privilege within the laxist casuistry we all use to get ourselves off the hook. This misuse would be far less common and useful for rationalizing if the basic idea behind the distinction were not very compelling.

I think it is compelling partly because there is a difference in the kind of responsibility we have for bad side effects and for what we intend: we can always refrain from an intentional action, but we cannot always, perhaps not ordinarily, refrain from causing harmful side effects. This means that if we think that a rational ethics includes prohibitions against inflicting certain kinds of harms on people, such as killing them, we cannot take these prohibitions as absolute unless they are limited to prohibiting intentional harming. A more broadly stated norm tells one to do what is often impossible: this is not the legalistic idea that such a norm would be too demanding but an application of the rationalist idea that ought implies can.[6]

If the case for the moral significance of the distinction between what is intended and what is brought about as a side effect can be made out along these lines (most of whose elements are in the tradition), then this significance holds more obviously within a sanctity-of-life normative view than within a more voluntaristic view. If harms to people are excluded because of the inherent dignity of the persons harmed, the limits on the exclusions cannot be based on the permissions of higher authority; the limits must be based on the values at stake in the action as a voluntary human initiative.

Keenan's question about a rescue that involves killing one who is to die so as to save another (which I take him to understand as not explicable in double-effect terms) puts all the weight on the value—the sacredness of the lives—involved. But it seems to me that Christian ethics, with its lively sense of divine providence, is too systematically agent-relative to allow the weight to rest on the value alone and not on a consideration of the value in light of the agent's limited responsibilities for the governance of the universe. As I indicated at the outset, sanctity of life indicates a moral argument, not simply a value. If I am right, the direct/indirect distinction, understood as a volitional distinction, marks one inevitable limit to an agent's responsibility: I can refrain from killing intentionally but not from being causally involved in bringing about death. The restrictive implication is primary: life is sacred; I can always refrain from intentionally taking life, so I must never do that. We cannot be so stringent when it is causing death as a side effect, but that does not mean we should be permissive. This reasoning may be a mistake, but it is not voluntarism.

NOTES

1. *ST* II–II, q. 64, a. 2. The discussion of capital punishment is the clearest example of what I call the ethics of authorization. The logic runs through q. 64. The first condition for justified warfare involves the same moral outlook; see q. 40, a. 1.

2. The texts I have in mind are respectively *ST* II–II, q. 64, a. 5; and a. 2, obj. 3 and a. 6.

3. See my "Sanctity of Life and Suicide: Tensions and Developments within Common Morality," in *Suicide and Euthanasia*, B. Brody, ed. (Dordrecht: Kluwer, 1989), pp. 240–47.

4. See J. Finnis, et al., *Nuclear Deterrence, Morality, and Realism* (Oxford: Oxford University Press, 1987), 309–19, for a development of this position with some qualifications.

5. *ST* II–II, q. 64, a. 7.

6. See my "Who is Entitled to Double Effect?" *Journal of Medicine and Philosophy* 16 (1991): 486–93.

Infallible Teaching on Moral Issues? Reflections on Veritatis Splendor and Evangelium Vitae

FRANCIS A. SULLIVAN, S.J.

The First Vatican Council defined that the Pope has the same infallibility that an ecumenical council has in defining doctrine of faith and morals. While at the Council of Trent the term *mores* had a rather broad meaning, including various Christian practices, by the time of Vatican I it had come to signify what we mean by "morals." It is certainly a dogma of Vatican I that the Church can define moral doctrine with infallibility. But this does not include all moral doctrine, regardless of its connection with revelation. The official explanation of the terms of the definition, given by Bishop Gasser, spokesman of the *Deputatio de fide*, made it clear that to be definable, a doctrine must be either revealed, or necessary for the defense or exposition of revealed truth.[1] In other words, it must belong either to the primary or to the secondary object of infallibility.[2]

This raises the question whether all matters of natural law morality are capable of being infallibly taught, as belonging at least to the secondary object of infallibility. Umberto Betti, a consultor for the Congregation for the Doctrine of the Faith, gave a positive answer to this question in his commentary that accompanied the publication of the new Formula for the Profession of Faith: "One can include in the object of irreformable definitions, even though not of faith, everything that pertains to the natural law, this also being an expression of the will of God."[3] The Congregation for the Doctrine of the Faith, however, in its 1990 *Instruction on the Ecclesial Vocation of the Theologian*, took a more restricted view: "Revelation also contains moral teachings which *per se* could be known by natural reason. Access to them, however, is made difficult by man's sinful condition. It is a doctrine of faith that these moral norms can be infallibly taught by the Magisterium."[4] It is obvious that "these moral norms" are the ones that are also contained in revelation. The same passage of the *Instruction* speaks of the "competence" of the magisterium with regard to "that which concerns the natural law," but "competence" does not necessarily include the capacity to teach with infallibility.

One can distinguish three levels of Church teaching on this question. It is a dogma of faith, defined by Vatican I, that the Church can infallibly define moral doctrine that is formally revealed. It is the teaching of Vatican II (though not solemnly defined) that the consensus of the ordinary universal magisterium would be infallible when it proposed a point of revealed moral doctrine as definitively to be held. It is official Catholic doctrine that the magisterium can teach with infallibility on moral doctrine that is not revealed but necessary for the defense or exposition of revealed truth. It is not certain, however, that it has actually done any of these things. Before taking up that question, it might be worthwhile to ask: what would be the effect of such infallible teaching if it did take place?

If it were certain that the Church had spoken with infallibility on some moral issue, it would mean that it had taken an irreversible stand, on which it could not be mistaken. There would be room for interpretation and further refinement of the Church's position, but there would be no room for dissent. So the practical effect for Catholic theologians would be the elimination of the possibility of legitimate and responsible dissent from the Church's teaching on that issue.

The next question is: has the Church ever taught any point of its moral doctrine with infallibility? I believe that there is no certain instance of a solemn definition of moral doctrine, even though some Catholic theologians did see such a definition in the condemnation of contraception by Pope Pius XI in *Casti Connubii*.[5] Nowadays those who claim that the Church has taught some moral doctrines with infallibility appeal rather to the infallible exercise of the ordinary universal magisterium. They say that on certain issues, the teaching of the Church meets the conditions laid down by Vatican II when it said, "Although the individual bishops do not enjoy the prerogative of infallibility, they do nevertheless proclaim Christ's doctrine infallibly even when dispersed around the world, provided that while maintaining the bond of communion among themselves and with Peter's successor, and teaching authoritatively on a matter of faith or morals, they are in agreement that a particular judgment is to be held definitively" (*LG* 25, my translation).

John C. Ford and Germain Grisez claimed that these conditions were fulfilled in the church's teaching on contraception.[6] More recently Joseph Boyle, John Finnis, and William E. May have joined Grisez in stating, "It is beyond reasonable doubt that the Church's teaching that contraception is always wrong has been infallibly proposed by the ordinary magisterium. This teaching ought to be accepted by every Catholic as a matter of faith."[7] William E. May has extended such a claim to the whole "core of Catholic moral teaching":

A strong case can be made that the core of Catholic moral teaching, as summarized in the Ten Commandments *as these have been traditionally understood within the Church* (for instance, by medieval theologians) and as set forth in such sources as the *Roman Catechism*, which was mandated by the Council of Trent and used universally throughout the world to instruct the faithful for centuries, has been taught infallibly. . . . In sum, Vatican II definitely teaches that the magisterium does teach infallibly on questions of morality when specific conditions are met, and I submit that these conditions have been met with respect to the core of Catholic moral teaching concerning the inviolability of innocent human life, the evil of adultery and fornication and similar issues. [8]

The claim that a doctrine has been taught infallibly by the ordinary universal magisterium is obviously seen as a way to put an end to dissent by Catholic theologians on the issue. Cardinal Ratzinger invoked this argument in the final letter of his correspondence with Charles Curran—the one in which he declared that Curran was "no longer suitable nor eligible to exercise the function of a Professor of Catholic Theology." In this letter Ratzinger said,

> Your basic assertion has been that since your positions are convincing to you and diverge only from the "non-infallible" teaching of the Church, they constitute "responsible" dissent and should therefore be allowed by the Church. In this regard the following considerations seem to be in order.
>
> First of all, one must remember the teaching of the Second Vatican Council which clearly does not confine the infallible magisterium purely to matters of faith nor to solemn definitions. *Lumen Gentium* 25 states . . . [here he cites the passage given above on the infallible exercise of ordinary universal magisterium]. Besides this, the Church does not build its life upon its infallible magisterium alone but on the teaching of its authentic, ordinary magisterium as well. [9]

While the cardinal did not give any specific example of a teaching that has been taught with infallibility by the ordinary universal magisterium, he obviously implied that some of the doctrines on which Curran claimed to express responsible dissent have been infallibly taught and hence allow no such dissent. In the following passage of the same letter, he did seem to propose the Church's teaching on abortion as an example of infallible teaching:

> In light of these considerations, it is clear that you have not taken into adequate account, for example, that the Church's position on the indissolubility of sacramental and consummated marriage, which you claim ought to be changed, was in fact defined at the Council of Trent, and so belongs to the patrimony of the Faith. You likewise do not give sufficient weight to the teaching of the Second Vatican Council when in full continuity with the Tradition of the Church it condemned abortion, calling it

an "unspeakable crime." In any case the faithful must accept not only the infallible magisterium.[10]

While Ratzinger asserted that the teaching on the indissolubility of marriage had been solemnly defined,[11] the last sentence implied that the doctrine on abortion had also been infallibly taught. The phrase "in full continuity with the Tradition of the Church" suggests that he saw it as fulfilling the conditions for the infallible teaching of the ordinary universal magisterium.

This brings us to the main question we are proposing: do the encyclicals *Veritatis Splendor*[12] and *Evangelium Vitae*[13] offer papal support to the claim that some moral doctrines have been infallibly taught by the ordinary and universal magisterium? I shall discuss the two encyclicals in the order of their publication.

VERITATIS SPLENDOR

In the first in the series of articles that the *Tablet* published on this encyclical, Germain Grisez offered an interpretation of the mind of Pope John Paul II that, if correct, would strengthen the case of those who look for infallible teaching on moral matters. The key points of his interpretation are as follows:[14]

> While nowhere treating the magisterium's infallibility, he [the Pope] everywhere teaches that the exceptionlessness of the relevant norms is a revealed truth—that is, a truth demanding from every Catholic the assent of faith. Thus the appeal is to God's authority in revealing, which is the source of the Church's infallibility in believing and the magisterium's authority in teaching.
>
> In claiming that the received teaching concerning intrinsically evil acts is a revealed truth, the Pope also implicitly asserts that it is definable.

Grisez has focused his attention on the key assertion of the encyclical, concerning the exceptionless norms that forbid intrinsically evil acts, and has interpreted the Pope to find this teaching in revelation. What I am concerned about is whether one might go further and interpret the encyclical to mean that all traditional Catholic moral doctrine is, in the final analysis, the Church's interpretation of the contents of the Ten Commandments as reaffirmed and further specified in the New Testament. If this truly reflects the mind of the Pope in *Veritatis Splendor*, then it would follow that the authority of the magisterium in teaching moral doctrine is really its authority to interpret revealed truth. This would mean that all moral questions fall within the primary object of the Church's infallibility. Furthermore, it could be argued that "traditional Catholic moral teaching," by virtue of being "traditional," would already satisfy the requirements laid down in Vatican II for the infallible teaching of the ordinary universal magisterium. In other words, Grisez and others could argue that not only the doctrine on artificial contraception but many other doctrines of traditional Catholic morality have already been infallibly taught, since they would fall within the primary object of infallible teaching and, as "traditional," would have been the common teaching of the whole episcopate together with the popes for many centuries. If this position were sustained by Church authorities, then no dissent on the part of Catholic theologians concerning the Church's traditional moral doctrine would be tolerated, since it would no longer be a question of dissenting from nondefinitive and possibly reformable teaching but, rather, from the Church's definitive and therefore irreformable interpretation of revealed truth.

It is obviously important, then, to try to determine whether this encyclical is correctly interpreted to mean that it is the mind of Pope John Paul II that the Church's authority on moral issues is effectively its authority to interpret revealed truth, in which it enjoys the assistance of the Holy Spirit that guarantees the infallibility of its definitive judgments.

I am not aware of any official document, prior to *Veritatis Splendor*, that based the authority of the magisterium in moral matters on the grounds that the whole moral law was contained in revelation. If this is what Pope John Paul really means to say, then in my opinion this encyclical would strengthen the position of those, such as William E. May, who claim that "the core of Catholic moral teaching . . . as set forth in such sources as the *Roman Catechism*" has been infallibly taught. Indeed, one could expect a similar claim to be made for the "core of Catholic moral teaching" as set forth in the new *Catechism of the Catholic Church*. What I wish to do, then, is to determine whether *Veritatis Splendor* is correctly interpreted to assert that the whole moral law is contained in revelation.

The following are some passages of the encyclical that suggest to me that this is indeed what Pope John Paul II means to say:

Consequently the decisive answer to every one of man's questions, his religious and moral questions in particular, is given by Jesus Christ himself, or rather is Jesus Christ himself. (*VS* 2)

The specific purpose of the present Encyclical is this: to set forth, with regard to the problems being discussed, the principles of a moral teaching based upon Sacred Scripture and the living apostolic tradition, and at the same time to shed light on the presuppositions and consequences of the dissent which that teaching has met. (*VS* 5)

Sacred Scripture remains the living and fruitful source of the Church's moral doctrine; as the Second Vatican Council recalled, the Gospel is "the source of all saving truth and moral teaching." (*VS* 28)

Because the Church has been sent by Jesus to preach the Gospel and to "make disciples of all nations . . . teaching them to observe all" that he has commanded (cf. Mt. 28:19–20), she today once more puts forward the master's reply, a reply that possesses a light and a power capable of answering even the most controversial and complex questions. (*VS* 30)

This eternal law is known both by man's natural reason (hence it is "natural law"), and—in an integral and perfect way—by God's supernatural Revelation (hence it is called "divine law"). (*VS* 72)

These are the goods safeguarded by the commandments, which, according to St. Thomas, contain the whole natural law. (*VS* 79)[15]

In teaching the existence of intrinsically evil acts, the Church accepts the teaching of Sacred Scripture . . . (1 Cor 6:9–10). (*VS* 81)

The doctrine of the object as a source of morality represents an authentic explicitation of the biblical morality of the Covenant and of the commandments, of charity and of the virtues. (*VS* 82)

In carrying out this task we are all assisted by theologians; even so, theological opinions constitute neither the rule nor the norm of our teaching. Its authority is derived, by the assistance of the Holy Spirit and in communion *cum Petro et sub Petro*, from our fidelity to the Catholic faith which comes from the Apostles. (*VS* 116)

In reading these passages, I find it difficult to avoid the conclusion that John Paul II is effectively basing the authority of the magisterium in all moral issues on its authority to interpret divine revelation. No doubt the encyclical contains a strong affirmation of the binding force of the natural moral law. It recognizes a distinction between moral law as knowable by human reason and moral law as revealed by God. It recognizes that "the moral order, as established by the natural law, is in principle, accessible to human reason" (*VS* 74). But human reason, clouded as it is by sin, is capable only of a partial knowledge of the moral law; it is revelation that provides an integral knowledge of the moral law. This is the conclusion I would draw from the following texts of the encyclical:

Some people, however, disregarding the dependence of human reason on divine wisdom and the need, given the present state of fallen nature, for divine revelation as an effective means of knowing moral truths, even those of the natural order, have actually posited a complete sovereignty of reason in the domain of moral norms regarding the right ordering of life in this world. (*VS* 36)

Man is able to recognize good and evil thanks to that discernment of good from evil which he himself carries out by his reason, in particular by his reason enlightened by divine revelation and by faith, through the law which God gave to the chosen people, beginning with the commandments on Sinai. (*VS* 44)

This eternal law is known both by man's natural reason (hence it is "natural law"), and—in an integral and perfect way—by God's supernatural Revelation (hence it is called "divine law"). (*VS* 72)

The conclusion seems clear: if it is only through God's supernatural revelation that the moral law can be known in an integral way and if this revelation has been entrusted to the magisterium for its authoritative and eventually infallible interpretation, then the Church's authority in moral matters is identical with its authority to interpret revelation.

Much as I regret to say so, I am afraid that Grisez's interpretation of *Veritatis Splendor* is probably the one that reflects the mind of John Paul II. I think it would be difficult to refute the contention that in this encyclical, without claiming to exercise infallibility, the Pope has laid the groundwork for that claim to be made about the Church's traditional moral teaching, by identifying the authority of the magisterium on moral issues with its authority to interpret divine revelation. This would insert all moral issues into the primary object of infallibility and make it that much easier to claim that many traditional Catholic moral doctrines have been infallibly taught by the ordinary universal magisterium. Among such traditional Catholic moral doctrines are those concerning murder, abortion, and euthanasia. And that brings us to the more recent encyclical, *Evangelium Vitae.*

EVANGELIUM VITAE

It surely came as no surprise that in this letter the Pope confirmed the Church's traditional condemnation of all direct taking of innocent human life. What does call for special comment, however, is the formula he used in specifically condemning murder, abortion, and euthanasia as grave violations of the moral law. In each case, the unusually solemn formula of condemnation concludes with the phrase "This doctrine . . . is transmitted by the Tradition of the Church and taught by the ordinary and universal magisterium" (*EV* 57, 62,

65). Each time a footnote refers to *Lumen Gentium* 25: the text that attributes infallibility to this exercise of the magisterium.

The question must surely be asked whether Pope John Paul II intends to say that the judgment on murder, abortion, and euthanasia expressed in this encyclical fulfills the conditions laid down by Vatican II for the infallible teaching of the whole episcopal college dispersed throughout the world. There are several reasons that would seem to favor an affirmative answer.

First, it is obvious that the morality of the taking of innocent human life is a "matter of faith or morals." While the Pope admits there is no *explicit* condemnation of abortion or euthanasia in Sacred Scripture (*EV* 44), he declares that his teaching on these, as well as on murder, is "based upon the natural law and upon the written Word of God" (*EV* 62, 65). There can be no doubt about the intention of the Pope to present the Church's condemnation of abortion and euthanasia as an authoritative interpretation of the biblical commandment "Thou shalt not kill." While he does invoke the natural law, the prevailing argument of the encyclical is based on the Judaeo-Christian revelation concerning the value of human life and its inviolability. Consistently with what we have already seen in *Veritatis Splendor*, the authority with which the pope proclaims the "Gospel of life" and pronounces his judgment on murder, abortion, and euthanasia is clearly identified with his authority as divinely appointed interpreter of revealed truth.

Furthermore, in each case, explicit reference is made to the fact that the Pope is teaching "in communion with the bishops of the Catholic Church," and in the case of abortion, the Pope refers to the consultation that showed them unanimous in condemning it (*EV* 62). Section 5 of the encyclical, entitled "In Communion with All the Bishops of the World," describes the consultation that preceded the writing of this encyclical: first with the cardinals in the extraordinary consistory of April 1991 and then with all the bishops by the personal letter that John Paul II wrote to each of them during that same year. Presumably the Pope had that consultation in mind when he repeatedly declared that the judgment he was expressing was "taught by the ordinary and universal magisterium."

According to canon 750 of the 1983 Code of Canon Law, the fact that a doctrine has been taught as divinely revealed by the ordinary universal magisterium will be manifested by the common adherence of Christ's faithful. The following passage of *Evangelium Vitae* suggests that Pope John Paul sees this criterion for recognizing infallible teaching of the ordinary universal magisterium as present in the case of the Church's doctrine on the inviolability of human life:

> In effect, the absolute inviolability of innocent human life is a moral truth clearly taught by Sacred Scripture, constantly upheld by the

church's tradition and consistently proposed by her magisterium. This consistent teaching is the evident result of that "supernatural sense of the faith" which, inspired and sustained by the Holy Spirit, safeguards the people of God from error when "it shows universal agreement in matters of faith and morals." (*EV* 57)[16]

The official "Vatican Summary" of the encyclical[17] also seems to favor giving an affirmative answer to our question:

The encyclical is presented with great doctrinal authority: It is not only an expression—like every other encyclical—of the ordinary magisterium of the pope, but also of the episcopal collegiality which was manifested first in the extraordinary consistory of cardinals in April 1991 and subsequently in a consultation of all the bishops of the Catholic Church, who unanimously and firmly agree with the teaching imparted in it.[18]

Here we are speaking of doctrinal affirmations of very high magisterial authority, presented with particular solemnity by the supreme pontiff. Exercising his own magisterial authority as the successor of Peter, in communion with the bishops of the Catholic Church, he "confirms" (or also, in the case of abortion, "declares") a doctrine "based upon the natural law and upon the written word of God" "transmitted by the church's tradition and taught by the ordinary and universal magisterium." In this connection, in the case of each of the three doctrinal formulations there is a significant reference in a note to the teaching of the Second Vatican Council's Dogmatic Constitution on the Church *Lumen Gentium*, which in Paragraph 25 declares that the bishops "even though dispersed throughout the world, but preserving for all that among themselves and with Peter's successor the bond of communion," when "in their authoritative teaching concerning matters of faith and morals, they are in agreement that a particular teaching is to be held definitively," "proclaim infallibly the doctrine of Christ."[19]

This official explanation of the doctrinal authority of the encyclical suggests that in pronouncing the Church's condemnation of murder, abortion, and euthanasia, Pope John Paul II intends to invoke the infallibility that Vatican II has attributed to the ordinary universal magisterium. One might, however, question this interpretation in the light of remarks that Cardinal Ratzinger is reported to have made at the press conference held on March 30 when the encyclical was released.

Cardinal Joseph Ratzinger said that Pope John Paul II considered making an infallible declaration against abortion and euthanasia in his latest encyclical "Evangelium Vitae," but the idea was dropped because the teachings were considered "so evident" in Christian faith and tradition. . . . Ratzinger, head of the Vatican Congregation for the Doctrine of the Faith, said the encyclical as published contains strongly worded formulas condemning abortion and euthanasia, while stopping short of the "formality of dogmatization." . . . Ratzinger confirmed rumors that the word "infallibly" had been considered for the formulas in earlier drafts. But experts researching the question found that in the past church pronouncements on dogma had never spoken of their own infallibility. Moreover, he said, it would have been "a little absurd" to solemnize teachings so clearly evident in Scripture and tradition, which is a main point of the encyclical.

Ratzinger said a formula used in the encyclical against the murder of innocent people is the strongest in the text because the pope points out that this teaching is contained in Scripture. The formulas used in the cases of abortion and euthanasia are more "toned down," the cardinal said, since the pope says these teachings are based upon but not explicitly mentioned in Scripture. In any case, Ratzinger said, these are authoritative teachings. "In the face of this text, one cannot seek refuge in formalistic discussions about what, when and where, and on what authority, all this is being taught," he said. [20]

Obviously, it is a bit risky to draw firm conclusions from a partial report of what was said at a press conference. One would want to know whether any question was asked about the significance of the repeated affirmation that what the Pope was declaring was "taught by the ordinary and universal magisterium." It is clear that it was decided not to issue any solemn papal definition in this encyclical and not to make an explicit claim to be speaking infallibly. Yet, to say that it would be "'a little absurd' to solemnize teachings so clearly evident in Scripture and tradition" could be taken as practically equivalent to saying that there was no need to define doctrine that was already so obviously the traditional teaching of the Catholic Church. And this is not very different from saying that the Church's judgment on murder, abortion, and euthanasia was a doctrine proposed by the ordinary universal magisterium as definitively to be held.

On the other hand, the cardinal's remarks, as quoted, suggest a reluctance to go so far as to claim that the Church's judgment on these three issues had been infallibly taught. If it really was the intention of the Pope to invoke the teaching of Vatican II about the infallibility of a consensus of the universal episcopate in proposing a doctrine as definitively to be held, one would expect the cardinal to have said so.

The following are some other points that have been, or could be, raised. The first is: "If the pope wanted to say something was infallible, he would have used the word."[21] In reply, I would recall the fact, mentioned by Cardinal Ratzinger, that even in their solemn dogmatic definitions, popes have not explicitly said that they were speaking infallibly. One has to judge, on other grounds, whether the conditions laid down by Vatican I for *ex cathedra* statements were fulfilled.

The second is that whereas *Lumen Gentium* 25 mentions, as a condition for the infallible teaching of the bishops together with the pope, that they concur in proposing a judgment "as definitively to be held," this expression was not used by the pope in *Evangelium Vitae.*[22] On the other hand, the formula that he used in this encyclical in condemning murder, abortion, and euthanasia would seem sufficient to remove any doubt as to whether he was expressing a judgment that he, along with the bishops, wanted all Catholics to hold definitively. It is hard to see how any other interpretation would do justice to the language that he used.

A third might be that this is an encyclical, and popes have not used encyclicals to speak with infallibility. I believe it is true that no dogma has ever been solemnly defined in a papal encyclical. It is also true that prior to *Evangelium Vitae*, no pope had ever declared that in preparing an encyclical he had consulted the entire episcopal college and gained their unanimous agreement on what he was going to say, or described the key points of his encyclical as "taught by the ordinary and universal magisterium." The fact that something has not been done before does not mean that it cannot be done.

To sum up: there are some good reasons for thinking that in this encyclical, Pope John Paul II intended to invoke not the infallibility that Vatican I attributed to papal definitions but the infallibility that Vatican II attributed to the teaching of the "ordinary and universal magisterium." On the other hand, questions remain, especially in view of the fact that Cardinal Ratzinger, while insisting that the encyclical's "strongly worded formulas condemning abortion and euthanasia" were "authoritative teachings," stopped short of saying that they met the conditions for infallibility.

In view of the present uncertainty, I would fall back on a thesis I defended in a note in *Theological Studies*, that a doctrine should not be understood as having been infallibly taught by the ordinary magisterium unless this fact is clearly established, and such a fact can hardly be said to be "clearly established" unless there is a consensus of Catholic theologians about it.[23] It is too soon to know whether there will be the consensus that would show that it is "clearly established" that the immorality of murder, abortion, and euthanasia has been infallibly taught. What this would mean is that the Church has taken an irreversible stand on these issues. But this would apply only to the three propositions that the encyclical declares are taught by the ordinary universal magisterium.

In dealing with conciliar decrees, theologians know how important it is to distinguish between the precise statements that a council intended to define and the rest of the material contained in its *capitula.* While everything in the decrees is taught with conciliar authority, only the defined dogmas are taught with infallibility. If it becomes certain that the immorality of murder, abortion, and euthanasia has been infallibly taught, I would insist on the necessity of distinguishing between those three statements and the rest of what is taught in *Evangelium Vitae.* Richard McCormick has stressed the important difference between moral principles and their application.[24] To say that the three *principles* affirmed in this encyclical have been infallibly taught would not mean that infallible answers have now been given to the many questions that concern their *application.* The statements that the encyclical makes concerning questions of this kind have been made with papal teaching authority but not with the infallibility that would make them irreversible.

It is particularly significant that this applies also to what is said in the encyclical about contraception. As we have seen above, Germain Grisez and some other Catholic moralists hold that the wrongfulness of any use of artificial means of contraception has been taught infallibly by the ordinary universal magisterium. While, in *Evangelium Vitae,* Pope John Paul again expressed the condemnation of contraception, there is no indication that he intended to invoke the infallibility of a consensus of the universal episcopate on that issue (*EV* 13). And he surely must know that on this question one cannot claim that a consensus on the part of the magisterium is "manifested by the common adherence of Christ's faithful." I believe that after *Evangelium Vitae,* the doctrine on contraception remains what it was: an authoritative but noninfallible teaching of the ordinary papal magisterium.

NOTES

1. Mansi, *Sacrorum Conciliorum Nova Collectio* 52:1226.

2. See my note "The 'Secondary Object' of Infallibility," *Theological Studies* 54 (1993): 536–50.

3. Umberto Betti, "Profession of Faith," *L'Osservatore Romano,* February 25, 1989, 6.

4. *Instruction on the Ecclesial Vocation of the Theologian* 16.

5. Among the best known of these were Felix Cappello, Francis Ter Haar, and Arthur Vermeersch. More recently, Ermenegildo Lio has written a book of almost a thousand pages, *"Humanae Vitae" e infallibilità* (Vatican City: Libreria Editrice Vaticana, 1986), to prove that the sinfulness of contraception has been solemnly defined both by Pius XI in *Casti Connubii* and by Paul VI in *Humanae Vitae.*

6. John C. Ford and Germain Grisez, "Contraception and Infallibility of the Ordinary Magisterium," *Theological Studies* 39 (1978): 258–312.

7. Germain Grisez and Joseph Boyle, John Finnis, and William E. May, "'Every Marital Act Ought to Be Open to New Life': Towards a Clearer Understanding," *Thomist* 52 (1988): 365–426, at 417.

8. William E. May, "Catholic Moral Teaching and the Limits of Dissent," in *Vatican Authority and American Catholic Dissent*, ed., William E. May (New York: Crossroad, 1987), 87–102, at 92–93.

9. Cardinal Joseph Ratzinger, letter of July 25, 1986, to Charles E. Curran, in Charles E. Curran, *Faithful Dissent* (Kansas City: Sheed and Ward, 1986), 268.

10. Ibid., 269.

11. Curran subsequently replied to the cardinal on this point, saying, "All Catholic theologians recognize that the teaching of the Council of Trent does not exclude as contrary to faith the practice of *economia* in the Greek Church. I have maintained that the position I propose on the indissolubility of marriage is in keeping with this tradition" (*Faithful Dissent*, 272).

12. *Veritatis Splendor*, English text, *Origins* 23, no. 18 (October 14, 1993):297–334.

13. *Evangelium Vitae*, English text, *Origins* 24, no. 42 (April 6, 1995): 689–727.

14. Germain Grisez, *The Tablet*, October 16, 1993, 1331.

15. A reference is given to *ST* I–II, q. 100, a. 1.

16. The reference in the text is to *LG* 12.

17. "The Vatican's Summary of *Evangelium Vitae*," *Origins* 24, no. 42 (April 6, 1995): 728–30.

18. Ibid., 728.

19. Ibid., 729.

20. *Origins* 24, no. 43 (April 13, 1995): 734.

21. Bishop Anthony Bosco of Greensburg, Pennsylvania, is quoted as having made this remark, in the *Pittsburgh Post-Gazette*, March 30, A–5.

22. He did use it in his apostolic letter on the ordination of women, where he said that his judgment that the Church has no authority to ordain women to the priesthood "must be held definitively by all the Church's faithful" (*Origins* 24, no. 4 [June 9,1994]: 51). In that letter, however, he did not invoke the infallible teaching of the universal magisterium, nor, as we have been informed by Cardinal Ratzinger, did he issue a solemn definition *ex cathedra*. See Cardinal Ratzinger, "The Limits of Church Authority," *L'Osservatore Romano*, English edition, June 29, 1994, 7; and my article "New Claims for the Pope," *The Tablet* June 18, 1994, 767–69. On November 18, 1995, however, the Congregation for the Doctrine of the Faith issued a "Response to a Doubt," which declared that the teaching that the Church has no authority whatsoever to confer priestly ordination on women "has been set forth infallibly by the ordinary and universal Magisterium." For a commentary on this, see my article "Guideposts from Catholic Tradition," *America* 173, no. 19 (December 9, 1995): 5–6.

23. Sullivan, "The 'Secondary Object' of Infallibility," 548–50.

24. Richard A. McCormick, "The Gospel of Life," *America* 172, no. 15 (April 29, 1995): 10–17.

Infallible Teaching on Moral Issues?
A RESPONSE

THOMAS P. RAUSCH, S.J.

On the difficult subject of the Church's magisterium, Francis Sullivan's voice is itself magisterial. Few Catholic theologians have done more to clarify and explain its intricacies. His present contribution raises the question, Do these two recent encyclicals of Pope John Paul II "offer papal support to the claim that some moral doctrines have been infallibly taught by the ordinary and universal magisterium?"

After carefully considering both documents and the way they were proposed, he concludes that in *Veritatis Splendor* John Paul II, "without claiming to exercise infallibility, . . . has laid the groundwork for that claim to be made about the Church's traditional moral teaching, by identifying the authority of the magisterium on moral issues with its authority to interpret divine revelation." In other words, the Pope seems to be moving towards claiming for the magisterium the ability to interpret revelation in terms of specific moral issues, even to do so infallibly. In *Evangelium Vitae*, the Pope moves further; Sullivan sees him as intending to invoke in regard to the Church's teaching on murder, abortion, and euthanasia "not the infallibility that Vatican I attributed to papal definitions but the infallibility that Vatican II attributed to the teaching of the 'ordinary and universal magisterium.'" Yet he notes in his conclusion that no less an authority than Cardinal Joseph Ratzinger, while acknowledging the encyclical's formulas condemning abortion and euthanasia as "authoritative teachings," stops short of saying that the conditions for infallibility have been met. Finally, Sullivan notes that without a "clearly established" consensus of Catholic theologians that these three propositions have been taught infallibly by the ordinary universal magisterium, one cannot conclude that they have been so taught.

Father Sullivan has clearly answered the question he so specifically posed. But his raising the question of infallible moral teachings from the ordinary universal magisterium suggests some further questions that I would like to consider. They are as follows: First, is the whole moral law contained in revelation? Second, what conditions must be present in order to judge that a teaching of the ordinary universal magisterium has been proposed infallibly?

And finally, is Pope John Paul II's attempt to extend the range of magisterial infallibility helpful at this particular point in the history of the Church? I'd like to explore briefly each of these questions.

IS THE WHOLE MORAL LAW CONTAINED IN REVELATION?

Sullivan offers a number of citations from *Veritatis Splendor* to show that John Paul II answers this question affirmatively. The Pope sees Sacred Scripture as "the living and fruitful source of the Church's moral doctrine" (*VS* 28).[1] The good to be done is established by the eternal law. "This eternal law is known both by man's natural reason (hence it is 'natural law') and—in an integral and perfect way—by God's supernatural Revelation (hence it is called 'divine law')" (*VS* 72). The Pope rejects any attempt to deny "that there exists, in divine revelation, a specific and determined moral content, universally valid and permanent" (*VS* 37). But if the natural law and the divine law have the one and the same God as author (*VS* 45), nevertheless, our understanding of "the purposes, rights and duties" of the natural moral law are based on our interpretation of "'the nature of the human person' . . . the person himself in the unity of soul and body, in the unity of his spiritual and biological inclinations and of all the other specific characteristics necessary for the pursuit of his end" (*VS* 50).

It is interesting to note that Cardinal Ratzinger points out the difference between moral teachings clearly contained in Scripture and others that are not so clearly present. After *Evangelium Vitae* was published, Ratzinger commented that "a formula used in the encyclical against the murder of innocent people is the strongest in the text because the pope points out that this teaching is contained in Scripture. The formulas used in the case of abortion and euthanasia are more 'toned down,' . . . since the pope says these teachings are based upon but not explicitly mentioned in Scripture."[2] Somewhat more critically, James Keenan observes that the pope's use of Scripture is "somewhat problematic." If he is calling upon Scripture not just in "a homiletic, exhortatory sense" but as a source of specific moral teaching, that use "requires more specific exegesis."[3] Of course, there are many questions today, such as birth control and those raised by modern medical science, that Scripture does not address.

How, for example, does all this work in the area of sexual ethics? In this area, many Catholic teachings that find constant support in the tradition rely more on natural law than on biblical revelation. Yet some traditional teachings appeal to, or have a source in, biblical texts that in their original context may have meant something quite different from the meaning seen in them by the tradition.

Take, for example, the question of homosexual acts. These are condemned in both the Old and the New Testament, but many commentators today do not see these as condemnations of homosexual relations as such, as the concept of a homosexual orientation was unknown until modern times. In the judgment of these scholars, the biblical condemnations are aimed at preserving ritual purity (Lv 18:22; 20:13) or against participation in idolatrous worship by consorting with male (and female) temple prostitutes (Dt 23:18), a common practice in the ancient near East (1 Kgs 14:24; 15:12), or against violating the duty of hospitality through homosexual rape (Gn 19:4–8), or against pederasty (1 Cor 6:9–10; 1 Tim 1:10). Romans 1:24–31 is a more difficult text, as Paul is clearly talking about homosexual relations in themselves, but the fact that he describes both men and women as giving up natural relations and choosing homosexual ones suggests that he did not understand homosexuality as a condition.[4] In recognizing for the first time that people do not choose to be homosexual, the *Catechism of the Catholic Church* moves Catholic teaching a step forward in this area.[5]

Is, then, the Church's traditional teaching on the universal immorality of homosexual acts contained in revelation? Though the claim that it is can be supported by appeals to both Scripture and the natural law tradition, the relevance of those biblical texts is questioned today by many biblical scholars and commentators, while others ask if the natural law arguments are sufficient to decide the question for those who are homosexual through no choice of their own. In neither case is it clear that this teaching comes to us from revelation. Without denying that the tradition gives full moral approval only to marital relations and to celibacy, Lisa Cahill observes, "A specific definition of 'human nature' proposed with excessive certainty, abstraction, rationalism, rigidity, and authoritarianism exposes the intrinsic liabilities of the method by which it is derived more readily than would a more cautious or provisional proposal."[6]

In his study of authority in morals, Gerard Hughes argues that the Christian tradition, whether in the Bible or as represented by the later writings, cannot be ultimately authoritative for moral reasoning: "The documents of this tradition are not simply limpid expressions of the mind of God immediately accessible to all men at all times. God's revelation of himself is not fundamentally a set of utterances, but the person of his son."[7] While many Catholic theologians would not exclude the possibility of the magisterium infallibly defining some doctrine regarding morals, there is wide agreement that the Church's charism of infallibility would not be exercised in decisions regarding particular norms of the natural law.

In an earlier work, Sullivan pointed out that the argument that the magisterium can speak infallibly on particular norms of the natural law "ignores the difference between what is revealed and what is not revealed with regard to morals. It presumes that the term 'matters of faith and morals' is rightly understood to include all moral issues, regardless of their relationship to the deposit of revelation."[8] Sullivan finds historical support for his argument here from Bishop Gasser, the *relator* for the official *Deputatio de Fide* of Vatican I. In rejecting a proposal to substitute the term "principles of morality" for the more familiar "matters of faith and morals," Gasser wrote that "principles of morals can be other merely philosophical principles of natural morality, which do not in every respect pertain to the deposit of faith."[9] In other words, the revealed truth that infallibility can define or safeguard does not include what may be merely philosophical principles of natural morality. Thus Sullivan argues that the magisterium is within its competence in applying the natural law understood in light of the gospel to particular, concrete moral issues but that the more common opinion today is that it cannot make these particular norms, based as they are on human nature as it exists in history, the objects of irreformable teaching.[10]

WHAT CONDITIONS MUST BE PRESENT IN ORDER TO JUDGE THAT A TEACHING OF THE ORDINARY UNIVERSAL MAGISTERIUM HAS BEEN PROPOSED INFALLIBLY?

In his summary, Sullivan argues that there are good reasons for thinking that in *Evangelium Vitae* Pope John Paul II intended to invoke the infallibility attributed by Vatican II to the ordinary and universal magisterium.[11] The Pope specifically condemns murder, abortion, and euthanasia as grave violations of the moral law, calling each time on the teaching of the ordinary and universal magisterium (*EV* 57, 62, 65). In each case, a footnote refers to *Lumen Gentium* 25, which states the following: "Although the individual bishops do not enjoy the prerogative of infallibility, they can nevertheless proclaim Christ's doctrine infallibly. This is so, even when they are dispersed around the world, provided that while maintaining the bond of unity among themselves and with Peter's successor, and while teaching authentically on a matter of faith or morals, they concur in a single viewpoint as the one which must be held conclusively."[12] According to the official "Vatican Summary" of the encyclical, the Pope, prior to its publication, consulted all the bishops of the Church, "who unanimously and firmly agree with the teaching imparted in it."[13]

What conditions must be present in order to judge that a teaching of the ordinary universal magisterium has been proposed infallibly? Joseph

Komonchak answers this question by applying the same three conditions used to describe the limits of the papal magisterium: first, a teaching must concern a matter of faith and morals, either divinely revealed or necessary to defend and explain what has been divinely revealed; second, it must be proposed by a moral unanimity of the bishops in communion with each other and with the pope; and third, it must be proposed as having to be held definitively. [14]

Are these three conditions sufficient by themselves for recognizing infallible teaching by the ordinary and universal magisterium? In asking if *Humanae Vitae*'s teaching on the sinfulness of artificial contraception has been proposed infallibly, Sullivan points out that according to canon law "no doctrine is understood to be infallibly defined unless it is clearly established as such" (can. 749.3). He then argues that it is equally true that no doctrine should be understood as having been infallibly *taught* by the ordinary universal magisterium unless this has been "clearly established," and it cannot be clearly established without a consensus of Catholic theologians that it has been so taught. [15] His argument is based on the theological consequences for the faithful of infallible teaching, whether by solemn definition or by the ordinary and universal magisterium; in either case, they must believe "with a divine and catholic faith" or be considered guilty of heresy. [16]

I would like to suggest a further reason for appealing to a consensus of Catholic theologians and indeed of the faithful, on the basis of the nature of the Church's charism of infallibility itself, for teaching authority and infallibility cannot be discussed in isolation from the community of the Church for which authority speaks. Thus, I would like to suggest two additional conditions.

First, the teachings of the ordinary and universal magisterium must be received by the whole Church. As Rahner has observed, it has often been incorrectly assumed that a doctrine is irreformable simply because it has been taught over a considerable period of time: "This view runs counter to the facts, because many doctrines which were once universally held have proved to be problematic or erroneous." [17] Today an increasing number of studies on reception illustrate how what has been the consistent teaching of the ordinary magisterium has been changed or even reversed because of the way in which it was received by the Church. In his study of infallibility, Luis M. Bermejo gives a number of examples of teachings of the ordinary magisterium, both papal and universal, repeated over the centuries but ultimately reversed; among them, the impossibility of salvation outside the Church, taught by Lateran IV (1215), Florence (1442), and Lateran V (1516); the tolerance of slavery, sanctioned by Lateran III (1179), Lateran IV (1215), Lyons I (1245), and Lyons II (1274), and the justification of the use of torture by Lateran III (1179) and

Vienne (1311).[18] In the last two cases, the Church accepted or justified practices it today considers immoral.

The statement of *Lumen Gentium* 25 on the infallibility of the ordinary universal magisterium, taken by itself, focuses only on authority rather than on the far more complex reality of how doctrine actually develops in the life of the Church. It falls too easily into the facile but difficult-to-maintain distinction between the teaching Church (*ecclesia docens*) and the learning Church (*ecclesia discens*), suggesting that the magisterium is an office placed over the Church rather than an instrument through which the faith entrusted to the entire Church comes to expression.[19] Such a view does not reflect the understanding of the Church present in its official documents. A footnote to *Lumen Gentium* 25, raising the objection that a pope might define something to which the rest of the episcopal college or the faithful did not agree, responded, "In practice, the Pope always consults the other bishops and the faithful before making a doctrinal decision."[20]

Thus, the need remains to see that a teaching reflects the faith of the Church and has been received. As Sullivan observes, referring to canon 750 of the 1983 Code of Canon Law, "The fact that a doctrine has been taught as divinely revealed by the ordinary universal magisterium will be manifested by the common adherence of Christ's faithful.[21]

Second, in light of his own study on reception, J. Robert Dionne suggests that the condition that a doctrine be propounded as definitively to be held needs to be qualified. He maintains that the conditions necessary for judging that the ordinary universal magisterium has infallibly taught a particular doctrine, as given in *Lumen Gentium* 25, are ambiguous. It is insufficient to suggest that a doctrine is infallibly taught merely because the bishops concur with the pope in judging that one view is to be held definitively, for their concurrence may be based more on obedience than on a judgment that the point in question pertains to the substance of the faith.[22]

Dionne shows how teachings of the papal magisterium upheld by the bishops over several generations as *definitive tenendum* were actually reversed by the bishops and pope of a later generation. He suggests that it may be necessary to add a phrase indicating that the bishops together with the pope teach infallibly when they judge that a single viewpoint is to be held definitively *as pertaining to the substance of the faith*. Otherwise, the magisterium remains faced with the dilemma posed by Hans Küng: either to acknowledge that the church's position on artificial contraception has been taught infallibly by the ordinary universal magisterium or to repudiate infallibility itself.[23] Thus, he suggests that "the conditions described in *Lumen Gentium* according to which the rest of the Catholic Church may judge that the ordinary universal magisterium has infallibly taught a particular doctrine may have to be revised by a future ecumenical Council."[24]

IS POPE JOHN PAUL II'S ATTEMPT TO EXTEND THE RANGE OF MAGISTERIAL INFALLIBILITY HELPFUL AT THIS PARTICULAR POINT IN THE HISTORY OF THE CHURCH?

Although Sullivan does not say so explicitly, his essay makes clear that the effect of John Paul's encyclicals *Veritatis Splendor* and *Evangelium Vitae* is to open the way for including a number of specific moral teachings, based on interpretations of Scripture and the natural law, as falling within the primary object of infallibility, thus extending considerably the range of the Church's magisterial infallibility. One might ask: Which is more important at this moment in the life of the Church, standing as it does at the threshold of the third millennium? Is it more important to extend the reach of magisterial infallibility on moral issues, an effort that remains dubious to many Catholics, let alone to other Christians? Or is it more important to rethink the way that the Church's teaching authority—and indeed, its charism of infallibility—is exercised, so that this important gift of Catholicism to tomorrow's Church might be gratefully received by other Christian communities? Pope John Paul himself has recently invited other Christians to help Catholicism rethink the way in which the primacy is exercised, for the sake of allowing it to perform its important function within a new and wider communion of churches.[25] Making additional claims for magisterial infallibility would not seem to be a helpful step in this direction.

NOTES

1. *Veritatis Splendor*, English text, *Origins* 23, no. 18 (October 14, 1993): 297–334.

2. *Origins* 24 (April 13, 1995): 734.

3. James F. Keenan, S.J., "The Moral Argumentation of Evangelium Vitae," in *Choosing Life: A Dialogue on Evangelium Vitae*, K. Wildes, S.J. and A. Mitchell, eds. (Washington, D.C.: Georgetown University Press, 1997), p. 47. John Conley characterizes the pope's exegesis as "spiritual-moral" rather than historical-critical; "Narrative, Act, Structure: John Paul II's Method of Moral Analysis," p. 5.

4. For a review of this discussion see Vincent J. Genovesi, *In Pursuit of Love: Catholic Morality and Human Sexuality* (Wilmington, DE: Michael Glazier, 1987), 262–73; also Victor Paul Furnish, "The Bible and Homosexuality," in Jeffrey S. Siker, *Homosexuality in the Church: Both Sides of the Debate* (Louisville, Ky.: Westminster John Knox Press, 1994), 18–35.

5. Cf. *Catechism of the Catholic Church*, no. 2358.

6. Lisa Sowle Cahill, "Homosexuality: A Case Study in Moral Argument," in Siker, *Homosexuality in the Church*, 79.

7. Gerard J. Hughes, *Authority in Morals* (London: Heythrop Monographs, 1978), p. 24.

8. Francis A. Sullivan, *Magisterium: Teaching Authority in the Catholic Church* (Mahwah, NJ: Paulist Press, 1983), p. 140.

9. Ibid; Gasser's comments can be found in Mansi 52, 1224.

10. Ibid., p. 152.

11. Francis A. Sullivan, "Infallible Teaching on Moral Issues? Reflections on Veritatis Splendor and Evangelium Vitae," in *Choosing Life: A Dialogue on Evangelium Vitae*, K. Wildes, S.J. and A. Mitchell, eds. (Washington, D.C.: Georgetown University Press), pp. 83–85.

12. In Walter M. Abbott, ed., *The Documents of Vatican II* (New York: America Press, 1966), p. 48.

13. "The Vatican's Summary of 'Evangelium Vitae,'" *Origins* 24 (April 6, 1995) 728.

14. Joseph A. Komonchak, "Humanae Vitae and Its Reception: Ecclesiological Reflections," *Theological Studies* 39 (1978): 247; in another article in the same issue John C. Ford and Germain Grisez add the additional condition that the bishops "agree in one judgment"; "Contraception and the Infallibility of the Ordinary Magisterium," 272.

15. Francis A. Sullivan, "The 'Secondary Object' of Infallibility," *Theological Studies* 54 (1993): 548–50; see also "Infallible Teaching on Moral Issues?" pp. 19–20.

16. Ibid., pp. 549–50.

17. Karl Rahner, "Magisterium," in *Sacramentum Mundi*, Vol. III (New York: Herder and Herder, 196) p. 356; cited by Sullivan in *Magisterium*, p. 126.

18. Luis M. Bermejo, *Infallibility on Trial: Church, Conciliarity and Communion* (Westminster, MD: Christian Classics, 1992), pp. 252–64; 309–40.

19. Komonchak refers to the former as the "classical view" of the relationship between the magisterium and the church, placing "the pope and bishops (the *ecclesia docens*) between Christ or the Spirit and the faithful (the *ecclesia discens*)"; "Humanae Vitae and Its Reception," p. 228.

20. *Lumen Gentium* 25, footnote 125; in Abbott, *Documents of Vatican II*, p. 49.

21. Sullivan, "Infallible Teaching," p. 84.

22. J. Robert Dionne, *The Papacy and the Church: A Study of Praxis and Reception in Ecumenical Perspective* (New York: Philosophical Library, 1987), p. 351.

23. Ibid., p. 353.

24. Ibid, p. 349; sentence italicized in original.

25. John Paul II, *Ut unum sint*, no. 96; *Origins* 25 (June 8, 1995), p. 70.

On Interpretation, on Infallibility:
A RESPONSE TO FR. SULLIVAN

LADISLAS ORSY, S.J.

ON INTERPRETATION

Horizon

As in any other act of interpretation, in the explanation of an encyclical, two horizons meet: that of the author and that of the interpreter. The first and foremost task of the interpreter is to enter into the horizon of the author and to re-create the meaning intended by the author and then, and only then, to formulate his or her own response.

Such a procedure demands on the part of the interpreter a great deal of initial restraint, a determination to discard any bias, and an effort to seek understanding. The absence of such dispositions would lead to a failure in perceiving the author's meaning and would allow the projection of the interpreter's views into the original text. Inevitably, the intended communication would break down, and any productive dialog would be foreclosed.

Christian Faith

The horizon in which this encyclical has been conceived and composed is that of Christian faith; its *full* meaning can be grasped only there. This is not to say that it does not carry any significance for those who are of other persuasions: it does. It is to say only that since the author is inspired by Christian faith, the integral content of his message can be understood and explained only within the context of the same persuasion and dedication. To give a concrete example: since for John Paul II every human person is an image, *ikon*, of God, all illegitimate destruction of human life is an invasion of the divine and amounts to a sacrilegious action.

Literary Form

Not all encyclicals are equal, not even when their creator is the same pope. One can be a powerful call to action, another an abstract instruction. The literary form of the document affects every part of it and assumes a governing role in its interpretation.

The literary form of the present encyclical is a blend of two seemingly opposite approaches: it contains an impassioned cry calling for action, and it provides a great deal of reasoning by way of instruction. It wants to be known by the title Gospel of Life, thus attaching itself to the original proclamation of the word of God and displaying the same urgency. It enters also into a reflective mood by providing extensive theological reasonings to promote understanding.

Meaning

There are clearly two levels of meaning in the encyclical: one in the concrete and existential order demanding action, another in the abstract and essential order giving doctrinal explanations.

In the Concrete and Existential Order

The publication of the encyclical can be seen as an *event* in the existential order, as a *deed* in the order of *esse* in Aristotelian-Thomistic terminology. If it is seen as such, the detailed and precise meanings of the words, sentences, and paragraphs recede: they are not lost, but their analyses must not take the first place. The *event* has its own significance that is easy to identify. It is a call: "Respect life!" This cry comes at the end of a century that has seen the destruction of human life by scientific means and methods—as never before. Through the encyclical, the Catholic Church proclaims its faith in the sanctity of human life and calls on all persons of goodwill to do what they can to protect and uphold it.

In the Abstract and Essential Order

The intention of the Pope is to communicate value judgments that must serve as norms of action. The authority of such judgments is rooted in the fact that they have been "transmitted by the tradition of the church and taught by the ordinary and universal magisterium." We are in the field of doctrinal affirmations and theological reflections. The primary aim is to communicate knowledge and promote understanding. Fr. Sullivan's analysis moves on this level.

ON INFALLIBILITY

The Meaning of the Word

"Infallibility" is a negative term, and a sweeping one at that: if not properly explained, it is bound to provoke and promote misunderstandings.

The term "fidelity" could do much better to convey the positive content of this Catholic belief. When Catholics speak about infallibility of the Church, of the bishops' college, or of the pope, they really want to state their belief in the fidelity of God: in matters of salvation he will not let his people fall victim to falsehoods and become captive to fallacies. If that could happen, so Catholics believe, the saving word of God would be dead.

In other terms, Catholics hold that through all the vicissitudes of history the Spirit of God keeps the original evangelical message in the Church alive and that this message is as fresh today as it was when the first disciples received it from their Master.

"Infallibility" is a poor human term to convey the doctrine of God's fidelity to his people. Because of our faith in his fidelity we know that we are not running after a fascinating dream but surrendering to a divine action.

It could be argued that the core of this doctrine is not specifically Roman Catholic: there is no Christian denomination that does not—in one form or another—believe in God's action to preserve his message among them. Every time the members of a community assert that the word of God is alive and known in their midst, they are proclaiming their faith in God's fidelity to his people.

The "Subjects" of Infallibility

Although in the Catholic Church the infallibility *of the pope* is most spoken of, his office is not the ultimate source of infallibility, nor is the manifestation of this gift restricted to his pronouncements.

Catholics hold that there are three "subjects" endowed with infallibility: the universal Church, the episcopal college, and the pope. These subjects are partly distinct, partly identical, because the Church cannot exist without the bishops and there is no episcopal college without its head, the pope.

(1) First and foremost, *the entire People of God* is infallible; that is, the Church as a whole: the faithful, the episcopate, the pope—all together. When they peacefully believe in, and celebrate, a mystery as an integral part of the revelation, there is no need to go further. In their belief and in their worship they proclaim their faith infallibly.

(2) When the faithful become divided or hesitant or are in need of an answer to new questions of great doctrinal importance, we believe, *the episcopal college presided by the pope* is competent to decide an issue and give an answer. The reason is that we hold that the evangelical message was entrusted to the apostles and that the bishops are their successors in office. This has been the Catholic position ever since the first ecumenical council, which was convened in the year 325 at Nicea. Vatican Council II formalized this traditional

belief by proclaiming—in carefully defined circumstances—the "infallibility" of the episcopal college.

(3) Further, we believe that the *bishop of Rome*, the Vicar of Peter (as St. Leo the Great, pope 440–61, claimed to be), is protected from misleading his flock when in rare and solemn circumstances he pronounces on matters concerning the doctrine of faith.

To sum up: Catholics believe that the fidelity of God can be manifest in the firm and quiet belief of the whole Church, or in the collective judgment of the episcopate, or in the judgment of the head of the episcopal college. For the "infallibility" to be operative, in every case certain strict conditions must be fulfilled.

FR. SULLIVAN'S PAPER

To appreciate correctly Fr. Sullivan's contribution both in its content and in its context, we need to reconstruct his questions and the horizon within which he set them and answered them.

Two questions appear to dominate in his paper. He asks in general terms, *Can the Church pronounce infallibly on moral issues?* Then he turns to particular issues: *Is the Pope's teaching in* Evangelium Vitae *concerning murder, abortion, and euthanasia infallible?* He raises these questions in the abstract and essential order; virtually all his conclusions are based on the analysis of the official texts. In them, he searches for, and evaluates, all potential evidence for papal infallibility. It was not his task to investigate the development of the same doctrinal points in the community at large or in episcopal declarations over so many centuries. In other words, in his conclusions we have the results of a well-focused and carefully limited inquiry.

After a hearing of his arguments, it remains conceivable that even if the present papal declarations do not satisfy all the technical requirements of infallible statements, the same doctrine—or the elements of it—is rooted in the infallible faith of the community.

Within such limits, I find myself in substantial agreement with Fr. Sullivan's position. Nonetheless, I wish he had given a greater scope to non-American moral theologians. After all, moral theology is an international science, and no matter how intense the disputes are on our continent, significantly more is being said and done overseas. Further, it seems to me that the weight that Fr. Sullivan has granted to the opinions of Vatican officials or Roman theologians in the interpretation of papal documents is out of proportion. While they may have more intimate knowledge of the process of the composition of a document, their very proximity to it may hamper them in collocating the doctrine proclaimed into a broader historical and systematic context.

A final remark: the exposition of Fr. Sullivan and my own comments move mostly in the abstract and essential order, in the world of doctrinal propositions. They are important, but the fullness of life is not there. The real challenge for all Christians is in the concrete and existential order: how to proclaim unceasingly that every human person is an image, *ikon*, of God and is, therefore, entitled to a reverence that is due the sacred. This challenge we know—infallibly.

PART 2

Thematic Considerations

Technology, Efficiency, and Gender in Evangelium Vitae

KATHRYN M. OLESKO

INTRODUCTION

Evangelium Vitae confirms the now routine observation that technology and society form a "seamless web."[1] The "culture of death," as Pope John Paul II has described it, weaves together technologies; values, especially moral and political ones; social practices, both of daily life and of the professions; marketplace economics; and political institutions associated primarily with democracies but not excluding those of communism and socialism. The result is an indictment of the technology-based practices that have become commonplace in what traditionally have been considered the most private moments of life: conception, birth, and death. By arguing for the integration, if not dominance, of spiritual values and considerations into the seamless web, the Pope restates what has for generations been a criticism of modern society: its spiritual depravity. As a statement on the relations between religion, science, and technology, *Evangelium Vitae* goes beyond the Pope's 1988 message to the Castel Gandolfo Conference on Physics, Philosophy, and Theology;[2] for in 1995 he not only called for dialogue and interaction between the two camps but also made specific recommendations on tasks and practices that highlight the values and goals of both sides of the divide.

The purpose of this essay is twofold. It first examines how *Evangelium Vitae* characterizes a technological system.[3] The Pope's understanding and depiction of technology are complex. Although the technologies mentioned in the encyclical are not all artifactual, they do all have a politics, in Langdon Winner's sense.[4] They embody power and authority, and they suggest, but do not unilaterally determine, a way of building order. They are also "forms of life" in that they map out or restrict ways of doing things in daily life.[5] Hence, although John Paul II strongly links these technologies to political democracy, its individualism, and its concept of rights, their political dimension could also be viewed more generally as organizing the activity of the members of the polis through the assignment or promotion of certain actions and values at the level of everyday practices. This latter perspective is not entirely absent from the encyclical, but its significance threatens to be lost amidst the encyclical's vilification of democracy. The broader context of everyday life is particularly important when considering the culture of efficiency, which the Pope holds especially responsible for the "culture of death."

The more general cultural dimensions of technology serve as a foundation for the second purpose of this essay, which concerns gender. The Pope's conception of gender and nature, of the natural and the supernatural, and of the contemporary culture of the body bear on his interpretations of science and technology in modern life. Yet the solution that he proposes to the contraception crisis—natural family planning—fails to take into account the ways in which the rational practices necessary for predicting periods of continence require a particular cultural environment to exist. Specifically, the rhythm method, as a technology, presupposes and may even require gender traits consistent with the culture of efficiency that John Paul II condemns.

TECHNOLOGY AND POLITICS

The principal material artifacts of the technological system identified with the "culture of death" in *Evangelium Vitae* are the modern technologies of reproduction and euthanasia. By casting them largely in a moral context, John Paul II not only highlights the choices and behavioral changes these artifacts have offered but also argues for narrowing considerably the paths they have opened. He condemns techniques of abortion, contraception, and euthanasia outright (*EV* 13–14, 22) but admits that techniques of artificial reproduction and prenatal diagnosis have more complicated moral dimensions for which "an accurate and systematic moral judgment is necessary" (*EV* 63).

In addition to material artifacts, other technologies are implicated in the "culture of death." The Pope identifies other features of modern civilization as "new threats to human life." Environmental crises "made worse by the culpable indifference and negligence of those who could in some cases remedy them" (*EV* 10) are one locus of technological foul play. Another locus is found in political institutions, which create undesirable ways of life by using rational means of planning to achieve "unjust distribution of resources," wars, and global arms trading (*EV* 10). And finally, the Pope implicates the medical and legal professions for utilizing what can only be called obfuscatory literary technologies[6] in the form of "innocuous" or "ambiguous" terminology, such as when the phrase "interruption of pregnancy" is used to signify abortion (*EV* 11, 58; see also 21). The "new" attacks on the dignity of the human being addressed by the Pope are thus not only greater in number and more varied in type than one finds in *Humanae Vitae*; they also constitute what seems to be a far more comprehensive technological system than one customarily associates with material artifacts in the history of technology.[7]

In two respects statements on the role of technology in *Evangelium Vitae* cannot be separated from a political context. Technology is, for instance, an integral part of the encyclical's statements on democracy, freedom, rights, and crime. Several dimensions of life in the (democratic) polis are transformed, according to John Paul II, by the technologies of life and death. The public and private spheres, for instance, coalesce when reproductive technologies are justified "in the name of the rights of individual freedom," which seek "authorization by the State" so that they can be used "with the free assistance of health care systems" (*EV* 4; see also *EV* 13, 18, 19). In contrast to the message of the Pope's story of Cain and Abel (*EV* 7–9), which emphasizes community, the Pope argues that technologies of death create a society of atomized persons whose individuality is reinforced by the structure of the democratic state (*EV* 18). The story that he tells of personal isolation and loss of meaningful values is thus strangely reminiscent of the incomplete narrative Sigmund Freud rendered in *Civilization and Its Discontents*, in which he embarked upon a journey in search of wholeness, solidarity, and social integration in an apparently over-civilized, technological world.[8]

Technology in the encyclical is also more broadly a part of the political dimensions of daily life. The technologies of life and death have transformed—not inevitably, but by choice—the routine habits, personal self-perceptions, social relations, and moral boundaries of ordinary daily action. The nonartifactual technologies, for example, create some of the meanings, symbols, and venues for the artifactual ones by providing a normative concept of nature, a context for rational action, and a style of communication. John Paul II's conclusion restates an oft cited dilemma of modern life by describing how reproductive and thanatotic technologies have reordered human action at the level of everyday experience: "Thus, in relation to life at birth or at death, man is no longer capable of posing the question of the truest meaning of his own existence, nor can he assimilate with genuine freedom these crucial moments of his own history. He is concerned only with 'doing', and, using all kinds of technology, he busies himself with programming, controlling and dominating birth and death" (*EV* 22).

Although made at the end of a lengthy commentary on the story of Cain and Abel stressing human responsibility for life, this conclusion, which juxtaposes meaning and "doing," more directly invokes the mysteries of Catholic culture—the birth, death, and resurrection of Christ—as the proper context for understanding the meaning of life and death. As the German sociologist Max Weber said a century ago of the "iron cage," the Pope too argues that rational action is inadequate for addressing the most important questions of value in daily life.[9] The order these technologies have helped to build thus goes beyond a narrow political context, for this order could exist and has existed in political cultures of types other than democratic. Or to put the issue in the apt words of Langdon Winner, "The map of the world shows no country called Technopolis, yet in many ways we are already its citizens."[10]

"A SOCIETY EXCESSIVELY CONCERNED WITH EFFICIENCY"

In reply to the question "How did such a situation come about?" (*EV* 11), John Paul II turns to what he believes to be the pervasive features of daily life in the industrialized world. Although he implicates the undesirable features of modern life—such as stress and the lack of time to think—he lays principal blame on a "larger reality." "This culture [of death]," he argues, "is actively fostered by powerful cultural, economic and political currents which encourage the idea of a society excessively concerned with efficiency" (*EV* 12). Efficiency is, in his view, the single greatest factor influencing decisions that constitute the "culture of death." Aiding and abetting the cultural popularity of efficiency are, in his view, the medical and legal professions, mass media, international institutions (*EV* 4, 17), and the scientific community, whose research, the Pope believes, "seems to be almost exclusively preoccupied with developing products [for abortion] which are ever more simple and effective" (*EV* 13). Efficiency is thus not only part of a large system dominated by rational actions; it is more broadly that which defines and guides those actions. But what does John Paul II mean by "efficiency"? How does his understanding fit into the history of the concept as well as its present use?

Efficiency in History

The concept of efficiency dates back to the seventeenth century, when it designated the fitness or power to accomplish a task.[11] A qualitative notion at first, efficiency was not initially subject to calculation, nor did it incorporate the concepts of work and energy, which did not yet exist. This early definition of "efficiency," which only rarely appeared outside scholarly contexts, was useful for absolute distinctions but not for comparative assessments. With the advent of more complex machinery (especially the steam engine), industrialization, and the quantification and clarification of key conceptual terms such as "work" and "energy," efficiency became in the nineteenth century the ratio of output to input. According to the engineer William Rankine and his colleagues in the late 1850s, "The EFFICIENCY of a machine is its economy or energy; that is the ratio of the useful work performed to the energy exerted . . .

The great end of improvement in machines is to diminish the lost work as to make the efficiency approximate to unity."[12] This quantitative notion of efficiency allowed for comparisons of performance and for hierarchies, rankings, or gradations determined by quantitative measures. The quantitative features of efficiency could also be used to signify deviations from an ideal and hence could be deployed to set up notions of the "normal"; but concepts from probability and statistics were much more culturally significant in this regard. The nineteenth-century quantitative notion of efficiency made it very difficult to establish the kinds of absolute distinctions that the earlier seventeenth-century notion allowed with ease. Unless one set up other distinguishing criteria (such as a definition of "waste" or a threshold for when "profit" kicked in), one simply did not have the freedom to make absolute, black-white distinctions when it came to judging performance that could only be accomplished by making comparisons along a quantitative scale.

Efficiency became a cultural value by way of its introduction into political economy and political philosophy, especially through utilitarianism. Although a part of the larger process of rationalization that has characterized the industrialized world since the nineteenth century, efficiency retained its cultural currency most strongly in the United States, where it became a "venerable tradition."[13] In the work of Frederick Winslow Taylor,[14] the time-and-motion studies that had employed the concept of efficiency to judge human performance (especially in the military) in the nineteenth century became in America the template for judging industrial performance. The goal here was not only to optimize the productivity of the worker but also to stress the worker's integration into the production process as a whole. Taylor's system of industrial management became the principal source of the "efficiency craze" of the Progressive Era. Historian Samuel Haber writes that "efficiency and good came closer to meaning the same thing in these years than in any other period of American history."[15] Haber demonstrates how efficiency became a highly valued personal attribute that placed hard work and discipline over feeling and sympathy and that compared individuals on the basis of how well they performed and produced. Efficiency could thus be promoted in an effort to increase production or output. The agencies responsible for planning in World War I created a single-mindedness of purpose that made efficiency "a patriotic duty." The strongly positive valuation of efficiency as a moral good was so thorough that even critics of efficiency, such as John Dewey, finally accepted its reign, and eventually the British and French allies took it seriously, too.[16]

In the political realm, the efficiency movement helped to transform American democracy. As Taylorites and other efficiency experts moved from business and industry to government service, the earlier idea that the rank and file ran the operation with little need of guidance from supervisors was eclipsed by an authority of experts equipped to criticize existing institutions.[17] "Efficiency provided a standpoint," Haber concludes, "from which those who had declared allegiance to democracy could resist the leveling tendencies of the principles of equality."[18] Acceptance of efficiency in the broader social and political realm created an aristocracy of experts, a technocracy that was enhanced considerably after World War II experiences in the management of goods, supplies, resources, and populations.

We tend to think of science and technology as universal constructs, but as the notion of a technological system has demonstrated, neither can be separated from its local cultural environments or from the political uses to which it is put. The attributes and valuation of efficiency are likewise culturally grounded. A quantitative notion of efficiency flourished in America but tended to languish elsewhere in the West until recently. England accepted it, but not for long. Terms for a quantitatively determined concept of efficiency are difficult to come by even to this day in France or Germany, where words closer to the seventeenth-century meaning of "efficiency" are still employed. National identifications with efficiency became vulnerable in times of conflict. Germany had been considered the "paragon of efficiency," but after America's entry into the war in 1917, the concept had to be cleared of its Prussian connotations.[19] It is worth emphasizing, too, that the cultural adaptation of quantitative efficiency was possible only in societies that had invested a considerable amount in their members to begin with. Finally, as has been the case for the process of rationalization since the late nineteenth century, efficiency, especially since World War II, has had its critics from within the cultures that seem to support it most.[20]

American society—and Western society as a whole—is certainly not as obsessed with efficiency as it was at the beginning of the century. Thanks largely to the perspectives of the environmental sciences, quantitative and mechanical notions of efficiency have been transformed. Waste, pollution, and recycling, for instance, are now a part of discussions concerning profit and utility. Quantitative determinations still remain, to be sure, but notions of scientific truth are tied more to probabilistic assessments than to absolute determinations. Probability has allowed for a certain amount of free play and even political manipulation of quantitative results.[21] And probability has also been effective in eliminating the notion that science and technology dictate absolute imperatives regarding their meaning and use. Statistically informed notions of efficiency and utility retain their greatest applicability today where the allocation of scarce resources is concerned; for example, in matters concerning energy and health care.

Evangelium Vitae's *Efficiency*

In order to understand John Paul II's use of the concept of efficiency in the argument of *Evangelium Vitae*, one must first appreciate his conception of the terms in which life can be discussed. A fundamental feature of his thinking is his deep-seated repugnance to quantification as a language or tool to assess or evaluate life. Early in the encyclical, he emphasizes the *"greatness* and *inestimable value* of human life even in its temporal phase" and the *"incomparable value of every human person"* (*EV* 2). Life, in the Pope's view, is beyond quantification. His rejection of quantification extends to utilitarian assessments and so, by implication, to those involving quantitative efficiency. "It is often claimed," the Pope writes in disdain, "that the life of an unborn child or a seriously disabled person is only a relative good: according to a proportionalist approach, or one of sheer calculation, this good should be compared with and balanced against other goods" (*EV* 68). He goes on to link this type of utilitarian and quantitative thinking to the democratic culture, especially its system of civil law. His rejection of quantitative thinking structures his views on how efficiency can be used in arguments concerning life and death.

Hence, in the overwhelming majority of instances where efficiency is invoked, the Pope either makes use of or alludes to a *qualitative* notion of efficiency. He can then set up a framework within which absolute differences between persons can be identified and absolute conclusions can be drawn. So, for instance, he argues that families and society "are organized almost exclusively on the basis of criteria of productive efficiency, according to which a hopelessly impaired life *no longer has any value*" (*EV* 64, emphasis added). Statements citing rejections of this sort are pervasive in the encyclical. John Paul II attributes this culture of exclusion to the replacement of the criterion of personal dignity as a guide for judging a person by "the criterion [*sic*] of efficiency, functionality, and usefulness" (*EV* 23). In this vein he further identifies a mentality "which tends to *equate personal dignity with the capacity for verbal and explicit*, or at least perceptible, *communication*" and which has "no place . . . for anyone who is a weak element . . . and can only communicate through the silent language of a profound sharing of affection" (*EV* 19). His use of military terminology in this context sharpens the perceived distance between those whom he believes are labeled efficient and those who are not. The *"war of the powerful against the weak,"* as the Pope describes this state of affairs, looks upon life requiring greater care "as the enemy to be resisted or eliminated" (*EV* 12). Thus, in the Pope's view, a society obsessed with (qualitative) efficiency is one whose social order is dominated by polarizations and negations.

Yet John Paul II himself cannot entirely abandon the usefulness of some kind of *quantitative* notion of efficiency in the complex and costly world of modern technologies, especially medical technologies. In three instances the Pope does mention quantitatively informed notions of efficiency or utility; all three cases concern euthanasia. The first two have direct and explicit negative connotations. Early in the encyclical (*EV* 15), he mentions that "euthanasia is sometimes justified by the utilitarian motive of avoiding costs which bring no return and which weigh heavily on society." He believes that euthanasia is advancing where there is an "attitude of excessive preoccupation with efficiency and which sees the growing number of elderly and disabled people as intolerable and *too* burdensome" (*EV* 64, emphasis added). The third instance, however, opens the door to a sensitive application of quantitative efficiency or utility. This occurs when John Paul II compares euthanasia to the case where "aggressive medical treatment" is withheld. In the latter case, utility—and so efficiency—justifies an otherwise morally questionable action because such treatments are "disproportionate to any expected results or because they impose an excessive burden on the patient and his family" (*EV* 65). He furthermore admits of a general guideline that is based explicitly on quantitative assessments of utility and efficiency. In such cases, he explains, "it needs to be determined whether the means of treatment available are objectively proportionate to the prospects for improvement" (*EV* 65). Presumably such cases could be the foundation for constructing a morally responsible culture of efficiency, as must occur in order to avoid the conundrum that results when, in the absence of "calculating" greater and lesser goods, not even the accepted notion of a "just war" would be possible. Moreover, a culture of life would seem to require that resources be allocated so that as many lives as possible be saved. Spending huge amounts of resources on marginal lives may prevent that.

Two versions of efficiency thus coexist in *Evangelium Vitae*. For the most part, the Pope condemns both. By claiming that certain judgments concerning persons in modern society are shaped by notions of qualitative efficiency, the Pope is able to make strong moral statements. But the basis of his judgment is, from a historical perspective, anachronistic. The result is, I believe, to close off discussion on certain moral issues raised by reproductive and thanatotic technologies. That discussion can begin, however, if the problems were cast more clearly in terms of quantitative notions of efficiency and utility. This alternative would seem to be more consistent with the Pope's positive valuation of ecological and environmental initiatives. Deeper discussion of these issues may furthermore provide the means for understanding how an equitable distribution of resources in a world of limited means might take place.

GENDER, NATURE, AND CULTURE

John Paul II's criticism of the culture of efficiency is essentially a criticism of rational principles applied to life. And as his depiction of a technological system suggests, his criticism is also more broadly one of the entire process of rationalization. Hence, it is surprising that the solution he proposes for the contraception crisis—natural family planning—is only possible, and can only survive, in a cultural environment where rational techniques are present. Moreover, the rhythm method also presupposes the acceptance of those techniques in shaping the discourse and culture of the female body and feminine gender traits.

John Paul II and the Natural

Near the end of *Evangelium Vitae*, the Pope reiterates the Church's sanction of natural family planning: "The moral law obliges [the married couple] in every case to control the impulse of instinct and passion, and to respect the biological laws inscribed in their person. It is precisely this respect which makes legitimate, at the service of responsible procreation, the *use of natural methods of regulating fertility*. From the scientific point of view, these methods are becoming more and more accurate and make it possible in practice to make choices in harmony with moral values" (*EV* 97). As he had done years earlier in his commentary on *Humanae Vitae*, the Pope advocates the study of the biological regularity of ovulation.[22] He also suggests that *"centers for natural methods of regulating fertility"* be established to promote "responsible parenthood" as well as "responsible procreation" (*EV* 97). The method, the Pope believes, has a utilitarian justification for its proper use, where "even [the good] of the whole of mankind" can be used as a reason for deploying it.[23]

One cannot help but notice that the rhythm method, which relies on a reading of signs, fits the Pope's notion of how nature, including human nature, should be studied in the first place: through the interpretation of signs.[24] He denies that the method is based simply on a biological regularity, a "natural law," for utilization of the method also involves fidelity to the "order of nature in procreation" and to the Creator-Person.[25] In the Pope's view, proper use of the method also relies upon reading the language of the body, which is expressed not merely sexually but more importantly through the expression of masculinity and femininity.[26] Deployment of the rhythm method is undeniably in part an attempt to find moral guidance in the signs of what is essentially a natural phenomenon, for these signs mark the onset and cessation of self-discipline and continence, which the Pope identifies as virtues.

Signs finally enable the Pope to set up distinctions that preserve the supernatural and the existence of miracles. In his view, miracles are "marvels and signs" or "deeds, wonders, and signs" that mark the suspension of the laws of nature or of their ordinary function. Miracles thus produce not only highly improbable results but also *impossible* ones: they extend the potential of nature "beyond the sphere of its normal capacity of action."[27] This combined system of both nature and miracle as sign is a point of no small importance when considering how the concepts and implications of science and technology, including the rhythm method, are treated throughout *Evangelium Vitae.* Case studies in the history of science have demonstrated that one way in which miracles were preserved in a scientific culture was to define sharply the ordinary course of nature; to allow for quantification, but not necessarily probability or probabilistic thinking; and to create a system of natural laws expressing absolute truth in which improbabilities have no role but impossibilities in the form of miracles do.[28] Hence, from a historical perspective, certain views regarding the laws of nature have been espoused by individuals who believe in them. The Pope's predilection for a qualitative concept of efficiency, for instance, fits within this framework. So do his claims concerning the rhythm method.

The Technology and Politics of the Rhythm Method

John Paul II's discussion of the rhythm method is extensive in places, but he never quite says what it is. A recent women's medical description reads,

> [The rhythm method] relies on close observation of a woman's cycle to detect when ovulation occurs. Women using this method note the temperature increase that occurs just after ovulation and the change in cervical mucus from dry to wet and slippery that occurs around the same time. It takes into account the fact that sperm live an average of five days in the uterus and that the lifespan of the egg after ovulation is 1–3 days. In general, a couple should not have sexual intercourse 7 days before and 3 days after ovulation. . . . It is less effective than other means of birth control . . . because of the difficulty in predicting exactly when ovulation will occur.[29]

A way to circumvent this difficulty is to keep a record of several cycles that the woman hopes will provide a pattern for the future behavior of her system. Still, the principal quantitative sign that ovulation has occurred—the temperature increase—appears only after the fact. It is furthermore well known that the menstrual cycle is sensitive to influences from any number of factors in the woman's life, thus always making "regularity" something less than absolute regularity. Ovulation could occur earlier or later. So no matter now accurate the methods of measurement or determination become, variations will still occur.

The rhythm method is a technology. It requires an accurate and sensitive thermometer, but one durable enough for home use. It is goal-oriented. It organizes, maps out, and restricts life. It organizes a small part of a woman's time on a daily basis and a larger portion of the interaction of a couple over the course of a month. For the woman, it promotes certain actions and values at the level of everyday practices: her temperature must be taken at the same time every day, and she must be as restful as she can be. For the couple, the method determines periods of continence, so it organizes their relationship. The method also requires a careful and learned reading of bodily signs, especially the consistency and elasticity of cervical (not vaginal) mucus. And it asks the woman to accept the rigid discipline of daily measurements that must be recorded.

The rhythm method has a politics. It settles a problem in modern marriage. It is not a neutral action, for it reshapes several different types of activities and their meaning. It may subject a couple to emotional constraints and redefines at least a part of the marriage. Finally, it makes the woman the vehicle of control in family planning; she is the one who has primary responsibility for "responsible parenthood" by taking, recording, and reading the signs of the ovulation cycle.

The rhythm method requires a particular cultural environment to exist. Viewed from an ethnographic perspective, the rhythm method requires that the routines that form the background of daily life be those that enable a person to act rationally and that those routines be so engrained in the culture that they can be taken for granted. The rhythm method can thus exist successfully only in a culture based on calculation, quantification, accuracy, and belief in the validity of instrumental readings; prediction, regularity, and punctuality; and finally deliberate action and the ability to select and project alternative plans. It must also be a culture where a woman knows what will influence her basal body temperature (restlessness, alcohol, and emotional or physical disturbances) and where she has the time to make and reason through the meaning of that quantitative determination. Finally, it must be a culture where women have running water to wash their hands and are accustomed to obtaining samples of cervical mucus. This culture is thus one that is overwhelmingly rational, and it is not one that exists worldwide. So although the Pope extols the appreciation of "the gestures and symbols present in the traditions and customs of different cultures and peoples" (*EV* 85), spreading the rhythm method would be to disseminate the core set of values and attitudes of rational efficient cultures he criticizes.

Gender Traits and the Rhythm Method

At least from the time of Aristotle, scientific theories have been applied to the woman's body. Historians have noted that, for the most part, no matter what those theories were, they have supported the hierarchies, control, and

domination inherent in a patriarchal society: man remained the measure—
and the master—of all things. These theories have also contributed to the formation of feminine gender traits.[30] For instance, although there are debates
on how to interpret the number of sexes in the Aristotelian system,[31] historians tend to agree that gender traits tended to be more fluid than they became
with the onset of modernity. By the late eighteenth and early nineteenth centuries, however, political and other factors helped to overthrow earlier
notions and put in their place a system of complementarity wherein male and
female as well as masculinity and femininity marked two separate and distinct
biological and gender entities.[32] As an example of how scientific theories
helped to create gender traits, consider the role of conservation of energy in
gendering the female body. This theory created a sense of bodily economy
where women had limited amounts of energy, as they did in the Aristotelian
tradition, but now that energy had to be conserved for reproductive purposes. Activities such as excessive thinking and reading "wasted" this finite
store of energy. So the more women tried to do more than have babies, the
more they put themselves into a state of nervous exhaustion. "Nervousness
was," according to Cynthia Russett, "synonymous with female sexuality."[33]
So was frailty, excitability, corporeal thinness, and mental exhaustion—traits
that were believed not to disappear until after menopause.

   This type of biological reductionism, which equates women with their
reproductive organs, has not entirely disappeared. It is present, for instance, in
John Paul II's thinking on gender. Although the Pope rejects the contemporary culture of the body wherein the body "is simply a complex of organs,
functions, and energies to be used according to the sole criteria of pleasure and
efficiency" (*EV* 23), he fails to extract his thinking from reductionism. *Evangelium Vitae*, which is not written in a gender-neutral language, projects an
image of women as vessels and vectors. They carry and give birth to life, an
earthly function that parallels that of the Church, which, as the vector to the
spiritual afterlife, is also engaged in maternal, feminine functions (*EV* 3). In
the Pope's thinking, pregnancy and birth furthermore make women emotionally privileged and morally responsible. Thus it is women who "bear witness to
the meaning of genuine love" (*EV* 99). And so women are the ones charged
with creating conditions for the authentic acceptance of the other person, "the
indispensable prerequisite for authentic cultural change" (*EV* 99). Femininity
and masculinity thus become little more than the bodily and psychological
expressions of biological women and men that constitute the "language of the
body."[34]

   The gender traits associated with the rational daily practices of the
rhythm method, however, contrast sharply with the emotional traits of femininity the Pope seems to favor. The rhythm method promotes a set of practices that, if adopted on a widespread scale, become potent resources for

gender characteristics. They are gender characteristics associated with rationality—such as calculation, punctuality, and regularity—but they have the potential to acquire connotations of power, too, since the purpose of the method is to regulate sexual intercourse in marriage. The woman, moreover, becomes associated with efficiency, for she becomes the efficient machine in daily routine but the reverse with respect to fertilization where the intent is to minimize output. Were we to view these rational practices in the context of the Progressive Era, we would be in a position to say, too, that they contributed to the masculinization of the feminine body and that they thus helped to promote (again, in their view) women's equality.[35] It seems sufficient to point out that via the rhythm method, especially its daily routine, the female body becomes incorporated as a topic within rational discourse. Hence, although John Paul II denies that the functional and utilitarian aspects are all there is to the method and claims that the method can only be understood in its ethical context,[36] the daily actions and their overwhelmingly rational cultural context remain. It might be argued that the Pope's inherently feminine conception of nature (as *mater*, not matter [*EV* 22]), which is not to be an object of manipulation, forecloses a rational reading of the rhythm method. But the fact remains that for the method to be successful, a rational culture must first exist.

CONCLUDING REMARKS

In the end this essay has largely concerned the cultural context of rationality in daily life, especially technology and efficiency as John Paul II views them. By pointing to a contradiction in the Pope's argument—that the rhythm method stands to instantiate the cultural characteristics that he largely condemns—this essay in essence has called for a deeper investigation of the role of rationality in daily life from several disciplinary perspectives as an aid to finding a solution to the vexing problems raised by the culture of death. The type of investigation it calls for must treat equally industrial and nonindustrial, or developed and underdeveloped, societies. For part of the problem of rationality is, in the words of the ethnographer Harold Garfinkel, to understand how parts of the world "can not only adopt the scientific attitude with impunity, but can, for their success in employing it, make substantial claims for living upon those to whom the attitude is foreign and in many cases repugnant."[37]

NOTES

I thank Kevin Wildes, S.J., for his support, patience, and good laughter; Wayne Davis for his support, advice, and friendly challenges; and Terry Pinkard and Julia Lamm for their superb and stimulating commentaries.

1. The phrase was coined by Thomas Hughes, *Networks of Power: Electrification in Western Society, 1880–1930* (Baltimore: Johns Hopkins University Press, 1983).

2. Pope John Paul II to the Reverend George V. Coyne, S.J., Director of the Vatican Observatory, June 1, 1988, in *John Paul II on Science and Religion: Reflections on the New View from Rome*, ed. Robert J. Russell, William R. Stoeger, S.J., and George V. Coyne (Vatican City: Vatican Observatory Publications, 1990), M1–M14.

3. As originally developed by Hughes (*Networks of Power*), a technological system expresses the unity of material artifacts, engineering and scientific practices, economic structures, political institutions, and social factors. A systems approach to the history of technology also makes no distinctions between macro and micro factors, such as what goes on in the economy and what goes on in the laboratory.

4. Langdon Winner, "Do Artifacts Have Politics?" in *The Whale and the Reactor: A Search for Limits in an Age of High Technology* (Chicago/London: University of Chicago Press, 1986), 19–39, esp. 19.

5. Winner, "Technologies as Forms of Life," 3–18. The phrase "forms of life" is also Wittgenstein's, but Winner criticizes Wittgenstein and Wittgensteinians for their traditionalism in the way they approach technological phenomena; their approach, Winner argues, "leaves much to be desired." He also criticizes Marxism for its "potential for equally woeful passivity" but acknowledges that both camps have done a good service in pointing out the connections between technology and "world-making" (p. 16).

6. By "literary technology" I mean the distinctive and controlled forms of writing practiced by members of the disciplines and the professions. Cf. Steven Shapin, "Pump and Circumstance: Robert Boyle's Literary Technology," *Social Studies of Science* 14 (1984): 481–520. Modern civilization, however, is not the only one to practice obfuscation when dealing with abortion. As a recent study by Tommaso Astarita demonstrates, early modern peasants had even more elaborate verbal means for turning abortion into something other than what it was ("Peasant Culture and Official Culture in an Early Modern Italian Village," essay presented to the Department of History, Georgetown University, October 18, 1995).

7. The technological systems associated with forms of energy, for instance, are far less encompassing; see Hughes, *Networks of Power*. Other comparisons, not all expressed in terms of Hughes's notion of system but relevant nonetheless, can be found in John Ellis, *The Social History of the Machine Gun* (Baltimore: Johns Hopkins University Press, 1975); Wolfgang Schivelbush, *Geschichte der Eisenbahnreise: Zur Industrialisierung von Raum und Zeit im 19. Jahrhundert* (Frankfurt am Main: Fischer Taschenbuch, 1989); idem, *Lichtblicke: Zur Geschichte der künstlichen Helligkeit im 19. Jahrhundert* (Frankfurt am Main: Fischer Taschenbuch, 1986); Otto Mayr, *Authority, Liberty, and Automatic Machinery in Early Modern Europe* (Baltimore/London: Johns Hopkins University Press, 1986); Michael Adas, *Machines as the Measure of Men: Science, Technology, and Ideologies of Western Dominance* (Ithaca/London: Cornell University Press, 1989); and especially Wiebe E. Bijker, Thomas P. Hughes, and Trevor Pinch, eds., *The Social Construction of Technological Systems: New Directions in the Sociology and History of Technology* (Cambridge: MIT Press, 1990). The works of Karl Marx are also relevant to this point.

8. Sigmund Freud, *Civilization and Its Discontents* (New York: W.W. Norton, 1959 [orig. publ. 1927]).

9. Max Weber, *The Protestant Ethic and the Spirit of Capitalism* (New York: Charles Scribner's Sons, 1958 [orig. publ. 1904]), esp. 182–83; "Science as a Vocation," in *From Max Weber: Essays in Sociology*, ed. H. H. Gerth and C. Wright Mills (New York: Oxford University Press, 1946), 129–56.

10. Winner, preface, *The Whale and the Reactor*, ix.

11. See, for instance, the numerous citations from the early modern period in *The Compact Edition of the Oxford English Dictionary* (New York: Oxford University Press, 1971), s.v. "efficiency," 1: 835.

12. James Robert Napier, Walter Neilson, and William J. M. Rankine, "Report on the Progress and State of Applied Mechanics," *Proceedings of the Glasgow Philosophical Society* 4 (1855–1860): 207–30, at 225–26, quoted in Ben Marsden, "Engineering Science in Glasgow: Economy, Efficiency, and Measurement as Prime Movers in the Differentiation of an Academic Discipline," *British Journal for the History of Science* 25 (1992): 319–46, at 343. Marsden argues strongly for the intertwining of the quantitative and economic dimensions of efficiency in the mid-nineteenth century: "Efficiency was thus analogous to precision; and since efficiency was essentially the accurate measure of economy, Rankine's academic engineering was essentially pure science regulated by economy" (p. 346).

13. Winner, "Technē and Politeia," 40–58, at 46. Though valued elsewhere, efficiency did not take hold so strongly due to an undercurrent of anti-technological sentiment. See, for instance, Kies Gispin, "National Socialism and the Technological Culture of the Weimar Republic," *Central European History* 25 (1992): 387–406.

14. Frederick Winslow Taylor, *The Principles of Scientific Management* (New York/London: Harper & Bros., 1911).

15. Samuel Haber, *Efficiency and Uplift: Scientific Management in the Progressive Era, 1890–1920* (Chicago/London: University of Chicago Press, 1964), ix.

16. Ibid., ix, 118–20.

17. Winner, "Technē and Politeia"; Jürgen Habermas, "Technology and Science as Ideology," in *Toward a Rational Society: Student Protest, Science, and Politics* (Boston: Beacon Press, 1970), 81–122; *Haber, Efficiency and Uplift*, 121, 127, 131.

18. Haber, *Efficiency and Uplift*, xii.

19. "What Edison Learned in Germany," *Literary Digest* 44 (1912): 1156–57; "Made in Germany," *Scientific American* 105 (1911): 550; Robert H. Davis and Perley Poor Sheehan, *Efficiency: A Play in One Act* (New York: Doran, 1917); Herbert F. Small, "The Legend of German Efficiency," *Unpopular Review* 7 (1917): 230.

20. Winner, "Technē and Politeia," esp. 54. Critics of the process of rationalization, from Max Weber to Herbert Marcuse to Jürgen Habermas, are also critics of efficiency.

21. Even a complex determination such as missile accuracy has been shown to have a political dimension. Donald MacKenzie, *Inventing Accuracy: A Historical Sociology of Nuclear Missile Guidance* (Cambridge: MIT Press, 1990).

22. John Paul II, *Reflections on "Humanae Vitae"* (Boston: St. Paul Editions, 1984), 40.

23. Ibid., 44.

24. Ibid., 42.

25. Ibid., 39.

26. Ibid., 42.

27. John Paul II, *Wonders and Signs: The Miracles of Jesus* (Boston: St. Paul Books & Media, 1990), 64.

28. See, for instance, Peter Dear, "Miracles, Experiments, and the Ordinary Course of Nature," *Isis* 81 (1990): 663–83; and William Ashworth, "Catholicism and Early Modern Science," in *God and Nature: Historical Essays on the Encounter between Christianity and Science*, ed. David C. Lindberg and Ronald L. Numbers (Berkeley/Los Angeles/London: University of California Press, 1986), 136–66. In this connection Ashworth conjectures that one of the reasons for the decline of Jesuit science was its overreliance on an interpretive strategy based on marvels and signs, rather than on theory.

29. American Medical Women's Association, Inc., *The Women's Complete Healthbook*, (New York: Delacorte Press, 1995), 225; see also 254–55 on basal body temperature and the cervical-mucus test.

30. See, for instance, Joan Cadden, *Meanings of Sex Difference in the Middle Ages: Medicine, Science, and Culture* (Cambridge: Cambridge University Press, 1993); David F. Noble, *A World without Women: The Christian Clerical Culture of Western Science* (New York/Oxford: Oxford University Press, 1992); Londa Schiebinger, *The Mind Has No Sex? Women in the Origins of Modern Science* (Cambridge/London: Harvard University Press, 1989); idem, *Nature's Body: Gender in the Making of Modern Science* (Boston: Beacon Press, 1993); Thomas Laqueur, *Making Sex: Body and Gender from the Greeks to Freud* (Cambridge/London: Harvard University Press, 1990); Cynthia Eagle Russett, *Sexual Science: The Victorian Construction of Womanhood* (Cambridge/London: Harvard University Press, 1989); Catherine Gallagher and Thomas Laqueur, eds., *The Making of the Modern Body: Sexuality and Society in the Nineteenth Century* (Berkeley/Los Angeles/London: University of California Press, 1987).

31. Cadden (*Meanings of Sex Difference*) has several arguments against the notion of the one-sex theory promoted by Laqueur (*Making Sex*), which views women strictly as immature males who in the uterus failed to receive enough heat to develop and distend their sexual organs.

32. On the systems of Aristotle and complementarity, see Schiebinger, *The Mind Has No Sex?* 160–70, 214–44.

33. Russett, *Sexual Science*, 118.

34. John Paul II, *Reflections*, 32, 86.

35. Haber, *Efficiency and Uplift*, 62.

36. John Paul II, *Reflections*, passim.

37. Harold Garfinkel, *Studies in Ethnomethodology* (Englewood Cliffs, N.J.: Prentice Hall, 1967), 282.

The (Ir) Rationality of Modernity? Critical Reflections on Evangelium Vitae—COMMENTS ON KATHRYN OLESKO'S ESSAY

TERRY PINKARD

Kathryn Olesko's fine, nuanced approach to some of the central issues raised in *Evangelium Vitae* has raised, to my mind, some of the crucial issues needing to be addressed in assessing *Evangelium Vitae*'s ideas. In particular, I was struck by the way in which she has located certain conceptions of rationality within certain types of cultural contexts and raised the issue of how this understanding of rationality impacts on our understanding of *Evangelium Vitae*. I shall expand on some of the points she has raised rather than raise questions about them per se. My comments fall into three parts: first, the idea of "false consciousness" at work in *Evangelium Vitae*; second, the idea of there being "spheres" of life; and, finally, the always present problem of "modernity" in *Evangelium Vitae*.

One of the striking features of *Evangelium Vitae* is the similarity in its view about the nature of technology and the way it shapes our lives with what can perhaps be loosely called the Frankfurt School conception of the relation of technology and culture. The Frankfurt School—typified best in Horkheimer and Adorno's *Dialectic of the Enlightenment* and extending through Habermas's theory of communicative action—has long held that modern technology is not neutral in its effects on people's self-conception and on culture. In particular, modern technology gives rise to a version of what in Marxian theory is called "false consciousness." False consciousness, in this conception, is not just a mistaken view on something or other but is a basic, fundamental way of taking certain items as authoritative that, first, is itself not ultimately justifiable and, second, serves to obscure or to shift towards invisibility various alternative ways of justifying and thinking about ourselves. To have false consciousness is to have a distorted view at the basis of how we understand ourselves and the world; more radically, it means that we see the world *as* such-and-such, and this seeing-as is "false" in the sense that it ultimately cannot be defended or it cannot make good on its claims to being the only way to understand ourselves and the world. Marxists—particularly Lenin—thought, for example, that under conditions of advanced capitalism and bourgeois culture, the proletariat was necessarily deceived about what the world was really like, unable to see that the capitalist market was not inevitable and that they alone were the source of the value of the commodities they produced.

In the line of thought represented by the Frankfurt School and appearing in *Evangelium Vitae*, technology produces a kind of false consciousness in that it moves to one side and hides what would otherwise be critical thought about the limits of technology. The idea is that modern technology with its paradigm of instrumental reason makes everything seem like a means to an end for something else. There are a variety of questions to be raised about this, not the least of which is why we think that technology is powerful enough to do this. (And to make what should be an obvious point: seeing that *Evangelium Vitae* has within it a notion of false consciousness and that Marxists have a notion of false consciousness does not warrant concluding that *Evangelium Vitae* is Marxist or that all views that have a notion of false consciousness at work in them are therefore Marxist views.)

But before we consider that, it is important to note just what such false consciousness obscures. *Evangelium Vitae* holds, as do a variety of political philosophers nowadays, that the social world comes divided into "spheres" and that norms that are appropriate in one sphere are inappropriate in another. For example, "family life" is a sphere unto itself, with its own set of norms that is appropriate to it and not necessarily to others, and it would be wrong to organize the family under the same norms that one might organize a modern high-tech business. Likewise, much of what is appropriate in the economy of buying and selling is inappropriate when applied to political participation. (It is appropriate to buy goods but not votes.) What is wrong with instrumental rationality, in this view, is that it encroaches upon spheres where it is not the appropriate norm and that it does so in a way that is not immediately apparent.

Part of the force of *Evangelium Vitae* is its notion that we not simply have made a mistake about the norms appropriate to family life, to birth and death, and to procreation but are *systematically* led to make such false characterizations by the nature of modern culture with its idea of the centrality—or, to use a more trendy word, *hegemony*—of instrumental reason: that is, we have trouble understanding—or, worse, we cannot even *see*—that there are alternative ways of thinking about procreation, birth, and death that do not appeal to instrumental reason (that is, to criteria of "efficiency"). To the extent that these alternatives are sufficiently obscured, other appeals (such as those offered in Catholic teaching) can only appear as irrational, dogmatic, and authoritarian (hardly things to commend them in modern culture). The alternative thus seems to be: either you are appealing to some notion of efficiency or you are appealing to some irrational or nonrational set of criteria.

Evangelium Vitae, like much modern "critical" thought, attempts to show that this either/or is not exhaustive of the possibilities, that there are *rational* ways to think about birth, death, and procreation that are not "instrumental" in character.

If there are naturally delimited spheres of life with norms appropriate to each of them—if, for example, social life is made of distinct ways in which human beings flourish—then it is irrational to apply the norms from one sphere into those of another sphere where they do not fit. In this view, what counts as rational is a *normative* notion of what it is appropriate to believe and infer and do. We act irrationally when we act on the basis of false norms, and instrumental norms, which may be perfectly appropriate in building bridges or cathedral walls, are false when applied to issues of birth and death. Now, on the one hand, this might seem to be compatible with instrumental reason; we might want the most efficient ways, for example, of securing the "loving care" that we take to be appropriate to family life (and that is perhaps out of place in large bureaucracies). Of course, what instrumental reason does is obliterate the distinction between such spheres; what counts is what efficiently produces a given end, and there can therefore be no *rational* deliberation of which ends we ought to be pursuing. The distinction between spheres thus appears arbitrary, not something subject to rational debate. This is made all the worse in that what is actually an *obscuring* of what are distinct normative spheres comes to look, to a culture that takes instrumental reasoning as authoritative, like a process of *enlightenment* itself.

Thus, we can sum up the argument of *Evangelium Vitae*: it tries to show not merely that certain modern practices are *incompatible* with some teachings of the Church but that modern practices are themselves *irrational* and that modern *culture* serves not merely to obscure their irrationality but, much worse, to make them appear as paragons of enlightened rationality itself.

It thus becomes crucial to see if there is in *Evangelium Vitae* or in other areas of Catholic or non-Catholic philosophy anything that can make good on that larger claim about the irrationality of modern life. This is all the more necessary if we accept Olesko's point about how certain aspects of *Evangelium Vitae* are themselves self-undermining. *Evangelium Vitae* teaches, for example, that only the rhythm method is acceptable as a means of family planning, seemingly ignoring thereby the fact that the habits of mind—of measuring, calculating, and so on—necessary to practice the rhythm method encourage the kind of acceptance of instrumental rationality that *Evangelium Vitae* otherwise thinks obscures the irrationality of modern life.

We might state the point in an admittedly oversimplified way in order to bring out one of the key issues at stake. If it really is irrational to apply instrumental rationality to matters of birth, death, and procreation, then how have we come to be fooled into thinking that it is instead eminently rational? We need an account of how technology—or perhaps, more generally, instrumental reason—has come to play such a crucial role in the creation of modern false consciousness.

There is, of course, a familiar story in some philosophical circles that say many of the same things. It roughly draws on Max Weber's account of the rise of capitalism. That story, in its most general form, goes like this: Before modernity, instrumental rationality was kept in check by various forms of social authority having to do with the authority of religious worldviews. But with the fracturing of Christianity and the rise of Calvinist Protestantism, a new form of economic activity took over in northern Europe, namely, capitalism. Capitalism, however, which put such a premium on instrumental rationality, quickly began encroaching into other spheres by virtue of the sheer wealth it created. Eventually, the religious worldviews ceased to have any social authority and became instead matters of private belief. The gap in social authority was thus filled in by instrumental rationality; social authority came to rest entirely on ideas about how efficient the "rulers" were in "managing" society and the economy. In place of the good life, we got instead a promise of an increasing supply of wealth, and gradually the only recognizable form of social authority had to do with the notion of efficiency.

Followers of Leo Strauss have supplemented this tale in something like the following way: The replacement of the noble sentiments with the "base passions" during this period made it mandatory that leaders be efficient managers. (Machiavelli and Hobbes are the two key players in this narrative.) People began to despair of politics as having anything to do with the good life, and politics therefore came to be judged in terms of how it produced more wealth (or national unity or whatever) most efficiently. But this continuous process of ever-increasing efficiency in the production of wealth requires a corresponding change in consciousness; we must acquire a conception of ourselves as consumers, and thus consumerist culture—with its associated ideas of efficient satisfaction of the "base passions"—becomes embedded in modern life, which itself serves to further obscure critical alternatives.

Common to all the critical accounts of instrumental reason that accept some version of this narrative is the idea that there is a natural normative division of spheres that is sufficiently obscured by this development. To attack the hegemony of instrumental reason is thus to attack the self-sufficiency and rationality of modernity itself. That the current pope would be attacking the basis of modernity itself surely is not surprising, since the contours of much of the recent so-called modernity debate has its origins in the Catholic rejection of modernity in the eighteenth and nineteenth centuries. But we should distinguish at least two different kinds of rejection of modernity. First, there is that espoused by people such as Heidegger, who see modern life as completely rational in all respects but as bereft of "spiritual" value. They do not condemn modern life for being irrational; they condemn it for ignoring certain alternatives that escape the dichotomy of rational/irrational. Second, there are the critics, from Jürgen Habermas to the current pope, who see social life as naturally divided into spheres and whose thus differentiated norms are irrational to deny; both Habermas and the Pope thus come down on the side of declaring modern life to be irrational, not just lacking something in some other dimension of value.

This raises an issue that *Evangelium Vitae* does not address but that is crucial for coming to terms with its key ideas. What if, we might ask, it were indeed *rational* for the moderns to reject the classical view of the world? What if, that is, the various crises and insufficiencies experienced by our premodern ancestors—with regard to conceptions of knowledge, political authority, scriptural and ecclesiastical authority, and so on—were exactly the kind of thing that at least provoked, if not required, the move to the modern outlook? That the move to modernity was not a mistake but was something itself thrust on us by the internal stresses and strains of premodern forms of life and authority that undermined all normative allegiance to those norms on our part? Unless an account of the normative sufficiency of those premodern ideals of the norms appropriate to various spheres demonstrates that the felt crises and insufficiencies of the early modern period did not *require* the kinds of moves to modern notions of reason and politics, we are just begging the question as to whether this move is in itself irrational. Indeed, the issue also has to do with what kind of account we can give of what it is that we have come to take as an authoritative reason itself. For the charge of irrationality to stick, it cannot beg the question as to what itself counts as rational; it must show that the instrumental conception or other alternative, noninstrumental conceptions of rationality are not merely incompatible with some other conception but are themselves insufficient with respect to something fundamental about its own claims. Otherwise, it can only appear as dogmatic and authoritarian to the other side, and its critical force would be lost. It would be at best merely an act of assertion, a "teaching" about things that is to be accepted or rejected on criteria external to the teachings themselves.

Indeed, the existence of alternative accounts of modernity, not in terms of the usual Weberian story of the gradual encroachment of instrumental reason but in terms of the growth of critical consciousness, of a reflective distancing of ourselves from all merely given norms, throws into question whether this idea—that there is such a thing as technology in general—has led us down the road to the false consciousness of instrumental reason, or whether there are, as Olesko suggests, only historically contingent technologies that must be understood in their specific historical contexts. It also raises the further issue that, although the rise of technology may be central to modernity, the issue of what modernity itself is and why technology may be central to it is another question. Other narratives stress other elements: the gradual application of reason to the study of the world led to the application of reason to human affairs, but the rise of that kind of critical consciousness gradually led to the unmooring of people from what had traditionally underwritten social authority. The result was that the process of "modernization" led us to gradually kick away the props that had traditionally held us up, until we were finally left free-standing. No longer could the voices of tradition *on their own* count as authoritative reasons; no longer could there be an unequivocal voice of nature simply telling us what to do; no longer was there to be immediate reliance on a sacred text (the higher criticism had to mediate it for us); and, finally and most controversially, there could not be an *immediate* awareness of what was divine for us—it too had to be mediated to us by virtue of cultural contexts and changing conditions, by what we had necessarily come to take as the authoritative norms that mediated knowledge for us. Finding themselves without immediate contact with any set of authoritative norms, the moderns had to reappropriate some traditional norms by giving them a new rationale, devise some of them anew, and make all of them subject to revision.

There have been, as we might put it, three typical responses to this state of affairs: one group sees this as nothing but a counsel of nihilism and despair; another group rejects modernity and wishes to return to the past; and a third group sees this as humanity's task of devising accounts of itself that meet its highest interests without at the same time falling back onto dogmatic bases, into uncritical acceptances of any kind of normative "givens." But the kind of critical consciousness that is characteristic of modernity makes returning to premodern modes of thought impossible; nihilism is not an attractive alternative; and we are thus left with the task of constructing accounts of what is to count for us as authoritative within the context of freedom, the only normative constraints that are acceptable being self-imposed constraints. (I happen to think myself that this requires a social, historical self-reflexive explanation, but that is another story.)[1] Failing such an account, we can only have dogmatic assertion.

NOTE

1. See Terry Pinkard, *Hegel's Phenomenology: The Sociality of Reason* (Cambridge: Cambridge University Press, 1994). Also see Robert Pippin, *Idealism as Modernism: Hegelian Variations* (Cambridge: Cambridge University Press, 1997).

Tensions in a Catholic Theology of the Body: A RESPONSE TO KATHRYN OLESKO'S ESSAY

JULIA A. LAMM

I would like, first of all, to thank Kathryn Olesko for a fresh and illuminating essay from which I have learned much. Regarding the sections on technology and efficiency, I can only let myself be informed, since they are beyond my area of expertise. Regarding the section "Gender, Nature, and Culture," I would like to express my fundamental agreement with her argument by supplementing it with some theological history.

I am especially interested in its final section, "Gender Traits and the Rhythm Method," because it addresses issues that, because they have to do with the meaning of the human body, are significant for the entire encyclical. In that section, Professor Olesko argues that present in Pope John Paul IIs thinking is a "biological reductionism [that] equates women with their reproductive organs," and she situates this in the context of late-eighteenth- and nineteenth-century constructions of gender. John Paul IIs "biological reductionism" is the consequence of "a system of complementarity wherein male and female as well as masculinity and femininity marked two separate and distinct biological and gender entities." I want to develop this basic point by examining the theological-historical background of the Pope's assumptions regarding body and gender. The tensions that Professor Olesko identifies in this encyclical are traceable not only to recent centuries but also, of course, back through the centuries to the fathers of the church, who enjoy a special place of authority in the Catholic tradition. In examining John Paul IIs thinking on the meaning of human embodiment, we also inevitably must address the history of a Catholic theology of the body.

In this encyclical, as in the wider Catholic tradition, we find a compelling, nonreductionistic view of the human body as "the site . . . of religious subjectivity."[1] The body is inseparable from personhood; the body, in its particularity, is inseparably part of the soul's journey to God. Although the "life of the body in its earthly state is not an absolute good" (*EV* 47), its irreducible goodness is theologically confirmed through the central Christian doctrines of the Incarnation and Resurrection. Some of John Paul IIs most moving passages are passionate expressions about the goodness and irreducibility of embodied humanity—for instance, when he refuses to "equate personal dignity with the capacity for verbal and explicit, or at least perceptible, communication" and refers to the bodily communication that takes place "through the silent language of a profound sharing of affection" (*EV* 19); when he speaks of the "bodily dimension" of the covenant between God and God's people (*EV* 48); and when he refers to those (bodily) gestures that are expressive both of our response to God and of our responsibility to others. This affirmation of the goodness of the human body is an inextricable part of John Paul IIs basic principle in the encyclical that human life is sacred and what is sacred is inviolable (see *EV* 40, 52, 81).

Yet also in this encyclical, as in the wider Catholic tradition, we find a dis-ease with the body, an uneasiness that is only intensified by the fact that the human body is always a gendered body and Christianity has never been comfortable with the female body. That John Paul II has inherited this discomfort with the female body is especially evident if one examines the theological sources he cites as being authoritative.

In making his three chief authoritative claims, the Pope appeals to the four pillars of natural law, Scripture, "the tradition of the church," and the magisterium (*EV* 57; cf. 62, 65). His case is weakened, however, because the tradition to which he appeals is more fractious and more problematic than he would like to admit. For instance, he appeals to Tertullian's condemnation of abortion (*EV* 61) and to Ambrose's reflections on the New Testament revelation regarding "*the value of life from its very beginning*" (*EV* 45). Yet the Pope borrows from these two thinkers not only their recognition of the value of life in the womb but also their associations of the female body with earth and their idealization of woman as mother and virgin. The question that must be addressed is whether he also shares their misogyny.

Tertullian (ca. 160–220), although he did not espouse a necessarily dualistic view of the human body, nevertheless viewed women as seductresses because of their connection to Eve: "And do you not know that you are (each) an Eve? The sentence of God on this sex of yours lives in this age: the guilt must of necessity live too. *You* are the devil's gateway: *you* are the unsealer of that forbidden tree: *you* are the first deserter of the divine law . . . *You* destroyed so easily God's image, man. On account of *your* desert—that is, death—even the Son of God had to die."[2] This is why he recommends that a woman dress as though in mourning, neglecting her appearance "in order that by every garb of penitence she might the more fully expiate that which she derives from Eve—the ignominy, I mean, of the first sin, and the odium (attaching to her as the cause) of human perdition."[3] This essential connection to Eve ought not be mistaken for a symbolically moral one that could be remedied through a moral life. For Tertullian, moral integrity is not enough to undo Eve's sin, because women are inescapably female; that is to say, it is an essential part of their nature to embody "beauty and glamour," thus to be vain and seductive.[4] To be woman is to be seductive because her female body is deemed beautiful by men; not even a life of moral and spiritual integrity can undo that.

Ambrose (339–97) is an especially favorite father of the Pope, in large part because of the honor that he gives Mary, the mother of Jesus. It was, after all, Ambrose who argued vehemently, against other Christians and against much of the tradition, for the perpetual virginity of Mary. Her virginity remained intact even *in partu*: her hymen was not broken in childbirth. This very literal interpretation of bodily integrity became for Ambrose the symbol of spiritual integrity—the integrity of the Milanese church in its refusal to be penetrated by Arianism, and the integrity of each individual believer. Of course, for the male believer, this symbol remained a symbol; for the female believer, the symbol was interpreted literally.

This emphasis on the literal integrity of the ideal female form reveals another aspect of Ambrose's thought that we find echoed in John Paul II—namely, his dualistic understanding of both body and gender. A neo-Platonic dualism such as Ambrose's is a hierarchical one according to which the body is lower, more base, and therefore needs to be transcended; it also involves a secondary dualism of male and female, according to which male is associated with the higher, spiritual levels of reality and female with the lower, material levels. It follows that the human soul has to transcend not only the body but also whatever is female.[5] Whatever is bodily or female is viewed as a hindrance to salvation and thus needs to be renounced. Therefore, in his *Exposition on the Gospel according to Luke*, the same text cited by John Paul II in *Evangelium Vitae*, Ambrose speaks of the "scar" (*cicatrix*) of human sexuality.[6] According to Peter Brown, "What was novel in Ambrose's unremitting exhortations to the virgin state was the cold shadow of perpetual withdrawal that fell across the family."[7] Ambrose and Jerome (ca. 347–419) both viewed virginity as a state superior to that of married life.

Other strands of the tradition, even though they share the basic hierarchical-dualistic metaphysics of Ambrose, nevertheless were able to view human sexuality and women in a more positive light. For example, Clement of Alexandria (ca. 150–215) recognized death, not sexuality, as the primary consequence of the Fall. Consequently, he insisted that marriage is on an equal spiritual footing with celibacy, and he even suggested that marriage may be more conducive to our soul's journey to God because, by immersing ourselves in the daily details of a Christian household, we have more opportunity to attune our souls properly.[8] Another example can be found in the work of the medieval scholar Caroline Walker Bynum, who reminds us that one symbol or symbolic system does not function in the same way for different people, cultures, or genders. In religious texts of the higher Middle Ages, she says, "We find not only that men and women use the image of woman differently, but that it is not simply misogyny in either usage."[9] In the recorded mystical visions of many medieval women, the earlier Christian notion of "becoming male" fades. Their own physicality represented to them not something to be renounced but something that connected them to Christ's humanity. By immersing themselves in their physicality, they identified themselves with the incarnate Christ and so shared also in his Resurrection. Bynum concludes, "Women thus asserted and embraced their humanity. They asserted it because traditional dichotomous images of woman and man opposed humanity-physicality-woman to divinity-rationality-man. Women stressed their humanity and Jesus' because tradition had accustomed them to associate humanity with the female. . . . Humanity is genderless. To medieval women humanity was, most basically, not femaleness, but physicality, the flesh of the 'Word made flesh.'"[10]

This, however, is not the strand of the tradition to which John Paul II appeals. For him, the tradition is adequately represented by Tertullian, Ambrose, and Augustine. Granted, the most extreme positions of these fathers are not found in this encyclical, which describes human sexuality as "the sign, place and language of love" (*EV* 23) and which celebrates the family as the "domestic church" and the "sanctuary of life" (*EV* 92). Still, a basic dualism is pervasive. Whereas Ambrose's anthropological dualism was severe, John Paul IIs is a mitigated dualism better described in terms of "complementarity" than in terms of "hierarchy."[11] It is a dualism that extends from the physical to the psychic. Again and again, the Pope describes the dignity of women in terms of their motherhood, which "profoundly marks the woman's personality" (*EV* 99).[12] This psychic dualism inevitably becomes a moral dualism. The virtues of "fidelity, chastity, sacrifice" are thus peculiarly female, rather than just Christian, because they define what it is to be a wife and mother (*EV* 86). And the moral comes full circle to the biological, since the two dimensions of women's vocation—motherhood and virginity[13]—are defined according to their biological status.

That the writings of the church fathers contain misogynist elements has all but been admitted by the Vatican: "It is true that in the writings of the fathers one will find the undeniable influence of prejudices unfavorable to women."[14] Yet it is not enough to make the passing admission that some elements of the tradition are misogynistic; rather, what is needed are clear interpretative principles by which we may determine what, precisely, may be accepted as authoritative in these sources and how that may be separated out from what is unacceptable—from what devalues women and from what therefore is inimical to the witness of the Gospel of life.

NOTES

1. Margaret R. Miles, *Carnal Knowing: Female Nakedness and Religious Meaning in the Christian West* (New York: Random House, 1989), 30.

2. Tertullian, "On the Apparel of Women," 1.1, trans. S. Thelwall, in *The Ante-Nicene Fathers* (Grand Rapids, Mich.: Wm. B. Eerdmans Publishing, 1956), 4: 14.

3. Ibid.

4. "For most women . . . either from simple ignorance or else from dissimulation, have the hardihood so to walk as if modesty consisted only in the (bare) integrity of the flesh, and in turning away from (actual) fornication; and there were no need for anything extrinsic to boot—in the matter (I mean) of the arrangement of dress and ornament, the studied graces of form and brilliance . . ." (ibid., 2.1.2).

5. For some early Christians, women had to "become male" in order to be saved; they had, in other words, to transcend their lower status in the hierarchy. See Miles, "'Becoming Male': Women Martyrs and Ascetics," chap. 2 in *Carnal Knowing*.

6. Ambrose, *Expositio evangelii secundum Lucam*, 5.24. In *Corpus Christianorum, Series Latina*, 14: 144, cited by Peter Brown, *The Body and Society: Men, Women, and Sexual Renunciation in Early Christianity* (New York: Columbia University Press, 1988), 350. See *EV* 45 36.

7. Brown, *The Body and Society*, 356.

8. See Clement of Alexandria, *Miscellanies*, book 3, "On Marriage."

9. Caroline Walker Bynum, "'. . . And Women His Humanity': Female Imagery in the Religious Writing of the Later Middle Ages," in *Fragmentation and Redemption: Essays on Gender and the Human Body in Medieval Religion* (New York: Zone Books, 1992), 156.

10. Ibid., 179.

11. In his *Letter to Women*, June 29, 1995, he writes, "Woman complements man, just as man complements woman: Men and women are complementary. Womanhood expresses the 'human' as much as manhood does, but in a different and complementary way. . . . Their most natural relationship, which corresponds to the plan of God, is the 'unity of the two,' a relational 'uni-duality' which enables each to experience their interpersonal and reciprocal relationship as a gift which enriches and which confers responsibility" (nos. 7, 8).

12. See John Paul II, *On the Dignity of Women; EV* 18.

13. John Paul II, *On the Dignity of Women* 6.17.

14. Sacred Congregation for the Doctrine of the Faith, *Declaration on the Question of the Admission of Women to the Ministerial Priesthood*, October 15, 1976, in *Origins* 6, no. 33 (February 3, 1977): 519.

The Limits of Ordinary Virtue:
The Limits of the Criminal Law in
Implementing Evangelium Vitae

M. Cathleen Kaveny

Law should be virtuous, just, possible to nature, according to the custom of the country, suitable to place and time, necessary, useful; clearly expressed, lest by its obscurity it lead to misunderstanding; framed for no private benefit, but for the common good."[1]

Pope John Paul II's encyclical *Evangelium Vitae* vigorously reaffirms the sanctity and inviolability of each human life as created in the image of God and passionately calls all persons in the name of God to "respect, protect, love and serve life, every human life" (*EV* 5).[2] Explicitly invoking the Second Vatican Council's condemnation of "whatever is opposed to life itself . . . whatever violates the integrity of the human person . . . and whatever insults human dignity,"[3] the encyclical contends that powerful technological, intellectual, and political currents threaten the sanctity of life in new and sinister ways. While many of these currents have their source in first-world countries, they undermine the sanctity of life across the globe, particularly in the third world.

Chief among the dangers identified by the Pope is the erosion of legal protections offered to weak and defenseless life such as the unborn and the elderly. Not only have many countries removed criminal penalties against the practices of abortion and euthanasia; they have also legitimated decisions to take such actions as an aspect of human autonomy. With respect to the United States, the Pope is no doubt contemplating the era of constitutionally protected abortion rights inaugurated in 1973 by *Roe v. Wade*, along with persistent and increasingly vocal calls to grant legal protection to a patient's decision in favor of physician-assisted suicide.[4]

According to John Paul II, the stakes are enormous: abortion and euthanasia are but two symptoms of an encroaching "culture of death" whose hallmarks are materialism, the depersonalization and commercialization of sexuality, and a distorted emphasis on autonomy and efficiency that corrodes the bonds of affection and responsibility between the productive and unproductive members of society. In the final analysis, the Pope views the "culture of death" as the war of the strong against the weak.

The Pope urges the creation of a "culture of life" to combat these death-dealing forces and to embrace each member of the human community with love and concern. He calls upon civil leaders to "make courageous choices in support of life, especially through *legislative measures*" (*EV* 90). The Pope urges lawmakers "not to pass laws which, by disregarding the dignity of the person, undermine the very fabric of society." At the same time, however, he acknowledges the difficulty of mounting "an effective legal defense of life in pluralistic democracies." While refusing to "give in," legislators must nonetheless "tak[e] into account what is realistically available" as they struggle toward the "reestablishment of a just order in the defense and promotion of the value of life (*EV* 90)."

The task of a legislator, then, involves a complex and morally precarious balancing act. How should we distinguish between censurable acquiescence in the culture of death and clear-eyed realism about concrete possibilities for legislative advancement of a culture of life? Does this elusive distinction require us to take advantage of every political opportunity to enact legislation prohibiting abortion and euthanasia, no matter how narrowly such measures are supported in the community, how ineffectively they may be enforced, and how quickly they might be repealed? Can the availability of the social support structures called for by the Pope for those individuals and families tempted by desperate or difficult circumstances to practice abortion or euthanasia legitimately affect our decisions about how to use the *criminal law* in order to prohibit or discourage such actions?

Evangelium Vitae does not provide clear and unequivocal guidance with respect to these issues. In many respects, such circumspection on the part of the Pope is appropriate and even welcome as he invites academics and legislators to make their own distinctive contributions to the culture of life by formulating nuanced answers to the questions falling under their particular sphere of expertise. At the same time, I believe that the encyclical's lack of clarity on these matters is also attributable to a fundamental ambiguity in the analytic framework it adopts.

On the one hand, certain portions of *Evangelium Vitae* focus on the absolute nature of the prohibition against taking innocent human life, along with its essential role in protecting the rights of vulnerable members of our society. Concentrating on the *victims* of abortion and euthanasia, this stance generates a straightforward jurisprudential approach. The most basic function of the state is to safeguard persons against infringements of their rights—if necessary, by using its coercive power. The state has a fundamental duty to use the criminal law to protect potential victims of abortion and euthanasia by prohibiting and punishing such activities. Governmental actions to institute social support programs may be pragmatically important, but they are purely secondary as a matter of jurisprudence.

On the other hand, other passages of *Evangelium Vitae* pay significantly greater attention to the potential *perpetrators* of these death-dealing activities, as well as the pressures that lead them toward such choices.[5] They also recognize that a negative moral obligation prohibiting the killing of the innocent is not sufficient to foster the culture of life but must be intertwined with positive obligations to assist the weak and the vulnerable. These themes lend themselves quite well to a legal theory that incorporates into the very heart of its legal draftsmanship the consideration of the concrete circumstances in which persons are led to commit morally objectionable acts.

I believe that this second jurisprudential approach is more congenial to the legal theory developed by St. Thomas Aquinas in the *Summa Theologica*, to which the Pope appeals more than once in *Evangelium Vitae*. For Thomas, the central goal of a system of positive law is not to protect the rights of the victims *but to lead potential perpetrators to virtue*, albeit slowly and haltingly. Furthermore, I believe that Thomas's theory of law not only is more capable than the rights-based approach of accommodating crucial concerns of the American legal system (particularly our system of criminal law) but also affords a more fruitful way of dealing with the question of American pluralism regarding the moral issues at the heart of *Evangelium Vitae*. I will elaborate upon these points in the remainder of this essay.[6]

THE INADEQUACY OF RIGHTS LANGUAGE AND NEGATIVE MORAL NORMS AS A SOURCE FOR POSITIVE LAW

In *Evangelium Vitae*, the Pope unequivocally reaffirms the teaching of the Church that "the deliberate decision to deprive an innocent human being of his life is always morally evil and can never be licit either as an end in itself or as a means to a good end" (*EV* 57). John Paul II construes this exceptionless moral norm as the guardian of last resort for "weak and defenseless human beings, who find their ultimate defense against the arrogance and caprice of others only in the absolute binding force of God's commandment" (*EV* 57).

The pivotal role played by the prohibition in the defense of the weak provides the Pope with a natural bridge to the alternative vocabulary in which he formulates his attack against the culture of death: the language of human rights. Contending that the purpose of the civil law is to "guarantee an ordered social coexistence in true justice," he maintains that "civil law must ensure that all members of society enjoy respect for certain fundamental rights which innately belong to the person, rights which every positive law must recognize and guarantee." The foremost of these is the "inviolable right to life of every innocent human being" (*EV* 71).

The Pope draws upon the vocabulary of exceptionless moral norms and upon "rights" language to articulate his conception of the proper stance of positive law toward abortion and euthanasia. Citing Thomas Aquinas for the proposition that a civil law opposed to the natural law (which prohibits all violations of exceptionless moral norms) is not really a law but a corruption of the same, the Pope proclaims that "laws which *authorize and promote* abortion and euthanasia . . . are completely lacking in authentic juridical validity." He also refers to a law "*permitting* abortion or euthanasia" as an "intrinsically unjust law" that calls for conscientious objection (*EV* 72, emphasis added). Turning to the language of human rights, the Pope rejects any attempt to characterize a choice for abortion or euthanasia as a competing right. "Public authority can never presume to legitimize as a right of individuals . . . an offense against other persons caused by the disregard of so fundamental a right as the right to life (*EV* 71)." His rejection encompasses voluntary as well as involuntary euthanasia.

Yet the Pope does not tell us precisely how the civil law must respect either natural law's absolute prohibition against intentional killing of the innocent or the fundamental rights claims of the weak and vulnerable. Are there jurisprudentially salient differences between 1) a law *permitting* abortion or euthanasia, 2) a law *authorizing and approving* abortion and euthanasia, and 3) a law declaring access to abortion and euthanasia to be a *fundamental aspect of human autonomy?* Where should we place the new "compromise" abortion legislation for unified Germany, which makes abortion within the first trimester illegal but imposes a penalty neither upon the women who obtain such abortions after receiving appropriate counseling nor upon the doctors who perform them?[7] For the reasons described below, neither the language of human rights nor that of absolute negative moral norms is adequate to address these questions.

Rights Language

Evangelium Vitae calls upon civil society to protect the fundamental right to life of all human beings. But in and of itself, the term "fundamental right to life" is essentially ambiguous. To invoke rights language does not tell us how conflicting rights are to be resolved or where to draw the limits of a right. For example, in Judith Jarvis Thomson's famous case of the hapless hospital patient who awakens "plugged into" an unconscious violinist dependent upon her for life support, we may very well say that the patient's right to autonomy trumps the violinist's right to life.[8] To draw this line, we invoke the moral distinction between an exceptionless duty to refrain from directly harming an innocent person and a context-dependent positive duty to assist that person. Taking another example, a right-holder may under certain circumstances waive that right by granting another person permission to do what he or she could not do without such permission. A patient's informed consent normally suffices to authorize a physician to perform medical procedures that would otherwise constitute battery. Yet some rights may not be waivable, such as the right not to be enslaved. To take a more controversial example, the Pope sharply contests the legitimacy of a person's decision to waive his or her "right" against euthanasia.

In short, rights language is underdetermined from a moral point of view. We draw the borders of our rights claims by reference to the landmarks of the background moral theory we believe to be decisive. The Pope's justification for denying that one can waive a right not to be euthanized does not arise from the internal logic of rights language itself but from his natural law arguments on the immorality of suicide. In his magisterial effort to fuse traditional natural law theory with contemporary human-rights language, John Finnis perceptively describes the necessary process: "How is this process of specification and demarcation [of rights] to be accomplished? . . . There is, I think, no alternative but to hold in one's mind's eye some pattern, or range of patterns, of human character, conduct, and interaction in community and then to choose such specification of rights as tends to favour that pattern, or range of patterns. In other words, one needs some conception of human good, of individual flourishing in a form (or range of forms) of communal life that fosters rather than hinders such flourishing."[9]

The status of rights language as a sort of "shorthand" for our unexpressed full-blown moral theory has two major consequences for the task of turning moral claims into legal claims. First, as theorists such as Alasdair MacIntyre, Mary Ann Glendon, and others have repeatedly noted,[10] rights language does not provide a basis for fruitful conversation about controverted moral issues, especially in a pluralistic society. The American experience with twenty years of often vituperative abortion debates has shown how rights claim meets its counterclaim in the relentless opposition of "life" and "choice." Any hope for dialogue, and a fortiori for the possibility of true moral conversion called for by the Pope, depends upon our willingness to offer our opponents the rich moral vision of human flourishing and the shape of our common life that animates rights claims in the context of abortion and euthanasia. In a democratic society such as our own, inability to forge consensus around these elements of the Gospel of life inevitably means that it will not be adopted as legislative and social policy.

Second, as alluded to above, conclusory claims of moral "rights" do not provide much guidance for discerning how the law should be used to protect such claims. Arguably, I have a right to expect that promises made to me will not be broken. I have a right to expect other persons will conduct their activities in a way that will not damage my property. I have a right to expect that products inserted into the stream of commerce will not harm me. For a panoply of reasons of the sort alluded to by John Finnis, our society has determined that these rights will be protected in quite different ways. Despite the moral wrong involved in promise breaking, contemporary contract law will not enforce even very important promises unless the promisee can show that he gave something in return for the promise (i.e., "consideration") or that he or she has demonstrably relied on that promise to his or her detriment. Moreover, even in cases where the court intervenes in favor of the recipient of a broken promise, its aim is not punitive but, at most, to put the promisee in the same position that he or she would have been in had the promise been fulfilled. Persons, however, who impede my right to enjoy the fruits of my consumerism by selling me a harmful and defective product, or who conduct their affairs in a way that foreseeably risks damage to my property, may be obliged to pay punitive damages in tort to me as a consequence of their wrongdoing.

The relevance of any moral fault or failing on the part of the "rights violator" also changes as we move from example to example. Since contract law is not fundamentally concerned with moral culpability, a person who breaches a contract without fault may still be liable to pay damages to make up for the breach. In tort law, whose very name proclaims its concern with moral rights and wrongs, I cannot ordinarily recover for damage done to my property unless it was the result of negligence or intentional wrongdoing. Under the theory of products liability, however, I can recover in tort from a manufacturer or retailer for damages caused by an unreasonably dangerous product sold to me, even if the manufacturer or retailer was guilty of no wrongdoing. To sort through the similarities and differences among the legal protections granted to these various rights claims, one needs to move beyond rights language itself into such issues as the nature and purpose of the relevant body of law, as well as the social import of the type of behavior at issue.

My next point about the limited usefulness of rights language in the task of legal draftsmanship follows closely upon the preceding one. Many of those who invoke the language of absolute human rights with respect to abortion and euthanasia, including the Pope, appear to believe that some sort of criminal sanctions are appropriate in these cases. More specifically, the Pope repeatedly refers to abortion as a "crime" and applies the term "murder" to apply to both abortion and euthanasia. He considers the fact that many countries have determined not to "punish" these practices against life to be a telling mark against contemporary culture.

Criminal law, far more than any other branch of our legal system, takes as decisive the moral status of the *perpetrator*. The indispensable core of legal culpability is moral culpability. In the United States, not everyone morally guilty of committing a certain act prohibited by the penal code will be found legally guilty; our system frequently sacrifices this sort of strict justice to other values, such as procedural fairness and due deference to liberty. Nonetheless, it is generally designed to insure that persons who are *not* morally guilty of a crime will not be found guilty under the law.

Without denigrating the equal worth of the victim as a human being, the crimes defined in the penal code take into account the subjective moral culpability of the *defendant*. For example, crimes involving the taking of human life commonly include first-degree murder, second-degree murder, and manslaughter. In many jurisdictions, a man who shoots his wife and her lover immediately upon discovering them in flagrante delicto would be guilty of manslaughter rather than murder. In effect, the law creates a presumption that most persons who commit such an act do so under extreme provocation that mitigates their culpability. More generally, the criminal law of most jurisdictions recognizes that extreme duress may completely excuse or partially mitigate the guilt of an agent who commits an act in direct violation of its strictures. At the extreme, the law recognizes that if a truly insane person commits an action prohibited by the penal code without understanding its nature or consequences, he or she cannot be morally or therefore criminally culpable.

Rights language is inadequate to capture the agent-centered approach of the criminal law for two basic reasons. First, in and of itself, rights language directs our attention to the needs and sufferings of the *victim* rather than to the capabilities and responsibilities of the *perpetrator*. To say that an individual has a right to life, or to food or shelter for that matter, is to highlight the crucial role that such a good plays in furthering his or her well-being. Moreover, language pertaining to the *violation* of rights focuses on the harm suffered by such a person when deprived of that good; it does not emphasize the intention, motive, and circumstances under which the agent causing that harm acted. A person's well-being is adversely affected to the same degree if he or she is 1) intentionally killed by an agent acting with full freedom and for entirely selfish motives, 2) killed by an agent acting under significant duress, or 3) killed as the unintended but foreseen effect of an action performed by an agent whose primary intent was to destroy a terrorist cell. Consequently, rights language by itself is highly unlikely either to generate or to support distinctions between these three situations when considering the question of what legal framework should be implemented. Such distinctions, however, are essential from the perspective of the criminal law, whose primary focus is the moral culpability of the agent.

Second and relatedly, the prevalence of rights language may be eroding the fundamental action theory commonly used by both Roman Catholic moral theology and the American legal system. As noted above, from the perspective of a rights-holder, there is no concrete difference between the harm suffered as a result of intentional wrongdoing and that suffered as the unintended but foreseen effect of a legitimate action. Consequently, for those who are not steeped in the action theory and the worldview that supports it, there appears to be no real reason to maintain the distinction between the intended effects of an action and its foreseen but unintended effects, particularly when the result to the rights-bearer is the same. A striking example of this phenomenon can be found in *Compassion in Dying v. State of Washington*. In pronouncing a constitutionally protected "right to die," the Ninth Circuit opinion entirely eradicated the distinction between intended and foreseeable effects of an action. The court maintained that there should be no ethical or legal difference between a physician who gives a patient painkillers that have the unintended but foreseeable consequence of greatly shortening his or her life, and a physician who prescribes a lethal dose of medication with the intention of killing the patient. A key element in the court's holding is that the concrete manner in which the two scenarios affect the rights-bearer is precisely the same.

Negative Moral Norms

Just as too great an emphasis on the rights of the victim can eclipse the necessary focus of the criminal law upon the moral capacities of the perpetrator, so too can a parallel emphasis upon the importance of exceptionless moral norms. In *Evangelium Vitae*, John Paul II continues the battle against proportionalism and ethical relativism that he began to wage in *Veritatis Splendor*. These norms, he contends, are always and everywhere binding because the actions they prohibit are "radically incompatible with the love of God and with the dignity of the person created in his image" (*EV* 75).

A key element in the theoretical justification of absolute negative moral norms is that in contrast with positive moral obligations, which may conflict with one another on occasion, it is logically possible for each person to obey all negative obligations always and everywhere. In fact, under most circumstances, it is fairly easy for most persons to refrain from violating the more serious negative moral prohibitions that are inscribed in our criminal law: do not kill, do not assault, do not steal. Yet there are circumstances where obeying a negative prohibition requires an immense amount of fortitude. In *Veritatis Splendor*, the Pope himself recognizes that in extraordinary situations, nothing less than the commitment of a martyr may be required in order to refrain from committing a morally evil act. "In raising [martyrs] to the honor of the altars, the Church has canonized their witness and declared the truth of their judgment, according to which the love of God entails the obligation to respect his commandments, even in the most dire of circumstances, and the refusal to betray those commandments, even for the sake of saving one's own life" (*VS* 91).[11]

From the point of view of the criminal law, it is the difficulty in obeying the obligation, not its absolute nature, that is crucial. Ethics can insist upon a duty to sacrifice one's own life rather than commit an intrinsically evil act, but such insistence is beyond the province of human law, which must take into account subjective capabilities as well as objective wrongdoing. Positive law in general, and a fortiori the criminal law, cannot require martyrdom on the part of its citizens. As the defenses of necessity and duress indicate, the criminal law should not attempt to punish even the most serious of intrinsically evil acts if the person who committed such an act did so under circumstances that severely compromised his or her free will.

Speaking of abortion and euthanasia, the Pope acknowledges that "decisions that go against life sometimes arise from difficult or even tragic situations of profound suffering, loneliness, a total lack of economic prospects, depression and anxiety about the future. Such circumstances can mitigate even to a notable degree subjective responsibility and the consequent culpability of those who make these choices which in themselves are evil" (*EV* 18). Yet his emphasis on rights language and the language of negative moral absolutes appears to obscure for him the necessity of taking these factors into account in drafting wise law.

There is a second problem with the Pope's emphasis on the applicability of negative moral norms in the context of euthanasia and abortion. As noted above, he believes these practices to be particularly disturbing because they target the most fragile members of the human community. Yet, as the Pope himself acknowledges, it is precisely in the case of the weak and the vulnerable that the distinction between positive duties and negative duties begins to break down. For the strong and well, general enforcement of negative duties suffices as protection. Almost by definition, however, the weak need assistance from the stronger in order to survive. How long and in what sort of condition will a person with advanced Alzheimer's live without someone to feed, clothe, shelter, and comfort her? How well will an unborn child fare if the woman who carries him refuses to put her body at his disposal by ensuring that he obtains proper nutrition while in utero and abstaining from drugs, alcohol, and other substances likely to do far more damage to him than to her? In these cases, a clear distinction between absolute negative duties and positive duties whose force can vary with time, ability, and circumstance is practically impossible.

Furthermore, as the Pope himself recognizes, the persons most tempted to kill the weak and the innocent are those upon whom the positive duties of continuing to care for them rest most heavily. For this reason, he emphasizes the responsibility of society as a whole "to ensure proper support for families and motherhood" by "rethink[ing] labor, urban, residential and social service policies so as to harmonize working schedules with time available for the family, so that it becomes effectively possible to take care of children and the elderly" (*EV* 90).

What is the status of this responsibility as compared with the societal obligation to eliminate laws declaring abortion or euthanasia to be fundamental rights? Is the creation of an equitable social policy regarding the care of society's vulnerable itself an obligation in justice, or is it merely a pragmatic support for laws recognizing the illicitness of direct attacks on innocent life? The Pope does not explicitly settle this question. An answer can be found, however, in the work of Thomas Aquinas. John Paul II invokes Thomas in order to emphasize that a law enacted in contravention of the moral order is an unjust law that "ceases to be a law and becomes instead an act of violence."[12] He might also have noted that Thomas uses precisely the same language to describe laws in which "burdens are imposed unequally on the community, although with a view to the common good." They too are labeled unjust, and hence "acts of violence rather than laws."[13]

To summarize my argument thus far: The Pope's emphasis on rights language and exceptionless moral norms has hindered his ability to address the fundamental jurisprudential question raised in implementing the culture of life within a legal system: in drafting law, how do we honor the moral claims made by the inviolability of the most vulnerable members of the human community, even while recognizing the moral limitations of those who must respect those claims in very difficult circumstances? In the second part of this essay, I will argue that the Pope's efforts to promote a culture of life in the midst of an encroaching culture of death are better served by viewing positive law as a teacher of virtue.

LAW AS A TEACHER OF VIRTUE

The Pope himself recognizes the significance of education in promoting the culture of life. A "first and fundamental step" is the formation of consciences with regard to the "incomparable and inviolable worth of every human life"; this in turn requires the adoption of a distinct scale of values recognizing the "primacy of being over having" and "of persons over things." Accordingly, he acknowledges the educational function of law, which "play[s] an important and sometimes decisive role in influencing patterns of thought and behavior" (*EV* 98, 90).

In this, the Pope stands at one with Thomas Aquinas. For Thomas, the central function of law is pedagogical: to lead persons to a state of virtue. This positive function stands at the core of even the most stringent prohibitions of the penal code. Thomas notes that for those persons who are "depraved, prone to vice, and not easily amenable to words, it was necessary for such to be restrained from evil by force and fear, in order that, at least, they might desist from evil-doing, and leave others in peace, and that they themselves, by being habituated in this way, might be brought to do willingly what hitherto they did from fear, and thus become virtuous."[14]

But what does it mean to be virtuous? For Thomas, answering this question requires understanding the nature and motivations of virtuous persons. They perform virtuous acts and refrain from vicious acts not because of any external motivation but "through love of virtue" itself. By contrast, the imperfect, who are not yet possessed of a virtuous habit, "are directed to the performance of virtuous acts by reason of some outward cause: for instance, by the threat of punishment, or the promise of some extrinsic rewards, such as honors, riches or the like."[15] Only acts performed *in the manner* of the virtuous person, that is, for the sake of virtue itself, are "virtuous acts" properly speaking. Consequently, in leading the imperfect to virtue, law must engage in a two-step process: 1) it must accustom the less-than-virtuous to refrain from the physical, external acts prohibited by virtue and to perform the physical, external acts required by virtue; 2) at the same time and no less essentially, it must illuminate for its subjects the reasons *why* its strictures support the flourishing of all persons in community and thus stand in accordance with the dictates of practical reason. Only in this manner will the less-than-perfect subjects of a given legal framework have the tools they need to begin the long journey to virtue.

Needless to say, a jurisprudence organized around the concept of law as a teacher of virtue must confront and surmount a number of difficulties. What tradition of human flourishing will be used to identify the virtues appropriate for the support of positive law? Are there limits to the range of virtues that are appropriately inculcated by the state? How does such a jurisprudence cope with the fact that in our pluralistic society, there are many competing visions of human flourishing that incorporate varied and sometimes conflicting conceptions of virtue and vice?

While an adequate response to the foregoing questions is beyond the scope of this essay, let me make the following brief points. First, the difficulties they identify pose problems not merely for a virtue-based theory of law but for a rights-based theory as well. As noted above, any conception of human rights sufficiently detailed to generate a legal framework must draw upon assumptions about the nature of human flourishing and human action. A rights-based approach must make the same choices as a virtue-based approach to law; the only difference is that it attempts to do so tacitly rather than explicitly.

Second, jurisprudence is the morals of law. No more in jurisprudence than in other spheres of morality is there a neutral, Archimedean point from which to arbitrate between competing conceptions of human flourishing. One needs to begin the process of moral reasoning squarely within the framework of a tradition. From the Pope's perspective, the Christian worldview supplies a richly detailed moral tradition with more than sufficient resources to specify a conception of the good life and the virtues or vices that either support or undermine it. Consequently, the primary virtues that he believes the law should inculcate will find their roots in that worldview.

There quickly arises, however, a second question: how does a jurisprudence of law as a teacher of virtue deal with the fact that there are many competing moral traditions in our pluralistic society? As discussed below, the limits of the (criminal) law of any given society must be set in terms of the limits of ordinary virtue in that society. This requirement places significant *moral* restrictions upon the ability of adherents of any one moral tradition to instantiate its vision in the law. The notion of "overlapping consensus" in a pluralistic society may be a helpful concept in explicating these restrictions.

Thomas's normative vision of law as a teacher of virtue is not likely to garner enthusiastic support from much contemporary jurisprudence. Liberal theorists of law such as Joel Feinberg see the function of the criminal law as essentially negative, as a sort of policeman protecting citizens from discrete and well-defined "harms."[16] In this view, it does not matter *why* persons refrain from committing harmful acts, as long as they do refrain from so doing. The law-and-economics school, represented most prominently by Richard Posner, contends that the underlying goal of the legal system should be to maximize economic efficiency. Many critical legal theorists, including Roberto Unger, believe that the function of law is one of continual *destabilization* of oppressive structures and institutions; they have to date devoted far less attention to the question of how to replace the destabilized elements of society.

A fully adequate contemporary defense of Aquinas's theory of law would need to enter into extensive conversation with the theorists noted in the preceding paragraph. For the more limited purposes of this essay, however, let me simply assert my belief that one can enlist the writings of such contemporary "post-liberal or "post-modern" philosophers as Alasdair MacIntyre, Jeffrey Stout, Richard Rorty, and Michael Sandel to defend the jurisprudential proposition that positive law always includes a pedagogical component, despite real differences among these thinkers. Furthermore, I believe that a moment's reflection upon the living tradition of the law in the present-day United States yields ample practical evidence of the pedagogical function of law. Clearly, the Americans with Disabilities Act of 1990 (42 U.S.C. 1210 et seq.), the Civil Rights Act of 1964 (42 U.S.C. 1971 et seq.), and the Family and Medical Leave Act of 1993 (29 U.S.C. 2601 et seq.) intend not only to prohibit and require specific actions but to inculcate a moral vision of how we should live our common life together.

How should positive law go about the process of inculcating virtue? For Thomas, law must lead persons to virtue gradually, not suddenly. Accordingly, lawmakers must take their starting point not from the abilities of those few persons in a society who are well advanced in virtue but from the capabilities of the majority of the citizenry, who are generally far from virtuous. "Otherwise these imperfect ones, being unable to bear such precepts, would break out into yet greater evils."[17]

Thomas includes this insight in an article entitled "Whether Human Law Should Be Framed for the Community Rather Than for the Individual," which is in turn gathered under a question devoted to "The *Power* of Human Law" (emphasis added). It is simply beyond the *power* of the criminal law of a community to prohibit or require actions that exceed the capacity of the ordinary virtue of the majority of its members. Laws that attempt to do so cannot be effectively or equitably enforced; no society can muster the resources necessary to police the behavior of a sizeable portion of the population. In the United States, juries are not likely to convict individuals charged with engaging in such behavior.

Taken together, the closely related Thomistic insights that the purpose of law is to lead persons to virtue and that the limits of the criminal law are the limits of *ordinary* virtue yield a realistic, gradualist approach regarding the use of the criminal law to implement the Gospel of life. Forging a pro-life jurisprudence for the United States requires that we take sober, clear-eyed account of the level of virtue our society currently possesses, not only of the virtue we earnestly hope that it will one day manifest. Societal habits, no less than individual habits, can be developed and strengthened only step-by-step. We cannot erase the damage done over many years with one vote of the legislature.

Our articulation of the limits of ordinary virtue—and thus the criminal law—in the case of euthanasia and abortion will involve two general sorts of considerations. First, the lawmaker needs to consider the concrete circumstances under which persons choose abortion or euthanasia. What types of pressure are they typically under; what sort of alternatives and assistance is available to them? As I argued in the first section of this paper, the criminal law takes as its central concern the subjective responsibility of the defendant. Lawmakers cannot ignore the unique nature of abortion and euthanasia from the perspective of the *perpetrators* of such actions. In many instances, making a decision not to commit a moral evil at the same time commits one to assuming significant positive duties toward a vulnerable human being who is unable to care for him- or herself.

One could object that the foregoing argument is precluded by the Pope's assertion in *Evangelium Vitae* that positive law cannot authorize actions prohibited by morality. In response, I would point to a helpful distinction drawn by Thomas himself. "Human law is said to permit certain things, not as approving of them, but as being unable to direct them. . . . It would be different, were human law to *sanction* what the eternal law condemns" (emphasis added). Applying this distinction to abortion and euthanasia, we can argue that there is a vast difference between a legal regime that declares such practices to be fundamental constitutional rights, on the one hand, and one that simply leaves such activities *unpunished*. The difference is rooted in the pedagogical function of the law itself. One can hardly be said to be teaching virtue if one's legal system treats a decision for abortion or euthanasia as an instance of autonomous self-actualization. The same charge, however, is not applicable to a legislature judging that in many if not most instances in a particular society, abortion and euthanasia are acts committed under such duress that criminal sanctions are generally not appropriate.[18] This does not mean, of course, that other types of law may not be used to discourage the practices.

The second set of considerations affecting the wise lawmaker's discernment of the limits of ordinary virtue pertains to the moral descriptions under which citizens view the acts in question. It is a feature of our pluralistic society that grave differences exist regarding the nature of the good life, the appropriate ethical theory according to which we are to distinguish licit from illicit actions, the proper use of moral-factual terms such as "personhood," and the correct way to describe acts such as abortion (e.g., an act of killing or the mother's refusal of life to extend her body to support the fetus) or define acts of euthanasia (e.g., any act or omission that is foreseen to cause death or any act or omission that intends to cause death).

For many persons, access to abortion or euthanasia is not simply a "convenient" solution to a difficult problem but an act that is morally justifiable from the perspective of the ethical framework in which they operate. In such instances, teaching someone to view abortion and euthanasia from the perspective of the Gospel of life is far from a simple matter. It may involve convincing a person to replace or significantly alter a well-worked-out and coherent worldview. In contrast, persons are likely to be more amenable to laws that impede their desired course of behavior if they do not believe they have a moral claim to engage in such behavior without interference.

It might be objected that *Evangelium Vitae* intends to preclude such consideration by its statement that "the legal toleration of abortion or of euthanasia can in no way claim to be based on respect for the conscience of others, precisely because society has the right and the duty to protect itself against abuses which can occur in the name of conscience and under the pretext of freedom." [19] There is an important difference, however, between saying that we must tolerate abortion and euthanasia because our duty to respect the consciences of others prevents us from judging their worldviews or interfering with their actions, and acknowledging that the widespread, even if erroneous, belief that certain courses of action are morally licit can greatly undermine the success of the criminal law in preventing such behavior.

Furthermore, I have argued elsewhere [20] that many American women who consider access to abortion to be a fundamental aspect of their individual freedom are *epistemologically justified* although tragically *wrong* in this belief. Abortion has been legal in this country for over two decades; its growth and promotion has been closely intertwined with the laudable moral goal of greater equality for women and participation in all spheres of society. Many persons simply do not see how that goal can be achieved without access to legal abortion.

Of what relevance is this fact for a Thomistic jurisprudence of virtue? First, given the greater knowledge that we now possess about the effect of broader societal beliefs upon individual moral sensibilities, it should at least be possible to consider some such persons to be inculpably "ignorant" of the true wrong caused by abortion in a manner that would render criminal sanctions inappropriate. Second and more generally, those of us who wish to develop a theory of positive law based on a Thomistic approach need to develop a way of honoring the honest, although mistaken, moral beliefs of others that is not reducible to pluralistic relativism or a callous disregard of the harmful effects of those beliefs when put into practice. From the perspective of a Thomistic approach, the considerable virtue that such persons *do* possess should focus our conversations with them.

My final point regarding the jurisprudential benefits of viewing law as a teacher of virtue is that it provides helpful guidance for judging whether the tools of criminal law are inappropriate or unlikely to be effective. A proper concern for law's pedagogical function forces us critically to reexamine our sanguine beliefs that the penal code affords ample protection to fragile human life.

For example, consider briefly the question of voluntary euthanasia. In many states euthanasia or the practice of "assisted suicide" falls under the letter of some aspect of the penal code dealing with homicide. Yet the criminal law has not proven an effective means of dealing with the question, for several reasons. First, unlike most types of homicide, where the "unnatural" cause of death is readily apparent, these actions are often practiced in situations where it is plausible to attribute the death to another factor, such as advancing illness. Second, to the extent that euthanasia is practiced by physicians within the walls of medical institutions, it takes place in a subculture that does not support reporting such incidents to external authorities. Third, as the saga of Jack Kevorkian attests, it is not easy to prosecute even flagrant cases of (sometimes questionably voluntary) euthanasia carried out with no procedural safeguards.

Finally, the penal code offers almost no tools enabling us to address the increasing pressures in favor of euthanasia as our health care system continues down the road from fee-for-service medicine to managed care. Under the quickly vanishing regime of fee-for-service medicine coupled with generous third-party indemnity insurance, health care institutions and physicians had no financial incentive to commit euthanasia. The more care they provided, the more money they made. By contrast, in a managed-care system in which health care providers are paid on a capitated basis, they have a significant financial motivation to eliminate the need for very expensive care to chronically or terminally ill patients. As the Pope recognizes, temptations toward evildoing are often exacerbated by social structures of sin. In my view, our rapidly expanding system of largely unregulated managed health care poses one of the greatest challenges to the Gospel of life. The legal tools likely to provide the most help in reshaping this social structure are not the blunt-edged tools of the criminal code but the more subtle and flexible instruments of administrative and regulatory law. It is to them that we must turn our attention.

NOTES

1. Isidore of Seville, *Etymologiae* 5.21, cited in Thomas Aquinas, *Summa Theologica*, trans. Fathers of the English Dominican Province (New York: Benziger Brothers, 1948), I–II, q. 95, a. 3, ob.

2. John Paul II, *The Gospel of Life (Evangelium Vitae)* (Boston: Pauline Books and Media, 1995), § 5.

3. *GS* 27, cited in *EV* 3. The full passage cited by the Pope reads,
   Whatever is opposed to life itself, such as any type of murder, genocide, abortion, euthanasia, or willful self-destruction, whatever violates the integrity of the human person, such as mutilation, torments inflicted on body or

mind, attempts to coerce the will itself; whatever insults human dignity, such as subhuman living conditions, arbitrary imprisonment, deportation, slavery, prostitution, the selling of women and children; as well as disgraceful working conditions where people are treated as mere instruments of gain rather than as free and responsible persons; all these things and others like them are infamies indeed. They poison human society, and they do more harm to those who practice them than to those who suffer the injury. Moreover, they are a supreme dishonor to the creator.

4. A constitutionally protected "liberty interest" in physician-assisted suicide was recently recognized by the U.S. Court of Appeals for the Ninth Circuit, *Compassion in Dying v. State of Washington*, 79 F.3d 790 (9th Cir. 1996) (en banc); the U.S. Court of Appeals for the Second Circuit, also gave assisted suicide constitutional protection. *Quill v. Vacco*, 80 F.3d 716 (2nd Cir. 1996).

5. This is a theological as well as an ethical and jurisprudential issue. The passage from *Gaudium et Spes* cited by the Pope and reprinted in note 3 above makes an important and often forgotten point: unjust and intentionally death-dealing actions harm their *perpetrators* far more than their victims.

6. In his response to an earlier draft of this essay, Kevin Quinn, S.J., of Georgetown Law Center asked whether my efforts to highlight the second set of themes is consonant with the fundamental spirit of the encyclical, which devotes far more attention to the first set. I believe that the primary question here is what constitutes an appropriate response to an encyclical on the part of a Catholic professional. In order to answer this question, it is in turn necessary to consider the genre to which an encyclical belongs. It is helpful to think of an encyclical as analogous to an authoritative judicial opinion situated within a broad and rich legal tradition. Through the work of attorneys and other judges, an important opinion does not merely decide the case before it; it is creatively incorporated into the ongoing life of the tradition to which it contributes. During this process of incorporation, some purposes and ways of approaching practical problems are highlighted, others are downplayed. The criteria used in this process are often internal to the tradition itself.

Similarly, a Catholic professional may be called not simply to respond to an encyclical in a narrow academic fashion but to work with the encyclical in a way that is creative, faithful to the tradition, and responsive to the concrete problems that the encyclical seeks to address. This is my goal in arguing that the second set of themes is more helpful than the first set, despite their relative lack of prominence. By contending that the second set is more consonant with the thought of Thomas Aquinas, who is repeatedly cited in the encyclical, I am deploying criteria internal to both the tradition in general and to the document in particular.

7. Bette-Jane Crigger, ed., "Germany's Compromise Abortion Bill," *Hastings Center Report* 25, no. 5 (1995): 48.

8. Judith Jarvis Thomson, "A Defense of Abortion," *Philosophy and Public Affairs* 1, no. 1 (1976): 47–66.

9. John Finnis, *Natural Law and Natural Rights* (Oxford: Clarendon Press, 1980), 219.

10. See, e.g., Alasdair MacIntyre, *After Virtue* (Notre Dame, In.: University of Notre Dame Press, 1980), esp. chap. 1.; and Mary Ann Glendon, *Abortion and Divorce in Western Law* (Cambridge: Harvard University Press, 1987), esp. chap. 3.

11. John Paul II, *The Splendor of Truth (Veritatis Splendor)* (Boston: St. Paul Books and Media, 1993).

12. *EV* 72 citing *ST* I–II, q. 93, a. 3, ad 2um.

13. *ST* I–II, q. 96, a. 5.

14. *ST* I–II, q. 95, a. 1.

15. *ST* I–II, q. 107, a. 1, rep. ob. 2.

16. See Joel Feinberg's four-volume work, *The Moral Limits of the Criminal Law* (New York: Oxford University Press, 1984–1988).

17. *ST* I–II, q. 96, a. 2, rep. ob. 2.

18. In this respect, the two most recent abortion decisions handed down by the Supreme Court, *Webster v. Reproductive Health Services*, 492 U.S. 490 (1989), and *Planned Parenthood v. Casey*, 505 U.S. 833 (1992), mark a small but significant positive shift in our constitutional jurisprudence. In these decisions, the Court moves away from its prior characterization of the abortion decision as protected by a woman's fundamental constitutional right to privacy, but instead describes it in the more circumscribed terms of a "liberty interest."

19. *EV* 71, citing Vatican II, *Dignitatis Humanae (Declaration on Religious Freedom)* 7.

20. M. Cathleen Kaveny, "Toward a Thomistic Perspective on Abortion and the Law in Contemporary America," *Thomist* 55, no. 3 (1991): 343–96.

Whose Virtue? Which Morality? The Limits of Law as a Teacher of Virtue—A COMMENT ON CATHLEEN KAVENY

KEVIN P. QUINN, S.J.

Cathleen Kaveny's purpose is to advance the view "that the Pope's efforts to promote a 'culture of life' in the midst of an encroaching 'culture of death' are better served by viewing positive law as a teacher of virtue." The project here is straightforward: to illustrate "the inadequacy of rights language and negative moral norms as a source of positive law" and then to champion the Thomistic insight that the "purpose of law is to lead persons to virtue." In particular, Kaveny gently chides John Paul II for his almost exclusive focus on the victims of acts opposed to the Gospel of life and invites the Pope to take into account the possible perpetrators of positive law.

I agree with Richard McCormick that the part of *Evangelium Vitae* covering the relation of civil and moral law "will remain its most controversial after the dust settles."[1] For this reason alone, I am sympathetic to Kaveny's enriching the discussion of this always controversial relation with Thomistic materials, and equally sympathetic to her call for a "realistic, gradualist approach regarding the use of the criminal law to implement the Gospel of life." Ungratefully, I am less happy with the way she uses the perfectionism[2] of Aquinas to make her case and, less significantly, with her deconstruction of the encyclical itself. It is these points of concern that I shall address.

LAW AND MORALITY

There is no denying that *Evangelium Vitae* is strong in the view that civil law must necessarily conform with moral law (*EV* 72).[3] And insistent that the proper (i.e., negative) functioning of criminal law ought to ensure the "inviolable right to life of every innocent human being" (*EV* 71). Kaveny's insight is to juxtapose this jurisprudential approach with another she says is present embryonically in *Evangelium Vitae*—namely, Aquinas's notion that "the central goal of a system of positive law is not to protect the rights of the victims *but to lead potential perpetrators to virtue*, albeit slowly and haltingly." A central target of Kaveny's essay then becomes a fundamental ambiguity in the encyclical itself, reflecting the unfortunate tension between two distinct juris-prudential stances. Not surprisingly, Kaveny defends Aquinas's theory of law as "not only more . . . capable than the rights-based approach of accommodating crucial concerns of the American legal system (particularly our system of criminal law) but also afford[ing] a more fruitful way of dealing with the question of American pluralism regarding the moral issues at the heart of *Evangelium Vitae*."

What, then, is troubling about Kaveny's project? An important omission lies at the heart of its exposition of the purpose of positive law. If the proper effect of law is to make human beings good (*ST* I–II 92, a.1)—"to lead persons to a state of virtue," in Kaveny's words—does this view of perfectionism not require a serviceable account of the good, of virtue, or of morality? In the rush to find a theoretical framework to accommodate the Pope's efforts to promote a "culture of life," Kaveny neglects to provide a clear account of any morality, much less the true morality. She simply does not ask what counts as morality. Absent any particular notion of what the good (or goods) might be, Kaveny's approach regarding the use of criminal law to implement the Gospel of life fails to equip John Paul II with a legitimate complement to his reliance on "the vocabulary of exceptionless moral norms and . . . 'rights' language to articulate his conception of the proper stance of positive law toward abortion and euthanasia."

This criticism, it should be noted, rests on very difficult questions posed by natural law theory, not unique to Kaveny's project alone. This, of course, is not the time to revisit these questions. My only point is a simple one: what is at stake here is the legitimacy of any attempt to develop a natural law justification for the state enforcement of moral standards within a liberal democracy. The essence of natural law theory is the belief that there exists a moral code that transcends the positive law of human beings. That transcending morality must, at a certain level, exist outside the politics that dominate human society. In turn, the determination of morality or immorality is fundamentally an act of reason. But as Alasdair MacIntyre piquantly reminds us, there exist competing rationalities.[4] The central conundrum of natural law theory, therefore, cannot be avoided: there has never been, and never will be, any commonly agreed content to moral-legal ideas that emanate from natural law.

How, then, is Aquinas's normative vision of positive law as a teacher of virtue to assist societal efforts in identifying the limits of the criminal law? Professor Kaveny answers, "The limits of the criminal law are the limits of *ordinary* virtue." At this point, it is fair to ask Kaveny, with a nod to MacIntyre, "Whose virtue? Which morality?" Even if one accepts her critique on the limited usefulness of "rights" language and negative moral norms in formulating positive law, as I do, it is the indeterminacy of the ethics of virtue that rankles, the fact that pedagogy without content is essentially question begging. Given the far-reaching implications of the proposition that positive law inculcates virtue, Kaveny must explain just how it is that the development of virtues makes sense, or the moral good life is defined. Not to engage in a concrete discussion of what constitutes virtue threatens to undermine much of what is good in her essay.

When a question like this is raised, one current response (which John Finnis and his fellow travelers find attractive)[5] is to say that the legal system cannot be used to enforce adherence to a univocal blueprint of the moral good life because there isn't one. Indeed, there are many different and incommensurable basic goods, not all of which can be tracked in equal degree in a morally good life. Knowledge of human goods, of course, does not *by itself* resolve moral questions because it does not exclude some choices that, while intelligible, are morally wrongful. Rather, our intelligent grasp of human goods is what makes moral *questions* possible. Other responses are possible, but a response is necessary. Otherwise, one could accuse Kaveny of sidestepping the really difficult questions posed by natural law theory.

Likewise, absent some notion of the shape of virtue, a "wise lawmaker's discernment of the limits of ordinary virtue," as required by Kaveny's legislature considering criminal sanctions against abortion and euthanasia, dissolves into bland relativism.

It is not possible to deploy prudential considerations—to temper overly coercive morals legislation—without implicating some substantive conception of the good. Again, my point is only that the matter needs to be addressed.

In any case, what about Kaveny's argument itself? There remains, of course, the decisive question of whether, in the American context, to advocate Aquinas's vision of positive law as a teacher of virtue is at all appropriate. In a culture such as ours, where many moralities compete with one another in the marketplace of ideas, to propose such a role for criminal law, as I shall try to show, is misguided.

Kaveny's approach cries out for a more complete exposition of the muddled relation between law and morality. This, of course, is not the place to analyze the relation at any length. Of relevance here is the social theory of John Courtney Murray, particularly in its useful insights concerning the proper *distinction* between law and morality and between public and private morality.[6] Murray, an American Jesuit who died in 1967, promoted a social philosophy rooted in the ancient and medieval natural law tradition, but with a decidedly American slant. He criticized the view that "what is moral ought by that fact to be legal [and] what is legal is by that fact also moral."[7] And he rejected as "foolish [the] position that all sins ought to be made crimes."[8] Yet Murray insisted that concerns of *public* morality should be addressed by the law. What matters here is that, in the Murray tradition, abortion and euthanasia are arguably concerns of public morality because "both involve at least the high probability that a human life is being taken."[9] We are left, then, with this question: how should the law address matters of public morality, including abortion and euthanasia?

Within the Murray tradition, the answer is, With caution. Here Todd Whitmore is most helpful. In a recent article "trying to discern what we might say [on abortion and euthanasia] in the context of the social theory [Murray] left us,"[10] Whitmore insists that "Murray was cautious about the degree to which law should lead public opinion."[11] The reason for Murray's caution is clear: "Law and morality are indeed related, even though differentiated. That is, the premises of law are ultimately found in the moral law. And human legislation does look to the moralization of society. But, mindful of its own nature and mode of action, it must not moralize excessively; otherwise it tends to defeat even its own more modest aims, by bringing itself into contempt."[12]

From such a point of view there is little ambiguity in applying Murray's distinction, as Whitmore does, to legislation limiting access to abortion services or maintaining anti-euthanasia laws already on the books. It follows that "simply changing the law will not be sufficient because of the problem of 'contempt,'" and "the only way to avoid the problem of possible contempt is to change public opinion."[13] For Murray insisted that "despite all the pluralism, some manner of consensus must support the order of law to which the whole community and all its groups are commonly subject."[14]

And law itself, as Whitmore explains, "is a bad vehicle"[15] to shape public opinion. While not denying the legitimacy of leading with efforts to change liberal abortion laws and to brace existing anti-euthanasia statutes, Murray would likely hold that prudence dictates that reformers should begin elsewhere, with efforts to shape (and change) public opinion on these controverted issues. And appropriate law would then follow. For this reason, it remains to the churches, particularly the Catholic Church with its teaching on objective morality, and other "voluntary associations" to shape public opinion by fostering greater harmony between law and that which is (objectively) right.

My point here is obvious enough. The use of criminal law to advance the Gospel of life, in the American context, is not the most prudent way to proceed. Reformers should not lead with coercive law but with systematic and evangelical efforts to promote the "culture of life."

EXCEPTIONLESS NORMS

But what about Kaveny's interpretation of the text? This is the second point of concern. She identifies a "second jurisprudential approach" present in *Evangelium Vitae*, labels it as "more congenial" to Aquinas's understanding of law as a teacher of virtue, and is off to the races in support of Aquinas's normative vision. What better way to make one's "own distinctive contribution to the 'culture of life'" than to counsel "that the Pope's efforts . . . are better served by viewing positive law as a teacher of virtue." At the very least, however, one might question if this complementary, albeit understated, jurisprudential approach is truly present in the text of the encyclical. Or if Kaveny is deconstructing *Evangelium Vitae* in search of an alternative moral theory, one that would play better in pluralistic America. In short, is Kaveny's essay a synopsis of the encyclical John Paul II should have written?

Kaveny reads John Paul II as "pay[ing] significantly greater attention to the potential *perpetrators* of these death-dealing activities [abortion and euthanasia], as well as the pressures that lead them toward such choices," than to the "prohibition against taking innocent human life" in the language of exceptionless moral norms. From this observation it follows, in Kaveny's argument, that these agent-relative themes "lend themselves quite well to a legal theory that incorporates . . . the consideration of the concrete circumstances in which persons are led to commit morally objectionable acts."

I read *Evangelium Vitae* differently. Chapter 3, entitled "You Shall Not Kill: God's Holy Law," is the climax of the encyclical. Here a vision of moral absolutism reigns defiantly: the Pope simply formulates three exceptionless moral norms condemning the killing of innocent human life, abortion, and euthanasia (*EV* 57, 62, 65). And Chapter 3 is wanting in the considerations, found elsewhere in the text, that are championed by Kaveny. Nary a glimpse of Kaveny's alternative jurisprudential approach is present in this critical chapter. This point, it seems to me, is telling.

One may think that Kaveny is attempting to smuggle into John Paul II's own work elements of proportionalism—an approach to morality he vigorously criticized in *Veritatis Splendor*.[16] A bold and creative move, but does it violate the text of *Evangelium Vitae*? To answer, permit me to appropriate two notions from first-year law school. The *holding* in the Pope's case arguing for the Gospel of life couldn't be clearer: the triple condemnation of killing, abortion, and euthanasia is the moral law. All else, it can be argued, is *dicta*—expressions that do not embody the Pope's determination and, therefore, are not binding in subsequent cases. Kaveny may stand accused of relying on *dicta* in making her elegant case, accused of the sin of faulty interpretation. But many judges responsible for the advancement of law in this country are guilty of the same offense. At the very least, in Kaveny's essay, there is hope for similar advances in moral and political theology.

NOTES

1. Richard A. McCormick, "The Gospel of Life," *America* 172, no. 15 (April 29, 1995): 10–17, at 12.

2. "Perfectionism" stands for the proposition that "laws have a legitimate subsidiary role to play in helping people to *make themselves* moral" Robert P. George, *Making Men Moral: Civil Liberties and Public Morality* (Oxford: Clarendon Press, 1993), 1.

3. John Paul II, *The Gospel of Life (Evangelium Vitae)* (New York: Random House, 1995).

4. Alasdair MacIntyre, *Whose Justice? Which Rationality?* (Notre Dame, Ind.: University of Notre Dame Press, 1988).

5. See, e.g., John Finnis, *Natural Law and Natural Rights* (Oxford: Clarendon Press, 1980), esp. chaps. 3–5; German Grisez, Joseph Boyle, and John Finnis, "Practical Principles, Moral Truth, and Ultimate Ends," *American Journal of Jurisprudence* 7 (1987): 99–151; George, *Making Men Moral*, esp. chap. 1.

6. See John Courtney Murray, S.J., *We Hold These Truths: Catholic Reflections on the American Proposition* (Kansas City, Mo.: Sheed and Ward, 1960), esp. chap. 7. See also J. Leon Hooper, S.J., *The Ethics of Discourse: The Social Philosophy of John Courtney Murray* (Washington: Georgetown University Press, 1986); Robert P. Hunt and Kenneth L. Grasso, eds., *John Courtney Murray and the American Civil Conversation* (Grand Rapids, Mich.: William B. Eerdmans, 1992); Robert W. McElroy, *The Search for an American Public Theology: The Contribution of John Courtney Murray* (New York: Paulist Press, 1989).

7. Murray, *We Hold These Truths*, 157.

8. Ibid., 158.

9. Todd David Whitmore, "What Would John Courtney Murray Say? On Abortion and Euthanasia," *Commonweal* 121, no. 17 (October 7, 1994): 16–22, at 21.

10. Ibid., 16.

11. Ibid., 19.

12. Murray, *We Hold These Truths*, 166; quoted in Whitmore, "What Would John Courtney Murray Say?" 19.

13. Whitmore, "What Would John Courtney Murray Say?" 19.

14. Murray, *We Hold These Truths*, 168.

15. Whitmore, "What Would John Courtney Murray Say?" 19.

16. John Paul II, *The Splendor of Truth (Veritatis Splendor)* (Boston: St. Paul's Books and Media, 1993).

PART 3

Moral Controversies

Evangelium Vitae: *Abortion*

LESLIE C. GRIFFIN

The Gospel of life proclaimed by Pope John Paul II in *Evangelium Vitae* opposes abortion with "dauntless fidelity" (*EV* 1). On the subject of abortion, the "good news" is old news.[1] The encyclical portrays its teaching on abortion as the standard that the Church has always taught. The Pope employs a traditional principle against direct killing of the innocent: "*I confirm that the direct and voluntary killing of an innocent human being is always gravely immoral*" (*EV* 57). He applies that principle to all abortions from conception onward: "Procured abortion is the deliberate and direct killing, by whatever means it is carried out, of a human being in the initial phase of his or her existence, extending from conception to birth" (*EV* 58). The embryo or fetus is by definition always an innocent human being. Finally, the principle is absolute: "These reasons and others like them, however serious and tragic, can never justify the deliberate killing of an innocent human being" (*EV* 58). The Pope is "*unconditionally* pro-life" (*EV* 28, my italics). Although self-defense may be an exception to the general prohibition against taking human life, the self-defense exception does not apply to abortion. "In no way could this human being ever be considered an aggressor, much less an unjust aggressor! He or she is weak, defenseless, even to the point of lacking that minimal form of defense consisting in the poignant power of a newborn baby's cries and tears" (*EV* 58).

Within the Church, the criticisms of this teaching are not new. The direct/indirect distinction has faced extensive criticism as an inadequate formulation of the Church's theological tradition.[2] "No direct killing of the innocent" has been described as a rule, not a principle, and so subject to exceptions.[3] On the subject of abortion, the direct/indirect distinction has been criticized for its excess physicalism. The principle allows, for example, the excision of the cancerous uterus and the ectopic pregnancy, but not other measures calculated to save the life of the mother. Moreover, in these two situations it requires that the woman's fertility not be spared.[4] In addition, theologians have questioned the abortion ban's extension to the time of conception. Some authors have argued, for example, that implantation, not conception, is

159

the significant developmental point and so the prohibition against abortion should not apply to the preimplantation embryo.[5] Moreover, theologians have argued that the Church's own tradition does not support an absolute ban on abortion from the time of conception. The history of ensoulment suggests a shifting assessment of the morality of early abortion and undermines John Paul's claim of an unchanging Catholic teaching on abortion.[6] Finally, in the past, some authors have suggested that abortion is at times an act of self-defense for the woman whose life or health is threatened by her pregnancy and so the general bar against abortion should not be absolute.[7]

Catholics have for years engaged in an extensive debate about the interpretation of the Church's tradition on abortion and about the formulation of the moral principles that regulate abortion. The encyclical is not noteworthy for its contribution to that discussion; it reiterates the official teaching of the magisterium. What is significant about *Evangelium Vitae* is not the substance but the style of its argument. The author prefers a distinctively Catholic, theological argument to a natural law style of reasoning. The analysis is predominantly scriptural and theological, not philosophical or scientific.

It is easy to identify both the advantages and the disadvantages of this style. The theological focus will be valuable to Catholics who inhabit the "culture of death" decried by the encyclical. Such teaching may inspire and reinvigorate Catholic commitment to the Church's moral teaching in a way that philosophical and scientific argument cannot. Theological language may serve as an important corrective to the excessively secular, antireligious language of our public culture.[8]

The disadvantages of this approach, however, are also evident in the encyclical's reasoning. By accentuating the theological argument, the encyclical urges Catholic moral principles upon all persons, non-Catholic as well as Catholic. It also recommends that Catholic moral teaching be inscribed into law. The result is a theory of civil law that is excessively entangled with theological doctrine. The retreat from natural law argument at the moral level undermines John Paul's arguments about the content of civil law in a democracy. Moreover, it burdens Catholic politicians with a moral obligation to vote their theological convictions into law.

NATURAL LAW

Even the encyclical's title, *The Gospel of Life*, encapsulates its theological and scriptural emphasis. Scriptural quotations provide the framework of the document. Much of the encyclical's prose is in the style of reflection and meditation on scriptural texts. In the first chapter, the initial focus is the story of Cain and

Abel, the story of an attack on human life. Such attacks must be condemned wherever they occur. The biblical story provides the basis for the encyclical's first extended treatment of abortion (*EV* 13–17). As Cain attacked Abel, so abortion is an attack on human life. The brothers' story is an appropriate analogy because the locus of abortion's attack on human beings is the family.

The rest of the encyclical also emphasizes the scriptural and theological basis of the document's moral principles. Even the general prohibition against killing is cast in theological terms. It is "God's holy Law" ("You Shall Not Kill") (*EV* 52). The prohibition against killing is a divine command (*EV* 52) revealed in Scripture (*EV* 54). Life is sacred; it comes from God, the "Lord of life" (*EV* 53). The distinctively Christian nature of the prohibition against taking human life is evident in the encyclical's contrast between the teaching of the Old and New Testaments. Although "the commandment regarding the inviolability of human life reverberates at the heart of the '10 words' in the covenant of Sinai . . . we must recognize that in the Old Testament this sense of the value of life, though already quite marked, *does not yet reach the refinement found in the Sermon on the Mount*" (*EV* 40, my italics).

When the Pope turns from Scripture, it is to the Church's tradition against killing. The scriptural argument and the church's tradition are consistent. "The church's tradition has always consistently taught the absolute and unchanging value of the commandment, 'you shall not kill'" (*EV* 54). Killing the innocent is a "serious sin" (*EV* 55). It is through "the very person of Jesus" that "man is given the possibility of 'knowing' the complete truth concerning the value of human life" (*EV* 29).

In the encyclical's second lengthy section on abortion (*EV* 44–45), the Pope's emphasis remains scriptural and theological. A verse from Psalm 139, "For you formed my inmost being," provides the section heading. It is from Scripture that we learn that the ban on abortion extends to every fetus from conception. The Pope concedes that "there are no direct and explicit calls to protect human life at its very beginning" (*EV* 44) in Scripture. Nonetheless the Old and New Testaments provide a normative argument against all abortion: "Denying life in these circumstances is completely foreign to the religious and cultural way of thinking of the people of God" (*EV* 44). The Pope's review of the relevant Old Testament texts demands, "How can anyone think that even a single moment of this marvelous process of the unfolding of life could be separated from the wise and loving work of the Creator?" (*EV* 44). Then the New Testament "confirms the indisputable recognition of the value of life from its very beginning" (*EV* 45). A passage in chapter 3 reiterates this argument: "The texts of Sacred Scripture never address the question of deliberate abortion and so do not directly and specifically condemn it. But they show such great respect for the human being in the mother's womb that they *require as a logical consequence* that God's commandment 'you shall not kill' be extended to the unborn child as well" (*EV* 61, my italics).

As in the case of Cain and Abel, another biblical story, of Mary and Elizabeth, is significant to the moral argument: "The value of the person from the moment of conception is celebrated in the meeting between the Virgin Mary and Elizabeth, and between the two children whom they are carrying in the womb" (*EV* 45). Jeremiah, Job, and Psalms provide similar evidence that fetal life must receive absolute protection from conception onward because it is created by God at that "moment." When the Pope turns from the scriptural argument, it is to another ancient text. The prohibition on abortion is "repeated" (*EV* 54) in the text of the *Didache*.

Throughout these arguments on killing and abortion, the natural law is not abandoned. Its role in the encyclical's argument, however, is not important. Instead, the natural law serves a theological purpose. The numerous references to natural law throughout the text of *Evangelium Vitae* reiterate the traditional description of the natural law, that it is shared by all human persons. For example, John Paul recognizes that "every person sincerely open to truth and goodness can, by the light of reason and the hidden action of grace, come to recognize in the natural law written in the heart . . . the sacred value of human life from its very beginning until its end" (*EV* 2). He states that "the voice of the Lord echo[es] in the conscience of every individual" (*EV* 24). He writes that the gospel is "written in the heart of every man and woman" and "can also be known in its essential traits by human reason" (*EV* 29). By these natural law references, John Paul is asserting that the moral teaching of the Gospel of life is a teaching for all human persons, not for Catholics only.

In one sense, this is a traditional natural law argument. It is significant, however, that John Paul argues that the *gospel* is inscribed in all human persons. "The church knows that this Gospel of life, which she has received from her Lord, has a profound and persuasive echo in the heart of every person—believer and non-believer alike—because it marvelously fulfils all the heart's expectations while infinitely surpassing them" (*EV* 2). In other words, the Pope is claiming that the Gospel of life proclaimed by him in this encyclical is a norm for all human persons. Yet the content of that Gospel is defined in theological, not philosophical or scientific, terms. There is, for example, no inductive reasoning from human nature.[9] Instead, Scripture and tradition provide moral principles while the natural law provides reasons for the Pope to urge all persons to follow those principles.

The role of the natural law in *Evangelium Vitae* is limited in part because of the general theological agenda of the document. The encyclical is prophetic, countercultural. Commentators on the encyclical have with good reason focused on *Evangelium Vitae*'s central theme of opposition to the "culture of death."[10] Natural law reasoning is not always useful when one argues that culture is morally corrupt. In that context, it is more important to claim, as John Paul does in this encyclical, that the natural law continues to exist even when majorities of human persons do not recognize it.

Complementing the traditional assertion that the natural law applies to all persons is the reminder that culture may prevent individuals—indeed whole societies—from recognizing the natural law. The encyclical focuses on the deterioration in society's morals. In modern society, "conscience itself, darkened as it were by such widespread conditioning, is finding it increasingly difficult to distinguish between good and evil in what concerns the basic value of human life" (*EV* 4). There is a "progressive darkening of the capacity to discern God's living and saving presence" (*EV* 21). "Nature itself, from being *mater* (mother), is now reduced to being 'matter,' and is subjected to every kind of manipulation" (*EV* 22). For this reason, the encyclical states that "when the sense of God is lost, there is also a tendency to lose the sense of man" (*EV* 21). "Moreover, once all reference to God has been removed, it is not surprising that the meaning of everything else becomes profoundly distorted" (*EV* 22). This "eclipse of the sense of God" (*EV* 23) has bred individualism, utilitarianism, and hedonism.

In an encyclical that emphasizes society's pervasive moral corruption, a natural law theory rooted in human experience is impractical. In response to this eclipse of natural law in the consciences of human persons, the encyclical offers the Church's privileged moral insight. If cultural influence has blinded human beings to the natural law, the best response is not more reason but more revelation.

Thus John Paul's steady references to the natural law do not mean that a natural law argument has been made. This does not mean, of course, that a natural law argument cannot be made. But it is noteworthy that the Pope has chosen not to make it. The natural law is not significant to the moral argument of the encyclical. Instead, the natural law serves another purpose: it provides reasons to apply the Pope's theological teaching to all human persons.

ABORTION AND NATURAL LAW

The theological role of the natural law is evident in the encyclical's treatment of abortion, where gospel and nature are intertwined. Catholic theology, of course, has traditionally claimed that the natural law and the gospel are consistent. But on the subject of abortion, the encyclical argues on the basis of the gospel and then asserts the consistency of the natural law with this gospel teaching. The natural law teaches us the "*sacred* value of human life" (*EV* 2, my italics). It is the "sacredness of life" that is the basis for life's invulnerability from attack (*EV* 40). We learn that "whoever attacks human life, in some way attacks God himself" (*EV* 9). The teaching on abortion is "based upon the natural law and upon the written Word of God" (*EV* 62), Church tradition, and the magisterium. The teaching invokes the authority of the magisterium: "*I declare that direct abortion, that is, abortion willed as an end or as a means, always constitutes a grave moral disorder*, since it is the deliberate killing of an innocent human being" (*EV* 62).

These arguments are of great importance to Catholics. Without the natural law argument, however, the encyclical leaves the impression that non-Catholics should accept the document's theological and magisterial arguments that abortion is a violation of God's commandment not to kill. There are three areas where the inadequacy or absence of the natural law argument is striking, especially when viewed from the perspective of readers who are not Catholic. These topics are the linking of the prohibitions on contraception and abortion; the encyclical's absolute, exceptionless ban on abortion; and the argument that the fetus is a person from conception.

First is the linking of the prohibitions on contraception and abortion. Contraception and abortion are recognized as "specifically different evils: The former contradicts the full truth of the sexual act as the proper expression of conjugal love, while the latter destroys the life of a human being; the former is opposed to the virtue of chastity in marriage, the latter is opposed to the virtue of justice and directly violates the divine commandment 'you shall not kill'" (*EV* 13). Nonetheless, the ethics of contraception and abortion cannot be separated. They are "closely connected, as fruits of the same tree." "The close connection which exists in mentality between the practice of contraception and that of abortion is becoming increasingly obvious" (*EV* 13). To those who argue that more or better contraception will decrease the occurrence of abortion (and thus that the Church should change its teaching on contraception), John Paul insists on the unity of the two teachings. He claims that the use of contraceptives leads to more abortion: "The pro-abortion culture is especially strong precisely where the church's teaching on contraception is rejected" (*EV* 13). The "negative values" of the "contraceptive mentality" "strengthen the temptation" to abortion (*EV* 13) and do not reduce its occurrence.

Moreover, John Paul rejects any demographic arguments for contraception. Overpopulation does not justify any artificial contraception. He states that it is better to share the world's resources than to encourage population control. The drop of the birth rate in developed countries is "disturbing" (*EV* 16): the solution to overpopulation is not contraception but redistribution of goods.

The magisterium's natural law argument against contraception has had a difficult reception among Catholics and Catholic theologians, many of whom have rejected *Humanae Vitae*'s artificial/natural distinction. There is no reason to expect that non-Catholics will accept the ban on artificial contraception as a universal moral principle. To argue that the bans on contraception and abortion are inseparable detracts from, rather than strengthens, a natural law argument about abortion.

There is a second area where the abortion argument of *Evangelium Vitae* would be strengthened by some natural law analysis. The encyclical's ban on abortion is absolute, exceptionless. Possible exceptions to "no direct killing of the innocent" are not treated in any detail, but the mother's health and a decent standard of living are clearly rejected as justifications for abortion (*EV* 58). An absolute ban, of course, also prohibits abortion where maternal life is at stake as well as abortion in cases of rape and incest. Moreover, no fetal indications may justify abortion.

The moral principle that bans all these abortions may be correct. But in our American culture, whether of death or not, this strict position requires some reasonable explanation. Rape, incest, and the life of the mother are commonly invoked as reasonable exceptions to prohibitions of abortion.[11] The theological rationale and the argument from papal authority may not be persuasive to those who do not share Catholicism's theological presuppositions.

The Pope does address in greater detail the argument about conception and implantation, yet this remains a third area of the encyclical where more natural law reasoning is necessary. John Paul mentions the argument that allows abortion for some short time after conception. His response is that genetic science demonstrates that this life is human from the time of fertilization. He then states, "The results themselves of scientific research on the human embryo provide 'a valuable indication for discerning by the use of reason a personal presence at the moment of the first appearance of a human life: How could a human individual not be a human person?'" (*EV* 60).

The quotation is from the Congregation for the Doctrine of the Faith's *Donum Vitae*. This rhetorical question avoids the difficult questions. The Pope does not address numerous arguments that the preembryo is not a human person. The philosophical and scientific challenges (e.g., on twinning or recombination or the nature of personhood) to the Pope's position are not examined.

This claim about the presence of the person from fertilization also implicates the second issue of the absolute ban on abortion. The encyclical states that the "mere probability" of human personhood at fertilization justifies an *absolute* prohibition on abortion (*EV* 60). The encyclical does not address the obvious question of how the "mere probability" of human life outweighs the actual life of the mother in all circumstances. Absent a philosophical or scientific analysis of this question, the Pope must return to the argument from the authority of the Church's tradition: "Over and above all scientific debates and those philosophical affirmations to which the Magisterium has not expressly committed itself, the church has always taught and continues to teach that the result of human procreation, from the first moment of its existence, must be guaranteed that unconditional respect which is morally due to the human being in his or her totality and unity as body and spirit" (*EV* 60). Catholic theologians have challenged, and will continue to dispute, whether the Church has always taught this. What is indisputable is that the argument that the Church has always taught something is not a compelling natural law argument.

Toward the end of the encyclical, the Pope does make a natural law claim about the prohibition on killing. He states, "The Gospel of life is not for believers alone: It is for everyone. . . . Life certainly has a sacred and religious value, but in no way is that value a concern only of believers. The value at stake is one which every human being can grasp by the light of reason; thus it necessarily concerns everyone" (*EV* 101). Once again, the Pope has made a natural law claim that the gospel teaching applies to everyone. He has not, however, constructed a natural law argument.

This absence or weakness of the natural law argument need not detract from the encyclical's goals. The Catholic pope has good reason to encourage Catholics to heed Scripture, tradition, and theology, and to remind Catholics that God cares for life in all its stages. But the encyclical proposes a standard for civil law; civil law should be consistent with the encyclical's teaching. It is standard Catholic teaching that civil law should reflect the moral or natural law. A weak natural law argument will affect the quality of the discussion of civil law. The encyclical would be a better document if it had either presented the church's theological teaching or provided a natural law argument along with its implications for civil law. Instead, we receive in *Evangelium Vitae* a theological rationale for changing civil law.

ABORTION LAW

Evangelium Vitae concludes that the civil law must conform to the Church's moral teaching, whether theological or natural. "The doctrine on the necessary conformity of civil law with the moral law is in continuity with the whole tradition of the church" (*EV* 72). On the subject of abortion, civil law must be in conformity with the moral conclusion that procured abortion is never permitted.

For abortion, as for the other life issues discussed in the encyclical, the Pope argues that civil law must reflect the moral law because life is a fundamental value at the heart of every society. John Paul is sharply critical of legal systems that do not enforce the Church's moral teaching. Earlier in this century, the popes lauded democracy for its encouragement of individual participation and its promotion of human rights.[12] This pope is ready to jettison democracy if it does not comply with the Church's moral teaching. John Paul acknowledges that in the past the magisterium developed a "positive" view of democracy as a "sign of the times" (*EV* 70). Once democracy permits moral relativism, however, it must be rejected: "The value of democracy stands or falls with the values which it embodies and promotes" (*EV* 70). Such values must not be relative because the values of democracy are based upon the "objective moral law which, as the 'natural law' written in the human heart, is the obligatory point of reference for civil law itself" (*EV* 70). The natural law is once again invoked as a reason to hold democratic institutions to the Church's moral teaching.

Democracy's moral relativism is evident in the abortion law of many nations. The encyclical identifies a "disturbing" trend in countries that have legalized abortion. Legalization of abortion has meant not only the decriminalization of abortion. Instead, abortion has been recognized as a legal right. "Crimes against life" have become "rights of individual freedom" (*EV* 4). States now approve or authorize abortion "indeed with the free assistance of health-care systems" (*EV* 4). It is bad enough to decriminalize attacks on human life. It is worse to label these attacks "rights" and to include them as part of free health services. Once abortion is a right, proponents ask for "safe and free assistance of doctors and medical personnel" (*EV* 68), thus challenging the consciences of health care providers.

In response to these developments, *Evangelium Vitae* argues that no law permitting any abortion, no matter how restricted the circumstances, is ever just. No democratic process, no democratic consensus can justify any law that allows abortion. Abortion laws are per se totalitarian, not authentically democratic because they unfairly impose the majority's will in violation of the fundamental human right to life. The majority's recognition of a right to abortion can never legitimate abortion; instead, the existence of laws allowing abortion calls democracy itself into question. "In this way democracy, contradicting its own principles, effectively moves towards a form of totalitarianism" (*EV* 20).

The encyclical focuses on the "majority rule" aspect of democracy, suggesting that human rights are not protected in abortion laws because the majority has imposed its will upon the minority. Such majority rule encourages relativism: "in the democratic culture of our time it is commonly held that the legal system of any society should limit itself to taking account of and accepting the convictions of the majority. It should therefore be based solely upon what the majority itself considers moral and actually practices. . . . [T]he only determining factor should be the will of the majority, whatever this may be" (*EV* 69). In the United States, of course, abortion law was not promulgated by a majority vote. *Evangelium Vitae* adds that countermajoritarian institutions may not legalize abortion. The constitutional recognition of a right to abortion is always wrong. Indeed the Pope asserts that some countries have violated their basic constitutional principles in order to legalize abortion; this is evidence of "grave moral decline" (*EV* 4).

The encyclical thus vigorously rejects the argument that the law in a democracy should respect moral disagreement about abortion by permitting individuals to choose in conscience that abortion is right or wrong. There is only one correct moral position on abortion: it is always wrong. The law must reflect that moral standard. If democracy leads to a different conclusion, it too is wrong. "The legal toleration of abortion or of euthanasia can in no way claim to be based on respect for the conscience of others" (*EV* 71) because the conscience that chooses abortion is wrong. Moral error has no rights. *Evangelium Vitae*'s conclusion is straightforward: "Abortion and euthanasia are thus *crimes* which *no* human law can claim to legitimize" (*EV* 73). Any law permitting abortion is "intrinsically unjust" (*EV* 73). "Laws which authorize and promote abortion and euthanasia are . . . completely lacking in authentic juridical validity" (*EV* 72).

Thus, civil law must protect life from its conception. Not just civil law. The encyclical's identification of abortion as a crime against human life suggests that abortion should be subject to criminal prosecution. The encyclical does not address questions of criminal law. We do not learn the extent of criminal sanctions, for example, for women who have abortions, for doctors, for all medical personnel who cooperate in abortions.

Evangelium Vitae demands a radical change in the current abortion law of the United States. Moreover, abortion is not the only legal issue implicated by the encyclical's argument. If contraception and abortion are closely linked in their morality and if democratic majorities and constitutional rulings have no legal status when they violate the moral law, then the logic of the encyclical demands a transformation of the law of contraceptives in the United States. If *Griswold* led to *Roe*,[13] then both should be overturned—for theological reasons. Such sweeping changes in the law demand a more compelling natural law argument than the one presented in *Evangelium Vitae*.

Laws that are inconsistent with the Church's teaching must be opposed by "conscientious objection" (*EV* 73), the duty left to Catholics in nations that permit abortion.

CATHOLIC COOPERATION WITH ABORTION

Given the discontinuity between Catholic moral teaching and laws that permit abortion, the only proper Catholic response to such laws is opposition, "conscientious objection." This duty of conscientious objection is cast in theological terms. "It is precisely from obedience to God . . . that the strength and the courage to resist unjust human laws are born" (*EV* 73). Catholics will need strength and courage because compliance with Church teaching may "require the sacrifice of prestigious professional positions or the relinquishing of reasonable hopes of career advancement" (*EV* 74). Conscientious objectors may suffer, but it is wrong that they suffer. They "must be protected not only from legal penalties, but also from any negative effects on the legal, disciplinary, financial and professional plane" (*EV* 74).

Some guidance to individuals who live in societies with unjust abortion laws is provided by the principle of cooperation. This principle gives Catholics "a right to demand not to be forced to take part in morally evil actions" (*EV* 74). The encyclical distinguishes formal from material cooperation with evil; the former is never permitted, and the latter is at times permitted. For the taking of life, formal "cooperation occurs when an action, either by its very nature or by the form it takes in a concrete situation, can be defined as a direct participation in an act against innocent human life or a sharing in the immoral intention of the person committing it" (*EV* 74).

In the manuals, the meaning of formal and material cooperation was illustrated in specific cases. *Evangelium Vitae* provides a minimal casuistry, with limited examples, and so leaves many specific questions of individual conduct unresolved. It tells us that doctors and other medical personnel should not participate in any abortions. "Doctors and nurses [should not] place at the service of death skills which were acquired for promoting life" (*EV* 59). "'Causing death' can never be considered a form of medical treatment, even when the intention is solely to comply with the patient's request" (*EV* 89), and certainly not, as in the case of abortion, where there can be no patient request. In addition, "the opportunity to refuse to take part in the phases of consultation, preparation and execution of these acts against life should be guaranteed to physicians, health-care personnel, and directors of hospitals, clinics and convalescent facilities" (*EV* 74). Beyond these statements, *Evangelium Vitae* does not provide any casuistry of cooperation to guide medical personnel as they conscientiously object to abortion. We do not know, for example, if it is wrong for Catholics to work in hospitals or in the offices of doctors who perform abortions. We do not know if Catholics may refer their patients to providers who perform abortions.

More specific guidance is provided in *Evangelium Vitae*'s statement that "in the case of an intrinsically unjust law, such as a law permitting abortion or euthanasia, it is therefore never licit to obey it, or to 'take part in a propaganda campaign in favour of such a law, or vote for it'" (*EV* 73). While all Catholic citizens face the moral obligation not to vote for abortion, the encyclical's focus falls upon the Catholic politician. Politicians should in most cases not vote for abortion laws; moral "responsibility likewise falls on the legislators who have promoted and approved abortion laws" (*EV* 59). As a rule, Catholics are never supposed to vote for "intrinsically unjust" abortion laws. But the encyclical identifies one exception to this rule; the Pope states that in some circumstances Catholic politicians may vote for laws that permit some abortion.

Evangelium Vitae examines a "particular problem of conscience . . . where a legislative vote would be decisive for the passage of a more restrictive law, aimed at limiting the number of authorized abortions, in place of a more permissive law already passed or ready to be voted on" (*EV* 73). *Evangelium Vitae* concludes, "When it is not possible to overturn or completely abrogate a pro-abortion law, an elected official whose absolute personal opposition to procured abortion was well known could licitly support proposals aimed at limiting the harm done by such a law and at lessening its negative consequences at the level of general opinion and public morality" (*EV* 73). Such a vote is not "illicit cooperation" with evil. It is material and not formal "to cooperate to pass less restrictive abortion laws." Here in the political realm is one exception to *Evangelium Vitae*'s absolute moral stance.

Catholic politicians will be left to calculate what "absolute personal opposition" is, what "limiting the harm" of abortion means, what "lessening its negative consequences" entails. For example, former governor Mario Cuomo made known his personal opposition to abortion ("I accept the bishops' position that abortion is to be avoided. . . . For me, life or fetal life in the womb should be protected, even if five of nine justices of the Supreme Court and my neighbor disagree with me.").[14] He supported legislation that would prevent abortion by "present[ing] an impoverished mother with the full range of support she needs to bear and raise her children."[15] He also stated that "legal interdicting of abortion by either the federal government or the individual states . . . wouldn't work" because these laws could not be enforced.[16] The Pope appears to reject this last argument about enforcement (*EV* 68). But it is possible, on one reading of this encyclical, that Cuomo's political stance, so criticized by the American bishops,[17] has been vindicated by the current pontiff.

Such vindication should not be consoling to many American Catholic politicians, however. While the encyclical recognizes the possibility of their casting a pragmatic vote for less restrictive abortion laws without violating their Catholic consciences, *Evangelium Vitae* imposes on them a more difficult dilemma of conscience. *Evangelium Vitae* forsakes the natural law and asks Catholic politicians to enact a theological teaching into law. Despite the absence of the natural law argument, the encyclical asks Catholic politicians to impose the Church's teaching on non-Catholics. For pragmatic reasons, Catholics may vote for less restrictive abortion laws when their absolute ban on abortion cannot be passed. Catholics may vote only to restrict abortion rights or to ban abortion altogether. Their goal must be for Catholicism's teaching on abortion to become the law for all citizens of the United States, so that no abortion is permitted. Moral error has no rights.

Without a natural law argument about abortion, American Catholic politicians (and, one presumes, justices) are asked to inscribe their religious beliefs into the law of the United States. In the past, American Catholic politicians have balked at this suggestion. So they should. Joseph Donceel has stated, "The church may in certain cases impose a philosophical doctrine upon her faithful, when that doctrine is essential to safeguard a revealed truth. But she has no right to impose it on non-Catholics and to expect the state (and therefore the politicians) to impose it." [18] *Evangelium Vitae* imposes a theological doctrine upon the Church's faithful, but theological doctrine should not be imposed on non-Catholics by the state and politicians, not even by Catholic politicians. It is not clear why *Evangelium Vitae* does not ask politicians to show their conscientious objection to unjust laws, or to a democracy without moral foundation, by leaving politics altogether. In the United States, that would be a better moral option than to ask them to object to the law by making the law theological and not secular. After all, as *Evangelium Vitae* reminds us, "laws are not the only means of protecting human life" (*EV* 90).

CONCLUSION

In the years before the Second Vatican Council, Roman pontiffs asked American Catholics to oppose their First Amendment because Catholicism, as the one true religion, was entitled to establishment. In *Evangelium Vitae*, the Polish pontiff asks American Catholics to oppose the constitutional protection of abortion because Catholicism, as the one true morality, is entitled to legal enforcement. In the former case, the magisterium was eventually dissuaded from its opposition to the separation of church and state by its acceptance of a natural law right to religious freedom. In the latter case, in *Evangelium Vitae* the magisterium has chosen not to address natural law arguments about abortion but instead to argue that the natural law requires that the Church's moral teaching become the civil law of all human persons.

NOTES

1. See, e.g., Bryan Hehir, "Get a (Culture of) Life," *Commonweal* 122, no. 10 (May 19, 1995): 8–9, at 9: "Neither the vision (chapter 2) nor the moral argument (chapter 3) breaks new ground; the power and value of the encyclical lie in its synthetic quality."

2. See Bruno Schüller, S.J., "Direct Killing/Indirect Killing," in *Readings in Moral Theology*, ed. Charles E. Curran and Richard A. McCormick, S.J. (New York: Paulist Press, 1979), 1: 138–57.

3. Richard A. McCormick, S.J., "The Consistent Ethic of Life: Is There an Historical Soft Underbelly?" in *Consistent Ethic of Life*, ed. J. Bernardin (Kansas City, Mo.: Sheed and Ward, 1988), 109–22; "The Gospel of Life," *America* 172, no. 15 (April 29, 1995): 10–17.

4. See Susan T. Nicholson, "The Roman Catholic Doctrine of Therapeutic Abortion," in *Feminism and Philosophy*, ed. M. Vetterling-Braggin et al. (Totowa, N.J.: Rowman & Allanheld, 1977), 385–407.

5. John Mahoney discusses these arguments in *Bioethics and Belief* (Westminster, Md.: Christian Classics, 1984), 62–67.

6. See Joseph F. Donceel, S.J., "Immediate Animation and Delayed Hominization," *Theological Studies* 31 (1970): 76–105; "Mediate v. Immediate Animation," in *Abortion: The Moral Issues*, ed. Edward Batchelor Jr. (New York: Pilgrim Press, 1982), 110–14.

7. For the history of the self-defense argument, see John Connery, S.J., *Abortion: The Development of the Roman Catholic Perspective* (Chicago: Loyola University Press, 1977), 124–224.

8. See Stephen L. Carter, *The Culture of Disbelief: How American Law and Politics Trivialize Religious Devotion* (New York: Basic Books, 1993).

9. For discussions of the inductive method in Catholic social ethics, see Marie-Dominique Chenu, La *"doctrine sociale" de l'Eglise comme idéologie* (Paris: Editions du Cerf, 1979); Charles E. Curran, "The Changing Anthropological Bases of Catholic Social Ethics," in *Moral Theology: A Continuing Journey* (Notre Dame, Ind.: University of Notre Dame Press, 1982), 173–208.

10. Many news reports highlighted the culture-of-death theme. See, e.g., Paul Baumann, "The Pope vs. the Culture of Death," *New York Times*, October 8, 1995, 4:13; Cal Thomas, "In America, Pope's 'Gospel of Life' Battles 'Culture of Death,'" *Dayton Daily News*, April 7, 1995, 19A; James D. David, "'Culture of Death' Encyclical Stirs Pope-Conscience Debate," *Sun-Sentinel*, April 1, 1995, 7D; Paul Galloway, "John Paul Condemns 'Culture of Death,'" *Chicago Tribune*, March 31, 1995, 1; Celestine Bohlen, "Pope Condemns a 'Culture of Death,'" *International Herald Tribune*, March 31, 1995, 8; Judith Lynn Howard, "'Culture of Death' Decried," *Dallas Morning News*, March 31, 1995, 1A.

11. See, e.g., Utah Code Ann. § 76-7-301.1(4) (1995); La. Rev. Stat. Ann. § 40:1299.34.5(B) (West 1995); *Harris v. McRae*, 448 U.S. 297 (1980) (ruling on 1980 version of the Hyde Amendment, Pub.L. 96–123, § 109, 93 Stat. 926); the Hyde

Amendment, Departments of Labor, Health and Human Services, Education, and Related Agencies Appropriations Act of 1994, § 509, 107 Stat. 1082; *Little Rock Family Planning Services, P.A. v. Dalton*, 60 F.3d 497 (8th Cir. 1995).

12. See, e.g., Pius XII, "Christmas Message, 1944," in *The Unwearied Advocate: Public Addresses of Pope Pius XII*, ed. V. Yzermans (St. Cloud, Minn: St. Cloud Bookshop, 1956), 1:54.

13. *Griswold v. Connecticut*, 381 U.S. 479 (1965); *Roe v. Wade*, 410 U.S. 959 (1973).

14. Mario Cuomo, "Religious Belief and Public Morality: A Catholic Governor's Perspective," in *Abortion and Catholicism*, ed. P. Beattie Jung and T. Shannon (New York: Crossroad, 1988), 209.

15. Ibid., 214.

16. Ibid., 212.

17. See, e.g., Kenneth A. Briggs, "Fight Abortion, O'Connor Urges Public Officials," *New York Times*, October 16, 1984, A27; Robert D. McFadden, "Archbishop Asserts That Cuomo Misinterpreted Stand on Abortion," *New York Times*, August 4, 1984, A1, A7.

18. Joseph F. Donceel, "Catholic Politicians and Abortion," *America* 152, no. 4 (February 2, 1985): 81–83, at 82. See also John Rawls, *Political Liberalism* (New York: Columbia University Press, 1993), pp. 224–26: Public reason "means that in discussing constitutional essentials and matters of basic justice we are not to appeal to comprehensive religious and philosophical doctrines—to what we as individuals or members of associations see as the whole truth . . ." Instead, public reasoning should "rest on the plain truths now widely accepted, or available, to citizens generally."

A Response to Leslie Griffin's Essay

Thomas R. Kopfensteiner

Practitioners of any scientific discipline know that problems may be of two kinds. The first is found within the normal scientific activity of the discipline. They are problems that are identified and solved within the classical paradigm utilizing the commonly accepted tools of the trade. The second kind of problem is of a more radical nature: the tradition itself may be the problem. Some practitioners of the discipline then engage in extraordinary scientific activity that, while attempting to render anomalies commonplace, results in the subtle but sure restructuring of the classical paradigm. Within this context, there are three areas of concern that I would offer for discussion on the issue of abortion from a fundamental moral perspective.

MORAL METHODOLOGY AND ABORTION

As Dr. Griffin points out, the "good news is old news" when it comes to the issue of abortion in *Evangelium Vitae*. The encyclical draws on arguments from revelation and the natural law tradition to support the condemnation of abortion. But there is a curious development when it comes to the context in which abortion is discussed. Abortion is part of a *culture* of death, not a culture of life. In placing the issue of abortion in the context of culture, the argument against abortion depends on a more nuanced treatment of the relationship of law and culture. The context of culture construes the problem of abortion not primarily in terms of individual rights (either of the fetus or of the woman) but in terms of the community, which strives "to show special favor to those who are poorest, most alone and most in need" (*EV* 87) and whose members are encouraged to bear each other's burdens (Gal 6:2). This context does not lessen the traditional argument against abortion as it was presented in the *Declaration on Abortion* issued by the Congregation of the Doctrine of the Faith in 1975, but extends and deepens it.

In the *Declaration on Abortion*, the argument against abortion is straightforward, syllogistic, and deductive. The major premise consists of the claim that human life is a basic good and the most fundamental right we have as persons is the right to life. The minor premise is that the fetus is a human person. And the conclusion is that denying an innocent person his or her life is prohibited absolutely. There is no doubt that this kind of reasoning is present in *Evangelium Vitae*. The Holy Father writes, "I confirm that the direct and voluntary killing of an innocent human being is always gravely immoral." When this is coupled with the minor premise, then "direct abortion, that is, abortion willed as an end or a means, always constitutes a grave disorder, since it is the deliberate killing of an innocent human being" (*EV* 57, 62).

It is only after the syllogism is stated and defended that the *Declaration on Abortion* addresses the broader economic, political, and cultural issues or calls for assistance for families, unmarried mothers or women in difficult situations, and children. Those concerns, however, are constitutive of the argument from culture found in *Evangelium Vitae*. The crisis of abortion is not primarily a crisis of law but a crisis of culture. This means that the Church's response to abortion is not limited to political or juridical measures but extends to the creation of what John Paul II calls an ethos of solidarity, where the dignity and equality of all persons is respected. An ethos of solidarity would not be limited to the recognition of the importance of the life and dignity of the fetus but would include the dignity and proper autonomy of the mother who is faced with the "tragic and painful" decision to abort the child not "for purely selfish reasons or out of convenience, but out of a desire to protect certain important values such as her own health or a decent standard of living for the other members of the family" (*EV* 58). An ethos of solidarity would not be limited to promoting strict abortion legislation but would include the promotion of "social policies in support of families, especially larger families and those with particular financial and educational needs (*EV* 59).

By creating a culture of life or an ethos of solidarity, the legitimate expectations of freedom of all are raised to a level below which we cannot fall and still hope to humanly shape our lives (*EV* 75). In this context we can recall the struggles outlawing slavery, bigamy, child labor, and the achievements of the suffrage and civil-rights movements. The creation of a culture of life unfolds into an axiom: the greater the solidarity we have with those in need, the less manifest will be the choices of a culture of death. The negative prohibition against abortion, then, is not given *simpliciter* but is meant to reflect and protect the culture in which those high standards of freedom are maintained.

THE THEORY OF INTRINSIC EVIL

When the encyclical labels abortion as "gravely immoral" (*EV* 57), "an act which is intrinsically illicit" (*EV* 62), there is an echo of the theory of intrinsically evil acts that has been discussed anew in recent literature. There are at least three meanings given to "intrinsically evil" in the encyclical. Intrinsically evil acts are those acts that no law or authority can legitimate (*EV* 62). Second, there are the negatively formulated precepts that reflect "the absolute limit beneath which free individuals cannot lower themselves" (*EV* 75); there is no possible situation or circumstance that can legitimate them. This is what the encyclical means when it equates abortion with murder. And finally there are those acts where there is a disproportion between the intention and execution; they are those actions that are evil no matter how good the intention of the agent may be (*bonum ex integra causa, malum e quocumque defectu*) (*EV* 62).

Recent Catholic moral theology has not doubted the theory of intrinsic evil but has offered a more nuanced understanding of it. Within the neo-scholastic manual tradition, the metaphysics of the act centered on the meaning of the moral object. The point of departure for the determination of the moral object was the *finis operis*. The determination of the object was made within an essentialist metaphysics of human nature and an epistemological realism. The intention of the agent was a *circumstantia principalis* and could modify the moral act accidentally. This traditional analysis of moral action had at least three effects. First, moral objectivity was attributed to the phenomenal structure of the act which, in turn, circumscribed the possible interpretations of the action. Second, while this circumspection protected a high level of communicability in conformity to the modern ideal of science, the price this communicability exacted was the impression that moral action no longer presupposed a human subject. There was a clear line drawn between the objective and subjective spheres of reality. Third, moral language had a univocal character whereby what was referred to by a proscription was clear to everyone in every place.

In a more personalist understanding of normative human nature and moral action, there is a more flexible relationship between person and nature. Nature is not infinitely malleable, but in such a way that the order of nature is subordinated to the order of reason and freedom. In this way, nature, as John Paul asserts in *Veritatis Splendor*, "acquires a moral significance in reference to the good of the person" (*VS* 50). Within this personalist context, theologians have sought to analyze the relationship between the subjective and objective spheres of morality or between intention, execution, and circumstances. The problem is: How flexible or malleable is the act in light of the agent's intention? Under a new metaphysics of action, can the intention of the agent—the *finis operantis*—be relegated to the psychology of action, or must it play a constitutive role in the determination of the moral object? Or can new historical circumstances open up new possibilities that must be accounted for in an adequate evaluation of the moral act? We can think of the history of the principle of totality and its interpretation in the debate over organ transplants *inter vivos* as an example of finding flexibility in the determination of the moral object.

A renewed analysis of moral action is important especially in the limit cases of abortion: those situations where the mother's life or other fetal life is threatened; tubal or ectopic pregnancies; the tragedy of an anencephalic fetus; or a fetus suffering from fatal anomalies such as Potter's syndrome. These cases and others like them do not question the validity of our traditional casuistic principles, such as double effect, totality, and material cooperation. Our moral reasoning about these cases, however, is severely limited when they are subsumed under the absolute proscription of abortion.

THE STATUS OF THE HUMAN EMBRYO

The Holy Father's condemnation of abortion includes "procedures that exploit living human embryos and fetuses—sometimes specifically 'produced' for this purpose by reproductive technologies such as *in vitro* fertilization—either to be used as 'biological material' or as providers of organs or tissue for transplants in the treatment of certain diseases" (*EV* 63). Though the encyclical does detail the scientific and philosophical debates concerning the moral status of the embryo, it argues tutioristically to assert that "what is at stake is so important that, from the standpoint of moral obligation, the mere probability that a human person is involved would suffice to justify an absolutely clear prohibition of any intervention aimed at killing a human embryo" (*EV* 60). There are always those who question this absolute prohibition. They argue that so long as the embryo is not to the point of biological individuation, it lacks the requisite substrata for personal existence. It is a matter of biological individuality. One cannot speak of the personal identity of the embryo, since it lacks the biological presupposition of somatic individuality. The issue is not human life; rather, the human life that is involved is only potentially a personal life. From this perspective, the embryo is not a thing, but not yet a person in the full sense. Consequently, before this is determined, one cannot speak of a bearer of rights—at least any time prior to the individuation of the embryo, which is by medical indications around fourteen days after conception. This view of the embryo would have the most immediate consequence on the protection of the embryo when in conflict with other goods.

Here is an issue where moral theologians need to question the adequacy of their philosophical tools. In the debate over the status of the embryo, it is common to have recourse to the classical definition of the person given to us by Boethius and adopted by Aquinas: *persona est naturae rationalis individua substantia*—the person is a rational and individuated substance. But is this definition suitable to the present discussion? It has a value only when it proceeds from a clear understanding of the meaning of "substance." The paradigm for the understanding of the person is substance as individuated.

Consequently, if there is a doubt about the substance as individuated, there is a doubt about there being a person.

But can this classical and biological concept of substance be readily transferred to modern molecular biology when it has been shown to be no longer valid in the area of physics? That is, is it not conditioned by a prescientific world view? Should not our conception of substance be inserted into a processual paradigm in such a way that individuation would not refer to any one temporal point? Within a processual paradigm, respect for an individuated substance would mean respect for an ongoing process. Then one could ask why this respect would not be accorded equally to all phases of this process—specifically to the earliest beginnings of human life. Is it not there that a new entity is formed and begins a development characterized by the achievement of ever higher stages? The process of embryonic development is programmed from the beginning and follows a clear linear structure or finality.

To fall back into the classical paradigm of substance would be to divide this whole into segments and risk falling into overly mechanistic categories. Are we not then obliged to justify the category of a human but potentially personal life? This clearly has sense in the classical paradigm, but within a more processual one, there is only a potency to reach higher stages of individuation; there is never a jump from prepersonal to personal life. The process of transcendence reaches ever new plateaus, but never jumps from a subpersonal to the personal one. In a processual paradigm, the distinction between human and personal life is put into doubt. Within a processual paradigm one cannot speak coherently of a "more or less" personal being; one either is or is not a person.

A Response to Leslie Griffin

HELEN M. ALVARE

In the world today, abortions occur at a rate of 40–50 million per year.[1] In the United States, they are legal throughout nine months of pregnancy and for any reason.[2] Most abortions in the United States are sought for reasons relating to lifestyle, not physical or even emotional health.[3] Abortion advocates defend abortion using notions of freedom and absolute autonomy that, if broadly accepted or exported outside the abortion context, would destroy our social contract as we know it.

Evangelium Vitae confronts this. The encyclical is a sweeping summary of centuries of Church teaching about abortion. It is replete with the lessons from Scripture and tradition that provide a thought-provoking context and guide to our current abortion problems. It is, at times, when speaking about the unborn, emotional, prayerful, inspirational. As a teaching document on abortion, it deserves a more generous, less cynical introductory critique than is found in the offhanded phrase "The 'good news' is old news."

Leslie Griffin advances many critiques of *Evangelium Vitae*. The first and general critique seems to be that the document is insufficiently "new." This is true in part, but not in any important way. It is also quite untrue in part. As a professional pro-life activist and policy advisor, I began to read *Evangelium Vitae* hoping, for the most part, to learn new and persuasive arguments against the act of abortion that would leave all hearers, Catholic and non-Catholic, convinced. By the end, I realized that the document reflected the fact that the foundational arguments against abortion have not changed and will not likely change. At the same time, I realized that the document was quite new in a variety of ways. It exposed the foundational philosophical principles used to justify abortion, and the gradual and harmful exporting of them outside of the abortion context. *Evangelium Vitae* also makes the case for the special danger posed to all human freedoms by an "abortion mentality." It also shows that the trajectory of Scripture and tradition in favor of life and against killing is so strong that future claims about the existence of a "Christian" argument for abortion could be laid to rest once and for all. That all of these things were done in a single document, that abortion was not treated as a solitary issue but also as a paradigm of the "culture of death," makes *Evangelium Vitae* "new" in a quite important way.

Like me, Griffin seems to have been seeking in *Evangelium Vitae* the definitive, rational argument that would convince even non-Catholics regarding the intrinsic evil of abortion itself. But unlike me, she appears disappointed by what *Evangelium Vitae* did deliver. Disappointed at the amount of summation of prior teachings and the lack of discussion regarding Catholic dissent from Church teaching on abortion. Disappointed at the amount of philosophical and scientific argumentation and the presence of so many scriptural references. And disappointed at the basis for, and the strength of, the call to lawmakers, for example, to act within their jurisdictions to realize the protection of unborn life.

I find that the Holy Father's decision to spend many paragraphs reviewing Church teachings is consonant with the document's purpose. The review is useful for demonstrating the weight and consistency of the Church's teachings over time and is an important foundation for the weighty condemnation of abortion—the weightiest in history—that comes from the Holy Father.

The absence of significant mention of dissent seems to me generally reflective of the relatively little dissent that has actually greeted Church teaching on abortion over time. From my perspective and experience—as a Catholic educator, public-policy analyst, and grassroots activist who travels to dozens of Catholic dioceses annually—it has become clear to me that there is a low level of informed dissent over abortion within the Catholic community. A noteworthy, but still limited, body of dissent exists within the community of Catholic theologians, but it is not widespread within the People of God generally.

Perhaps most disappointing to Griffin, however, is what she characterizes as the document's "distinctively Catholic, theological argument," as opposed to what she would call a "philosophical or scientific" argument. She characterizes this as a "retreat from natural law argument." This critique is closely related to her final claim that the encyclical "asks Catholic politicians to enact a theological teaching into law" and that politicians and non-Catholics can rightly be angry about this.

Treating first the claim that the document "forsakes the natural law." While Griffin is not explicit about her standards for making a natural law argument, it appears that she requires the presence of arguments that are sourced specifically to various scientific and philosophical authorities. Herein seems to lie the foundation of her claim, as well as the source of its flaws: she seems to understand natural law as mutually exclusive of arguments based upon divine law as well as upon basic human instincts about the morality of killing. She seems to have ignored the traditional understanding of natural law as our participation in divine law. She recognizes later in the paper that the Church understands reason and revelation to be consistent, but does not seem willing to accept some of the consequences of that understanding.

Again, while it is not precisely clear what "natural law" evidence Professor Griffin is seeking, it seems that she may have in mind a recitation of the biological evidence about the precise moment when human life begins, the twinning mechanisms of very young embryos, the philosophical traits necessary for "personhood," and so forth. But this is to make natural law argumentation synonymous purely with scientific or philosophical evidence. (I would note here that even were these the accepted standards for natural law argumentation, the Pope incorporates by reference all of the prior Church documents on abortion, including the most scientifically detailed, the *Declaration on Procured Abortion* and *Donum Vitae*; these ought to satisfy even such standards.) But natural law, while it does not contradict these, is more. It is also evident in the quite basic human understandings that it is wrong to kill another human life, or that developing human life ought to be respected.

In *Evangelium Vitae*, there are a fair number of references to, and expressions of, human beings' basic intuitions and expressions of the preciousness of all human life. These form a powerful natural law argument. The Pope notes "Life is always a good (*EV* 34). This is an instinctive perception and a fact of experience and man is called to grasp the profound reason why this is so." He also notes (*EV* 11 and 58) that evidence of a divine law against killing, written in the human heart, is evident even from within the argument for abortion itself. Advocates defend abortion with euphemisms, he says, and refuse to call things by their proper names when they make the argument for abortion. Their methods, their discomfort are evidence that the human mind and heart have not lost a sense of the evil of killing.

Evidence of an international consensus against violations of human rights is also cited in *Evangelium Vitae*: "A long historical process is reaching a turning point. The process which once led to discovering the idea of 'human rights'—rights inherent in every person and prior to any Constitution and State legislation—is today marked by a surprising contradiction" (*EV* 18). The Pope goes on in the same paragraph to note, "On the one hand, the various declarations of human rights and the many initiatives inspired by these declarations show that at the global level there is a growing moral sensitivity, more alert to acknowledging the value and dignity of every individual as a human being, without any distinction of race, nationality, religion, political opinion or social class."

The Pope also makes a kind of natural law argument when he reflects on the philosophical and ideological foundations of the arguments in favor of killing (*EV* 18, 26). He identifies those foundations: excessive notions of subjectivity, a quality-of-life ethic, corrupted ideas about freedom that deny its relationship with others' or with truth, and excessive secularism. He draws out the consequences of these ideas. One primary consequence is the domination of the weak by the powerful. In the grim picture that the Pope paints of societies living by these precepts, Catholics and non-Catholics alike can easily see themselves, their families, and their communities. Similar laments about American culture and politics are made every day by politicians and social observers without referring explicitly to Christian revelation. Similar foundational problems are exposed. By describing the journey from harmful premises to harmful actions and by relating the causes of abortion to the causes of other human-rights violations, *Evangelium Vitae* makes a powerful argument from reason, likely to be heard inside *and outside* the Church, that abortion violates our human nature.

Even abortion advocates find themselves regularly making arguments about abortion against the backdrop of the moral analysis rendered by the Pope in *Evangelium Vitae*. In several recent and noteworthy pieces, feminist abortion advocates such as Naomi Wolf,[4] Elizabeth Fox-Genovese,[5] and Camille Paglia[6] have acknowledged the concerns articulated from pro-life quarters. They are now urging fellow pro-choice advocates to seriously consider, for example, whether they have wrongly conceived of "freedom" as unmitigated license, whether they can continue to turn a blind eye to scientific developments deepening knowledge about the unborn, and whether the rampant individualism inherent in the "choice" rhetoric will not be self-destructive in the end. All of these developments are touched upon in *Evangelium Vitae*, the first and the last most prominently. Griffin's failure to recognize the significance of the Holy Father's exploration of these weakens her claims regarding the document's treatment of natural law.

Even members of the secular media covering the document heard this argument and seemed to have little difficulty understanding its moral force. They tended even to sympathize with *Evangelium Vitae*'s reading of modern moral trends. "He caught us with our rationalizations down and our contradictions showing" (*Chicago Tribune*). "For the first time [he] set out an overarching moral rationale by which Catholics and all 'persons of good will' should judge a wide range of decisions involving human life" (*Los Angeles Times*). "The clearest, most impassioned and most commanding encyclical of his 16 year reign. Something new and hopeful—a sweeping evangelical plea for the creation of an alternative 'culture of life' that respects human dignity from conception to the moment of death"; a "human rights encyclical" *(Newsweek)*. The *New York Times*' Peter Steinfels noted Jewish sympathy with the Pope's reading of the culture of death.

In addition to my disagreement with Griffin's claims about the absence of natural law argument, I also find troubling her worries about those who might be affected by Catholics' acting on their convictions about abortion. Her argument seems to proceed on the suspicion or presumption that, indeed, natural law could contradict revelation on this point. And if it does, non-Catholics affected by Catholic legislators have been harmed, *and* harmed under false pretenses. If Griffin really believes that natural law does not support a right for the unborn not to be killed, this ought to be stated squarely. It should not be hidden behind an argument that it is procedurally unfair for Catholic legislators to vote even good laws into practice if they are acting out of purely theological beliefs. If, on the other hand, we are dealing with a situation in which legislators pass pro-life legislation affecting citizens who have less than full knowledge of the detailed embryological and philosophical arguments that do indeed support such a law, then there is no grave moral conflict here. But Griffin does not engage in a direct argument for or against the existence of a credible natural law case against abortion. Rather, by allusion to several writers who doubt the existence of such a case, she merely places it in doubt.

Also relevant to Griffin's expressions of dismay regarding *Evangelium Vitae*'s advice to legislators is the fact that when the Pope pleads for the moral exercise of legislative authority in the abortion arena, he is not proposing a sledgehammer approach. On the contrary, his approval of an incrementalist approach to improving bad abortion laws shows a quite sophisticated knowledge of the political process, a respect for the politics and culture of different societies and for democracy. He recognizes that it takes time to educate a public whose most elite institutions have supported abortion and that it is better to pass a law saving some lives than—in a situation of abortion on demand as we have in the United States—leave all prey to abortion (*EV* 73).

Griffin also speaks as if there does not already exist a plethora of scientific and philosophical evidence about the presence of a human being in the womb, weighing against the assertion of a right to kill the unborn. The reason such evidence is not all restated in *Evangelium Vitae* (though some is incorporated by reference) is that the Pope did not apparently intend *Evangelium Vitae* to be that sort of teaching instrument. But Griffin seems to suggest that its absence here could be fatal for the pro-life project of convincing non-Catholics. Theologians, scientists, philosophers, and other scholars whose work precedes *Evangelium Vitae* have written of this evidence for decades. It is certainly valid, not to mention necessary, also to have a document that exhorts Catholics regarding their particular obligations to vulnerable life. A document that also inspires them to action.

Finally, Griffin expresses the suspicion that the Pope shortchanges the natural law because he would find it hard simultaneously to argue that the conscience of the culture is having difficulty discerning abortion's immorality and that abortion contravenes the natural law. This line of reasoning, too, reveals a strange understanding of natural law—as if majority sentiment at any particular point in history could be clearly indicative of the truth of a matter. On the one hand, this is entirely too narrow an understanding of natural law. On the other hand, it is not without some truth. If the great majority of people, throughout history, has held a certain principle of human rights as true, it might be a rough indication of natural law.

The recent acceptance by modern societies of abortion, however, is quite a historical aberration. Perhaps best detailed in Marvin Olasky's *Abortion Rites,*[7] the history of recorded abortion opinion usually stays within boundaries marked by almost universal moral condemnation, almost universal legal condemnation, and some little tolerance for cases where a woman is the victim of rape or incest or would lose her life if the pregnancy continues. Furthermore, legal toleration of abortion today, now fairly widespread on an international level, exists simultaneously with moral intolerance of most abortions and with apathy born of tremendous ignorance about the permissiveness of the law or the reality of abortion procedures. In short, even if public-opinion polls could help us discern natural law principles from fakes, such polls would not contradict our understanding that abortion is wrong.[8]

Furthermore, the Pope is not claiming that human persons have utterly lost touch with their abhorrence of killing, including abortion. He points out, rather, that they are aware of it but often refuse to apply it to matters such as abortion and euthanasia. That is why they justify euthanasia to themselves in the name of "compassion." It is why they refuse to "look the truth in the eye and to *call things by their proper name* without yielding to convenient compromises or to the temptation of self-deception" (*EV* 58). He also notes that international support for universal human rights still lives in modern times, but in coexistence with blatant violations (*EV* 18). "Although man instinctively loves life because it is a good, this love will find further inspiration and strength and new breadth and depth, in the divine dimension of this good" (*EV* 38).

CONCLUSION

Evangelium Vitae's handling of abortion deserved a less narrow reading and critique than offered in Griffin's essay. Even if it consisted only of its lengthy treatment of Old and New Testament teachings about life, it would be a very valuable document. In a world where lofty human-rights pronouncements do coexist with some of the worst violations in history, human beings need to be reinspired about the origins, the dignity, and the destiny of the human person. Some may be convinced by the scientists and the philosophers, and that is good. Some may be turned around by exposure to the results of awful human-rights abuses or by a growing understanding of the philosophical and political errors that propel us toward all of these. Many, however, will respond as did the first apostles. They will ask, "Where will we go Lord? You have the words of everlasting life!" For them, and for those uplifted by them, the Gospel of life speaks powerfully.

NOTES

1. Stanley K. Henshaw and Evelyn Morrow, *Induced Abortion: A World Review* (1990 Supplement) (New York: Alan Guttmacher Institute, 1990), 10.

2. *Roe v. Wade*, 410 U.S. 113 (1973).

3. Aida Torres and Jacqueline Darroch Forrest, "Why Do Women Have Abortions?" *Family Planning Perspectives* 20, no. 5 (July/August 1988): 169–76.

4. Naomi Wolf, "Our Bodies, Our Souls: Rethinking Pro-choice Rhetoric," *New Republic*, October 16, 1995, 26–35.

5. Elizabeth Fox-Genovese, *Feminism Is Not the Story of My Life* (Chapel Hill: University of North Carolina Press, 1994).

6. Camille Paglia, *Vamps and Tramps* (New York: Vintage, 1994).

7. Marvin Olasky, *Abortion Rites* (Wheaton, Ill.: Crossway Books, 1992).

8. See "A National Survey of Public Attitudes toward the Issue of Abortion," prepared for the United States Catholic Conference by the Wirthlin Group (June 1991).

In the Service of Life: Evangelium Vitae and Medical Research

KEVIN WM. WILDES, S.J.

Few people will dispute the importance of advances in medical science in this century. From the development of high-technology interventions such as organ transplants to low-technology interventions such as vaccinations and drug therapy, the lives of men and women have been changed for the better by contemporary medical science. In *Evangelium Vitae* Pope John Paul II addresses the positive advances of scientific medicine when he writes, "*Medical science*, thanks to the committed efforts of researchers and practitioners, continues in efforts to discover ever more effective remedies: treatments which were once inconceivable but which now offer much promise for the future are today being developed for the unborn, the suffering and those in acute or terminal stages of sickness" (*EV* 28).[1] While medical science has been responsible for dramatic changes and improvements in the lives of men and women, it has also been the source of great and numerous moral offenses. From the horrors of Nazi Germany[2] to studies conducted by the U.S. government,[3] there is a history of moral failure as medical research has taken place under coercive circumstances and justified in the name of progress and saving lives.

The moral issues of research are not relics of the past. In his recent presidential address to the Society for Health and Human Values, Baruch Brody argued that there are numerous ethical issues raised in contemporary medical research that are being neglected by the field of bioethics. Many of these issues emerge because of the complex relationship between the clinic as a place of therapy and the clinic as a place of research, and the complex roles of the physician as both clinician and as researcher.

In this essay I want to examine the implications of *Evangelium Vitae* for contemporary ethical issues in medical research. As a specific topic, medical research is not part of *Evangelium Vitae*. Yet it is clear that the themes of the encyclical have implications for medical research that are relevant particularly for Catholic researchers, scholars, and health care institutions at a time when medical research is focusing on reproduction, genetics, and early human life. The general theme of the encyclical is "to reaffirm with the authority of the Successor of Peter the value of human life and its inviolability, in light of present day circumstances and attacks threatening it today" (*EV* 5). The repeated emphasis on the dignity and inviolability of human life provides a view of the limits and moral direction for medical research. This essay argues that the appeal to human dignity is at the heart of many of the moral positions announced within the encyclical. The encyclical argues that in light of inherent human dignity there are deontological boundaries that restrict human actions such as research. The encyclical clearly seeks to extend these deontological boundaries to protect the earliest stages of human life.

There seem to be two arguments at work in the encyclical. These arguments overlap and cannot be completely separated. For the sake of analysis and clarity, however, it is worthwhile to try to separate them. One argument can be called the "external argument." Since the encyclical is addressed to all men and women of goodwill, presumably one can examine its arguments in a philosophical framework. That is, the argument should be intelligible without the particular commitments of the Christian faith. The second argument can be labeled an "internal argument" insofar as it takes a stand regarding certain disputed areas in Roman Catholic moral theology. This internal argument faces questions about how it resolves certain tensions within Roman Catholic thought and how it supports the external argument.

Before proceeding, it is worth pointing out that the arguments in *Evangelium Vitae* cannot be a matter of indifference to Catholics or institutions that identify themselves as Catholic, since it is a statement from the Holy Father. As other essays in this volume argue, however, the judgments expressed in *Evangelium Vitae* need not be understood as so definitive as to preclude all discussion.[4] Within the Roman Catholic community questions about authority and institutional identity cannot be absent from considerations of the moral arguments of the encyclical. Nonetheless, it is possible to set aside the ecclesiological questions of authority in order to better understand the arguments of the encyclical on their own merits. This does not mean that the ecclesiological questions are unimportant, only that the merits of *Evangelium Vitae*'s moral arguments call for separate examination. Such an undertaking is done in light of the words of the Second Vatican Council's document *Gaudium et Spes*: "For the proper exercise of this role [theological research], the faithful, both clerical and lay, should be accorded a lawful freedom of inquiry, of thought, and of expression, tempered by humility and courage in whatever branch of study they have specialized" (*GS* 62).[5]

RESEARCH

In this century there have been, and continue to be, concrete examples of research abuse, such that there has been widespread efforts in many nations to regulate and oversee medical research.[6] One may well ask, in light of these harms and abuses, What are the justifications for research? One justification is based on an appeal to the principle of nonmaleficence. If those in medical practice are to know how treatments will affect patients and are to limit harms that may come with therapy, research is required. The history of medicine is filled with examples of treatments—such as blistering, bleeding, and purging—that were harmful to patients. Yet at the time such treatments were considered the standard of care according to the medical knowledge that was available. In the age of Thomas Syndeham (1624–89), Harvey (1578–1657), and Vesalius (1514–64) the developing scientific method became part of medicine. One reason for the ascendency of the scientific method was the need to test medical knowledge so as to minimize harms to patients and identify treatments that were actually beneficent. The need for research and testing is also supported by an appeal to a principle of beneficence. If physicians have an obligation to benefit the patient, it follows that knowledge and therapies must be tested and studied to understand the possible benefits.

The appeals to beneficence and nonmaleficence have been part of the general secular discussion, and there are similar discussions within Roman Catholicism. The Roman Catholic moral tradition frames its view of science and medicine within a comprehensive view of knowledge as a good in itself. The justification for research is founded in a general philosophical and theological anthropological framework long a part of Roman Catholic moral thought. One element of this theological anthropology is a view that knowledge is a good and the human person is, in part, a knower. Indeed, the pursuit of knowledge is understood by Aquinas as one of the primary goods of the natural law.[7] Pope Pius XII spoke of the search for truth as one of the basic moral commitments of human life that informs scientific research. In an address to physicians in 1953 he said, "In your research you seek for truth, and it is on this that you base your conclusions and build your systems."[8] This emphasis on the human person as a knower is joined with the view of the human person as free and as one who chooses. Karl Rahner wrote of "self-determination as the nature and task of man's freedom."[9] Indeed, Rahner characterizes the human person as the being who manipulates himself.[10] Medical research, as part of the quest for knowledge, fits well within the broad framework of traditional Roman Catholic anthropology insofar as it brings together the central human desire to know with the task of freedom in the application of knowledge.

While the tradition supports a positive obligation towards the pursuit of truth, it also limits and constrains medical research. The pursuit of knowledge is not an absolute good in its own right. Rather, it is one good situated among other goods. Pius XII wrote, "Nevertheless one cannot let pass the following affirmation: Given that the intervention be determined by scientific interests and that it observe the professional rules, then there are no limits to the methods of advancing and deepening the knowledge of medical science."[11] For Pius XII, the professional rules were not simply the rules about good scientific research; they also included moral rules. What are these rules?

One restraint, essential for understanding *Evangelium Vitae*, is a prohibition against the intentional taking of innocent human life. This restraint has ancient roots in Christianity. Another restraint comes from an assumption against mutilation—the willful destruction of any part of the body. This prohibition relies upon a broader view, that a person does not have an absolute right over his/her body. Pius XII wrote, "As far as the patient is concerned, he is not absolute master of himself, of his body, or of his soul. He cannot, therefore, freely dispose of himself as he pleases. . . . Because he is the beneficiary, and not the proprietor, he does not possess unlimited power to allow acts of destruction or mutilation."[12] In the seventeenth century Cardinal de Lugo articulated this view in regard to medical decisions of life and death: "[Man] cannot, however, receive dominion over himself, because from the very concept and definition, it is clear that a master is something relative, for example, a father or a teacher; and just as no one can be father or teacher of himself, so neither can he be master of himself, . . . he can be master of his operations. . . . Therefore a man can dispose of his own operations of which he is master, not of himself or (to say the same thing) of his own life, over which he is not master."[13]

For the good of the whole self, however, a person may undergo medical treatment that would otherwise, in healthier circumstances, be considered mutilation. Pius XII wrote that "in virtue of the principle of totality, of his right to employ the service of the organism as a whole, he can give individual parts to destruction or mutilation when and to the extent that it is good for the being as a whole, to assume its existence or to avoid, and naturally to repair, grave and lasting damage which could otherwise be neither avoided or repaired."[14]

The tradition has disallowed, however, an appeal to the principle of totality as a justification for the use of state power to coerce the participation of individuals in research. The concern in this century, of course, has been the protection of people from the coercion of the totalitarian state. Pius XII wrote, "It must be pointed out that man, as a person, in the final reckoning does not exist for the use of society; on the contrary, the community exists for man."[15] Society is not a unity that subsists in itself but is a medium to regulate exchanges by which mutual needs are met. The principle of totality, used by individuals who are unities, cannot be deployed by societies or the state. Because of a concern to limit the legitimate use of the principle of totality and the coercive force of the state, an emphasis is placed on the voluntary nature of participation in research.

Medical research, then, is limited by the taking of life, mutilation, and coercion. What, then, justifies medical research? First, the goodness of knowledge itself; second, the interests of patients under treatment; and, finally, the good of the community.[16]

THE EXTERNAL ARGUMENT

In much of his writing, particularly *Evangelium Vitae*, John Paul argues from the dignity of the human person for constraints on human action in research. In writing about human dignity and autonomy, John Paul seems to work from a Kantian understanding of autonomy insofar as he thinks that the idea of human dignity carries within it its own constraints. The appeal to dignity works as a restraint not only on what others may do to an individual but also on what an individual can do to himself or herself. A person's autonomy is controlled by the truth of one's human dignity.

For John Paul, the absolutizing of autonomy, understood as preference satisfaction, is the death of true freedom (*EV* 20). Why? The absolutizing of autonomy is the loss of God, and such a loss represents the denial of the truth of the human condition. The rebellion of Adam and Eve was a denial of creaturehood and an attempt by creatures to "be like God," that is, to view themselves as having the authority of the Creator, not as creatures. In this, human dignity, rooted in the relationship with the Creator, is lost because of a false view of the human person. Once this fundamental relationship has been altered, there is a real danger about how other human beings are perceived and treated. They can easily be treated as objects without dignity. Throughout *Evangelium Vitae* John Paul appeals to human dignity as justifying constraints on how a person acts towards others and self. "Human life is thus given a sacred and inviolable character, which reflects the inviolability of the Creator himself" (*EV* 53). This appeal to "dignity" is often mixed with appeals to inviolability and sanctity.

How dignity is understood, however, is crucial for the moral constraints derived from it. In the appeal to dignity in *Evangelium Vitae* one sees that the danger to any research is that the research subject may be treated as an object, not as a person. By acknowledging this risk and taking precautions against it, one can conduct research within the parameters of human dignity. Dignity calls for a person to be treated with honor or esteem. A difficulty is, however, that there are different views about what characteristic is the source of human "dignity." There are also differing views about the extent and implications of the appeal to dignity. Some accounts of dignity depend on a person's social worth.[17] Other accounts argue that human dignity is founded in the capacity for freedom. Another line of thought situates human dignity in the capacity for rationality. Still another view of dignity is rooted in a balance of pleasure and pain. In the debate over physician-assisted suicide (PSA), for example, there are those who argue that to forbid PSA is to condemn the dying to unnecessary pain and suffering, which is an offense to human dignity, while others argue that to engage in PSA is an offense to human dignity. These different uses of human dignity illustrate the problem with appealing to the concept: the appeal to dignity, by itself, often fails to inform the moral analysis because it informs too much. There are many different ways to understand dignity, and it is not clear which is the most appropriate.

A counterargument to these objections might be that there are certain formal elements to the concept of dignity. For example, there is an egalitarian structure to human dignity, insofar as dignity is used as a human quality and not just a special quality belonging to some men and women. Furthermore, human dignity is often understood as an inalienable characteristic. Yet these formal conditions of equality and inalienability lack content and do not give a clear grounding for constraints on human freedom.

In the Christian traditions, human dignity is rooted in the relationship of the human being to God (*GS* 3, 19, 26, 27, 29). Because men and women "possess a rational soul *and* are created in God's likeness, . . . have been redeemed by Christ, and enjoy the same divine calling and destiny, the basic equality of all must receive increasingly greater recognition" (*GS* 29). Created in the image of God, human beings are not simply isolated selves but selves in relationship with God and others. It is the self-giving of God to every person that is the basis for the reverence and dignity owed to a person.

John Paul writes, "Human life is thus given a sacred and inviolable character, which reflects the inviolability of the Creator himself" (*EV* 53). To understand John Paul's use of the appeal to dignity, one has to look beyond *Evangelium Vitae* to his first encyclical, *Redemptor Hominis*, which provides a more complete basis for the argument. There he argues that human beings are incomprehensible to themselves or others without love (*RH* 10). It is only by their relationship with the Creator, who is love, that human beings can become comprehensible to themselves and others. That link, broken by sin, is restored in Christ (*RH* 10). Human dignity comes from God's love for the human person (*RH* 10) and from God's divine adoption. He argues that our natural awareness of this dignity is but a glimmering of a full, robust account of dignity (*RH* 11). Furthermore, the concern of the Church for social structures, and human rights is a concern for this fuller account of human dignity (*RH* 12, 16, 17).

This view of the basis of human dignity leaves a puzzle, however, for the reader of *Evangelium Vitae*. *Evangelium Vitae* is addressed to "all men and women of good will." Yet one of the central arguments of the letter is rooted in the Christian experience of God and is articulated in very particular, theological categories. There is no clear connection from the theological discourse to the public square. In *Evangelium Vitae* John Paul argues that the Gospel of Life should be proclaimed by "emphasizing the *anthropological reasons* upon which respect for every human being is based. In this way, by making the newness of the *Gospel of Life* shine forth, we can also help everyone discover in the light of reason and of personal experience how the Christian message fully reveals what man is and the meaning of his being and existence" (*EV* 82). Given that reason begins in very different places and often reaches very different conclusions, however, one might well be puzzled as to why the arguments of *Evangelium Vitae* should be accepted by those who do not share these assumptions. The Stoics, for example, held a view that human dignity was grounded in human rational capacities. One could well imagine an argument that without rational capacity there is no human dignity. Yet many of the groups John Paul seeks to protect in his appeal to human dignity have diminished rational capacity. Given his concern for the handicapped, the unborn, and the vulnerable, it is clear that John Paul does not accept this account of dignity as sufficient. The fundamental problem is, How are men and women of goodwill to know the correct account of human dignity?

It seems clear that John Paul thinks that sufficient common points of agreement about human dignity are expressed in the language of human rights and that one can move from the language of rights to a wider, richer framework. Yet the language of human rights does not provide necessarily the fuller account for which he hopes. Rights of privacy, which are often the easiest to establish, will not ground the kinds of constraints John Paul wants. One will have to address such issues as who is included in the class of rights bearers. The language of rights may only provide a bare minimum, a starting point, rather than the fuller account of dignity in which John Paul seeks to ground the constraints of *Evangelium Vitae*.

The search for a common natural starting point is limited in another way. That is, it is not clear that by an appeal to reason we can reach agreement on who is to be counted as "human" and who has human dignity and human rights. John Paul speaks of embryos and fetuses as having "dignity as human beings who have a right to the same respect owed to a child once born just as to every person" (*EV* 73). This assertion bears directly on many issues in medical research. One will need more of an argument to make the case and draw strong conclusions for all men and women.

While endorsing medical research, John Paul wants to constrain it by an appeal to human dignity. The argument from human dignity in *Evangelium Vitae*, however, is built on a particular theological anthropology that gives rise to deontological constraints and limited dominion. Short of conversion, rational, moral, or spiritual, men and women will not be moved by the argument. The appeal to natural insight falls short of the mark for the precise points John Paul wants to address: early human life and the issues at the end of life.

THE INTERNAL ARGUMENT

In attempting to extend the general line of thought in *Evangelium Vitae* to embryo and fetal research, one encounters a point of dispute within traditional Roman Catholic thought. The point of discussion is the moral and metaphysical status of early human life. The encyclical simply assumes the personhood of embryo and fetus. But the moral and metaphysical status of the preimplantation embryo is an evaluative, moral question, not a scientific one. Both *Donum Vitae* and *Evangelium Vitae* make two mutually inconsistent assertions (*EV* 60) on this point. First, there is the assertion that the preimplantation embryo is a person. In *Donum Vitae* the Congregation for the Doctrine of the Faith wrote, "The conclusions of science regarding the human embryo provide a valuable indication for discerning by the use of reason a personal presence at the moment of this first appearance of human life: how could a human individual not be a human person?" (*DV* 1.1).[18] Simultaneously, the assumption is made that the preimplantation embryo must be treated as a person because of its *potential* to be a person (*DV* 1.1). The two positions yield different moral constraints. In the first position it is clear that (1) *X is A.* The second position holds that (2) *X is not A but X should be treated as A.* In the second position it is not immediately clear why X should be treated as A. Furthermore (1) and (2) are contradictory about the status of A. These assumptions are also made in *Evangelium Vitae*.

Indeed, the personhood of embryos and early fetal life has been a topic of moral controversy in the life of the Church. The long-held position has been that the human person is the integration of matter and spirit. There is also a long tradition that prior to twinning, or some later stage of development, there is insufficient material condition for ensoulment. The assumption has been that ensoulment is essential to personhood and that God is the creator of souls—they are created immediately by God.[19] The logical problem is that a soul could not be infused prior to twinning, since what was one must now be two. There are philosophical accounts that try to overcome this problem. The relevant point here, however, is that the question of the moral status of early human life is not an area of settled moral opinion. Indeed, in the *Declaration on Procured Abortion* the Congregation for the Doctrine of the Faith acknowledges that there is dispute about the metaphysical status and moral claims of the embryo.[20] It acknowledges the idea that there is a period of time when the living being is not a person. Despite assertions to the contrary there are clear questions within the tradition about the moral status of the nonensouled, nonpersonal human being.[21] The debate is not resolved or clarified by introducing the category of "potential," since it simply extends the fundamental position.

Karl Rahner points out that there exists a highly probable opinion that the preimplantation embryo is not a human person. In the tradition of probabilism, Rahner argues that since personhood is disputed, then reasons for experimentation might carry greater weight than the uncertain rights of a human being whose existence is in doubt; "It would be conceivable that, given a serious positive doubt about the human quality of the experimental material (i.e. *the embryonic material*), the reasons in favour of experimenting might carry more weight, considered rationally, then the uncertainties of a human being whose existence is in doubt."[22]

Others may raise serious questions about the role of consent in such research. That is, much of the focus in research ethics has been on the role of informed consent by the research subject. In the case of embryonic fetal life, the place of consent attracts special concern. The first argument can be formulated as follows: research subjects ought to be treated as persons, which involves consent, and since they are unable to consent, they ought not to be subjected to research (and institutions ought not be involved). Consent then becomes a necessary condition for moral licitness. This position is not entirely consistent with John Paul's own views and traditional Roman Catholic thought. If one assumes that embryonic life and fetal life ought to be treated as persons, then it would seem that, in principle, the duties and obligations of persons fall to them. It is clear that Roman Catholic moral tradition does not conceive personal life individualistically. Rather, personal good is conceived in a social context. One can argue that it is by participation in the social context that a human being becomes more fully human, in activities such as organ donation or involvement in research and experimentation. Such participation instantiates a Christian concern for others through the advancement of medicine.[23] Certainly throughout *Evangelium Vitae* there is the constant assumption that human beings are part of the human community and this membership creates certain obligations toward one another.

Furthermore, it is possible to miss the fact that the clinical setting often plays two roles: a center for therapy and a center for research. In *Donum Vitae*[24] the Congregation wrote that "as with all medical interventions on patients, one must uphold as licit procedures carried out in the human embryo which respect the life and integrity of the embryo and do not involve disproportionate risk for it but are directed towards its healing, the improvement of its condition of health, or its individual survival." Experimentation is justified insofar as it has a therapeutic purpose (*DV* 1.3). Three elements create the moral space for research: consent, possible therapeutic value, contribution to the human community. In research involving adults, these three elements create a wide latitude for participation in research. Why not for early human life?

Another objection to much of contemporary research is that it alters human nature. But it becomes crucial to determine what is meant by human nature. Karl Rahner wrote, "The question arises as to *which* 'nature' of man must be the guide for man's categorical self-manipulation, lest he be put in a situation of radical, destructive self-contradiction." Rahner went on to argue that if one regards the "essence" of the human to be "the personal spirit which, in freedom and radical self-possession, is confronted with the absolute mystery of God (as the One Who communicates Himself in love), and if this essence were *nothing else*, it seems initially at least as thought—in the biological, physical, social and institutional dimensions—man's categorical self-manipulation would be unable to come into really serious conflict with nature."[25] The essential nature of the human person is in freedom and creation. Thus, "man forms and molds his own nature through culture."[26]

Any appeal to nature as the basis of moral constraints depends on how nature is understood for the constraints that will be developed. Outside the context of any particular moral framework, there will be numerous ways to understand nature. Absent a commonly held view of human nature, we will not be able to develop content-full moral constraints by an appeal to nature.

At first glance many people will think that an appeal to nature is sufficient for moral guidance. Yet, as one investigates, it becomes apparent that to understand the meaning of an appeal to nature, one must situate the term in the context of moral language. Outside a particular context of a moral language, terms such as "nature" can take on multiple meanings so as to become meaningless. One can call to mind the thirty-year debate in Roman Catholic moral theology about the moral evaluation of birth control. There are those who evaluate the physical act of intercourse and see artificial contraception as illicit, while those who argue for a person-centered ethic see the act as morally neutral and put the evaluative emphasis on the intention of the agent. Yet both arguments appeal to nature.

The problem, then, is clear. If people agree that an appeal to nature is paramount in our moral analysis, that will depend on which understanding of nature is brought to bear on the issue. Appeals to nature are embedded within the context of a moral worldview. Different appeals will often be incommensurable with one another even though they appeal to nature. We lack a view above the particular views to enable us to pick out the correct particular view.

Even if we could resolve the first fundamental question about the nature of "nature," we are left with a second, perhaps more difficult issue: why should nature be morally normative at all? That is, unless one begins moral analysis by viewing nature, however defined, as morally normative, then there is no reason why one should think of nature as morally normative. We are caught in a vicious circle. This objection revisits the concerns raised by Hume's analysis of the is/ought distinction and G. E. Moore's concern about the naturalistic fallacy. Hume argued that simply because we can describe how something is, this does not mean that we can deduce an "ought" from the "is." Even if we could establish a common understanding of human nature, we would still face the question of why nature should be normative morally. If one sees nature as the outcome of random chance, there will be no reason to view nature as normative. Indeed, one may well hold the view that the natural moral imperative justifies rational, human control of the designing process.

This circle is not simply a philosopher's game. In a morally pluralistic world the assumptions with which one begins moral argument are significant. That is, unless men and women share the same assumptions about nature, they will not follow arguments that hold that nature gives us moral constraints.

In light of the arguments in *Evangelium Vitae*, the door seems to be open for research involving early human life. First, the extent to which the appeal to human dignity creates deontological constraints is not clear. Second, the basic conditions of consent, therapeutic value, and social good can be present in such research. Third, there are different internal arguments, within the tradition, about the moral status of early human life, and these differences are not resolved simply by the assertion of a position. Finally, the argument from nature to constrain human research and experimentation is a dog that "don't hunt no more."

CONCLUSIONS

There are many who will argue that *Evangelium Vitae* sets out important constraints on medical research. Upon investigation, however, it does not appear to be the case. *Evangelium Vitae* makes assertions about human dignity, but the content of this appeal is particularized in a way that undercuts the argument's effectiveness in the secular context. This argument, addressed to men and women of goodwill, needs crucial assumptions and premises that are not necessarily shared outside the context of the Christian faith. The lack of clear argument leaves little hope that the encyclical will address the concerns of different moral cultures in a secular society. *Evangelium Vitae* also asserts that from its earliest stage human life is (1) a person or (2) ought to be treated as a person. But it is unclear why such assertions, even if accepted, should constrain research. One could assume that, as with children, so with embryos and fetuses, parents can consent to experimental research when there is some therapeutic hope. Furthermore, one can argue that, insofar as embryos are members of the human community, parents have the obligation to consider seriously participation.

NOTES

1. John Paul II, *Evangelium Vitae* (Vatican City: Libreria Editrice Vaticana, 1995).

2. George Annas and Michael Grodin, *The Nazi Doctors and the Nuremberg Code: Human Rights in Human Experimentation* (New York: Oxford University Press, 1992).

3. Advisory Committee on Human Radiation Experiments, *The Human Radiation Experiments: Final Report of the Presidential Advisory Committee* (New York: Oxford University Press, 1996).

4. See the contributions of Sullivan, Orsy, and Rausch, this volume.

5. *Gaudium et Spes*, in *Documents of Vatican II*, ed. Austin Flannery (Grand Rapids, Mich.: W. B. Eerdmans, 1975).

6. See National Commission for the Protection of Human Subjects (Washington: U.S. Government Printing Office).

7. *ST* I–II, q. 94, a.1

8. Pius XII, "Primum Symposium Geneticae Medicae," September 7, 1953, in *Papal Teaching on the Human Body*, ed. Monks of Solesmes (Boston: Daughters of St. Paul: 1960), no. 455.

9. Karl Rahner, "The Experiment with Man," in *Theological Investigations* (Herder: 1972), 9: 212.

10. Ibid., 212.

11. Pius XII, "The Intangibility of the Human Person," September 13, 1952, in Monks of Solesmes, *Papal Teaching on the Human Body*, no. 356.

12. Ibid., 359.

13. Cardinal de Lugo, *De Justitia et Jure* (Paris: Vives, 1869).

14. Pius XII, "Intangibility of the Human Person," 359.

15. Ibid., 370.

16. Ibid., 353.

17. Thomas Hobbes, *Leviathan* (New York: Cambridge University Press, 1991), 63.

18. English text: Congregation for the Doctrine of the Faith, *Instruction on Respect for Human Life in Its Origin and on the Dignity of Procreation* (Vatican City: Libreria Editrice Vaticana, 1987).

19. Pius XII, *Humani Generis*, in Denzinger-Schonmetzer, *Enchiridion Symbolorum* (Freiburg: Herder, 1965), no. 3896, 779.

20. Congregation for the Doctrine of the Faith, *Declaration on Procured Abortion*, 1974.

21. See John Mahoney, *Bioethics and Belief* (London: Sheed and Ward, 1984), chap. 3.

22. Karl Rahner, "The Problem of Genetic Manipulation," in *Theological Investigation*, 9: 236.

23. There was a vigorous discussion about the Christian views on the role of children in experimentation between Paul Ramsey and Richard McCormick in the 1970s. See Paul Ramsey, *Fabricated Man* (New Haven: Yale University Press, 1970); and Richard McCormick, "Genetic Medicine: Notes on the Moral Literature," *Theological Studies* 1972. See *DV* 1.3.

24. Since Pius XII the episcopal magisterium has held a position condemning the use of reproductive technology outside the conjugal union. Pius set the framework for both *Humanae Vitae* and *Donum Vitae* in arguing that the conjugal act has a natural God-given design that conjoins the unitive and the procreative. This view forms the basis for the prohibition against contraception as both separate the unitive and procreation use of technologies such as IVF. This view is affirmed in *Evangelium Vitae*.

This view, however, has not gone unchallenged. One of the earliest challenges came from M. Zalba, a traditional moralist, who argued that the papal analysis was too physicalist in that it focused on the materiality of the act rather than its moral significance. In recent years other moralists have taken up the same viewpoint. They have argued that Vatican II's view of the human person moved away from focusing on the use of faculties and shifted to focusing on the whole person. The argument is that in looking at the whole person, one moves away from a physicalist account of sexuality toward the realm of relationships. Seen in this way, the unitive and procreative ends of marriage are not limited to the physical act.

25. Rahner, "The Experiment with Man," 215.

26. Ibid., 216.

On the Justification and Limits of *Medical Research:* A RESPONSE TO KEVIN WILDES

JOHN W. CARLSON

We are all in Kevin Wildes's debt for focusing light on an important topic left underdeveloped in the encyclical and most of the commentaries on it—the justification and limits of medical research, especially at life's earliest stages.

PRELIMINARY REMARKS

Father Wildes makes at least four significant contributions: (1) He relates John Paul II's brief but positive reference to medical research (*EV* 28) to a long tradition of Roman Catholic thought. (2) He shows how the Pope's reflections on human dignity—both in the present encyclical and in earlier writings—are crucial for his thinking on this topic. (3) He sketches a theoretical justification for medical research in terms of general principles and values—nonmaleficence, beneficence, the value of knowledge, and the common good. (4) Finally, he offers an assessment of *Evangelium Vitae*'s modes of presentation, taken as arguments designed to appeal to all persons of goodwill and/or to the specifically Catholic community.

Before discussing Wildes's assessment, I wish to make two preliminary observations. It is not clear, first of all, to what extent *Evangelium Vitae* should be interpreted as offering arguments in the standard academic sense. (This issue, as has been widely noted, also affected the reception of the prior encyclical, *Veritatis Splendor*.[1]) Note, for example, John Paul II's opening remark (*EV* 1) that the Gospel of life "is to be preached with dauntless fidelity as 'good news' to the people of every age and culture." And while he notes with appreciation that the "development of bioethics is promoting . . . reflection and dialogue" both within and between communities (*EV* 27), he does not say that he intends the present encyclical to be, formally speaking, a contribution to that dialogue. Moreover, of course, he pauses at key points to make formal declarations "by the authority which Christ conferred upon Peter and his successors"—regarding the direct and voluntary killing of innocent human beings (*EV* 56), regarding abortion (*EV* 62), and regarding euthanasia (*EV* 65).

The second preliminary observation is that there is significant overlap between what Wildes calls "external" and "internal" lines of thought. In particular, questions about the natural and about the status of early human life turn up under both headings in his essay. This overlap should not be surprising, however, for moralists within the Catholic tradition endeavor to think, at least to some degree, in terms and patterns that are in principle available to all. Let us now turn to the treatment of the arguments.

THE "EXTERNAL ARGUMENT"

Wildes applauds the Pope's intention to speak to all persons and to do so in terms of natural moral insights and reasoning. But he has grave difficulties with the manner in which this intention is carried out, and perhaps with the very possibility of doing so. After all, dignity, for example, is concretely understood in "many different ways"; reason "begins in very different places and often reaches very different conclusions"; and "moral frameworks" and "appeals" are often "incommensurable." Thus, "short of conversion, rational, moral, or spiritual," men and women who do not share John Paul II's assumptions will fail to be moved by his arguments. This is more especially the case since, while he speaks a common moral language, he roots this language in a particular theological anthropology.

As Alasdair MacIntyre has recently remarked, issues such as this now seem "inescapable and central" to contemporary thinkers.[2] This does not mean, however that such issues cannot be addressed. I believe they can and should be by thinkers in the "natural law" tradition—although not necessarily by the Pope in every teaching—and this through at least three mutually supportive lines of thought.

First, it needs to be shown that there are, or that there can be plausibly elicited, a core of moral sentiments, perceptions, and judgments—for example, as noted in *Evangelium Vitae* 101, concerning the value of human life. Second, there should be developed a supporting theory in terms of the natural—that is, an account of our human end, of authentic human functions and relations, and of types of acts that promote or that are incompatible with the values these contain. (This account, as we are now aware, must take note of the historical development of moral insight,[3] and of the roles of human freedom and culture. In the Catholic tradition this account also is deepened by specifically theological reflection.) Finally, there needs to be mounted a critique of traditions and currents of thought that are inimical to—and, indeed, could cloud people's natural perceptions of—the common moral core.[4]

None of these tasks is easy, but I believe they all can be undertaken. Thus Wildes's old "dog" may yet live to hunt another day!

Concerning the statement that an "appeal to natural insight falls short of the mark" concerning early human life and the end of life, I can only suggest, on the contrary, that at this point we have the wherewithal to establish about as firmly as one can a philosophical position that the career of a human being—as a complete structure with unified functioning and active potentiality for self-development—begins at the time of fertilization (not later than syngamy) and continues until unified functioning irreversibly ceases. Questions about twinning, recombination, and the like are, I think, puzzles that can be answered.[5] Of course, this alone doesn't settle the issue of dignity or the moral status of human life at these stages. But I would point out (*pace* a common philosophical view) that to suggest that the early embryo has "full moral status" is *not* to say that it has a full range or panoply of rights but, rather, to say that whatever rights it has—for example, a right not to be killed, or simply used for experimental purposes—it *has fully.*

Pope John Paul II says that dialogue is taking place "between believers and non-believers as well as between followers of different religions—on . . . fundamental issues pertaining to human life" (*EV* 27). While I think this is true (and is exemplified in the present volume), I wish to offer certain cautions about the process of dialogue, as well as comments on some of the ways in which Father Wildes's essay may conceive it.

To begin, while it is clearly true that we operate in a "morally pluralistic world" and thus that we must (some of us) work out a "philosophical framework" in which arguments are "intelligible" and, one hopes, persuasive to those outside the Christian faith,[6] it is more worrisome to read that our arguments must have "effectiveness in the secular context" or "address the concerns of . . . a secular society." Would the latter require a *foreswearing* of religious insight, which, according to John Paul (following the long tradition of Catholic thought), provides a fuller, more complete account of human dignity?[7] More important, perhaps, would it require the accepting of a competing ideology? These questions tie in with the Pope's deep ambivalence—detailed in Father Conley's contribution—concerning the cultures of liberal democracies. On the one hand, the Pope expresses confidence that the "Gospel of life . . . has a profound and persuasive echo in the heart of every person—believer and non-believer alike" (*EV* 2). On the other hand, he finds a widespread acceptance of unsound notions of human freedom and value—ones that are separated from "the very truth of the human being," including our relations with our fellows (*EV* 70–71).

I am concerned as well when I see Wildes give credence to a question such as "*what characteristic* is the source of human 'dignity'" and when he notes answers to it such as "social worth," the "capacity for freedom," or "a balance of pleasure and pain" (emphasis added)—as though the Catholic tradition's answer will be on a par with these. To accept this mode of discussion, as Oliver O'Donovan noted some years ago, is tantamount to agreeing that the source of dignity "is something qualitative, something that an individual [human] being may or may not turn out to possess."[8] In framing the issue this way we risk putting altogether out of play the metaphysics of personhood, on which, I believe, adequate Christian accounts of dignity must build. In so doing, we would abandon a crucial element of our intellectual tradition; we also would fail to make a distinctive contribution to the contemporary dialogue.

THE "INTERNAL ARGUMENT"

I now turn to features of what Father Wildes calls *Evangelium Vitae*'s "internal argument." I also will comment on two specific issues in medical research, related to human embryos and germ cells.

Father Wildes notes that a concern for "authority and institutional identity" should inform Catholic considerations of the encyclical. Nonetheless, he believes that certain of its formulations and arguments are problematic within as well as beyond the community of faith. First of all, John Paul's continuing appeal to "nature" is underdeterminative of specific moral positions. For outside a particular context the term "can take on multiple meanings so as to become meaningless"—as is seen in the perduring debate over artificial contraception.

Now I myself believe that progress has been made in recent years in specifying an appropriate understanding of the "natural" and thus in shedding light on issues of contraception.[9] But this does not mean that these issues have been finally and definitively resolved. More generally, as Richard McCormick noted in his review of *Evangelium Vitae*,[10] there indeed are a number of important issues, especially at the concrete level, that remain surrounded by "complexity . . . and uncertainty." Among these would be what counts, for example, in certain concrete situations as euthanasia. Further, John Paul does not try to resolve, for instance, the ethics of gamete intrafallopian transfer as a means of assisting fertilization, or (at the other end of the lifespan) the ethics of withholding or withdrawing artificial nutrition and hydration in selected extreme cases.[11] In light of this, it should not surprise us (and it should not be taken as a defect of the encyclical) that concrete issues in medical research also are left unsettled—especially since, as Wildes notes, these do not form a specific topic in the document. Like the others, these require further reflection and analysis.

Wildes pursues two lines of thought within the Catholic tradition that should prove helpful in assessing issues in research. The first concerns the relation between the individual and the community. "Personal good," Wildes writes, "is conceived in a social context"; and as members of the human community we have "obligations toward one another"—which may include "involvement in research and experimentation." It is suggested that, "as with children, so with embryos and fetuses, parents can consent to experimental research when there is some therapeutic hope" and indeed that "they have obligations to . . . consider participation."

It is not clear whether Wildes intends the last remark to include participation in nontherapeutic research. Following Ashley and O'Rourke, I would say that proxy (or, perhaps better, vicarious) consent to nontherapeutic experimentation is acceptable when there is no, or virtually no, risk to the child. [12] *In principle*, this point might be extended to the fetus and embryo. Regarding the latter, however, it would seem that *in fact any* research or manipulation will involve at least some risk. Thus, there are clear, if not altogether compelling, grounds for the Congregation for the Doctrine of the Faith's recent rejection of "experimentation on embryos which is not directly therapeutic" (*DV* 1.4). [13] A fortiori, the laboratory creation of embryos specifically for research—which was proposed for funding by an advisory committee to the National Institutes of Health [14]—should be unacceptable within the Catholic tradition. Nonetheless, as research protocols for embryos emerge having a therapeutic aspect, these indeed may be acceptable; and parents could legitimately give vicarious consent.

The other line of thought Father Wildes explores concerns the implications of human freedom for the ethics of genetic research. With reference to Karl Rahner, he considers the position that the "essential nature of the human person is in freedom and creation"; if such is the case, there would seem to be virtually no moral limits on genetic intervention, for our "self-manipulation would be unable to come into really serious conflict with nature."

As most readers of this volume will be aware, the bioethical community was surprised to learn in November 1994 that genetic modification of germ cells (in particular, early-stage sperm cells) would likely be possible in the near, rather than the intermediate or distant, future. [15] The resulting possibilities, by common agreement, are awesome. It seems to me that the Catholic tradition should accommodate germ-line manipulation related to what LeRoy Walters terms the "cure or prevention of disease"; it is not so clear, however—even given our proper sharing, through intelligent freedom, in God's own creativity—that it should accommodate what Walters calls the "enhancement of capabilities." [16] At the very least, careful standards would need to be developed to prevent the suppression, by intention or accident, of fundamental human functions. Do we really have the wisdom or the technical knowledge or the effective capacity to generate and enforce such standards? [17]

CONCLUSION

Toward the end of *Evangelium Vitae,* John Paul II expresses the hope—indeed, a prediction—that the Christian community, including its scholars, will "find important points of contact and dialogue with non-believers in our common commitment to the establishment of a new culture of life" (*EV* 81). As can be gathered from my comments, I share this hope, albeit with reservations and cautions. Since I have said more about the cautions than the hope, I will close with a comment on the latter. Wildes notes in his introductory section that there is general agreement about "the importance of advances in medical science," and also about significant instances of "moral failure" that have taken place under the guise of such advances. Now the work of critical moral reflection is difficult, and it is, in the modern world, subject to a variety of legitimate approaches.[18] But when it can be related to common perceptions such as the ones just indicated, there indeed is reason to anticipate that its practitioners will find their interaction both fruitful and mutually supportive. (A "natural law" thinker might even suggest that there is thus indicated a recognition, however dim, of our natural end and the means to attain it.) What remains to be seen is the extent to which such commonality of perception can be refined, rationally articulated, and expanded.

Although I have questioned some aspects of Wildes's treatment of the present topic, I believe it has been well articulated; and I again applaud him for bringing it to our attention.

NOTES

1. For a representative selection of commentaries, see Michael Alsopp and John O'Keefe, eds., *Veritatis Splendor* (Kansas City, Mo.: Sheed and Ward, 1995).

2. Alasdair MacIntyre, "A Partial Reply to My Critics," in *After MacIntyre,* ed. John Horton and Susan Mendus (Notre Dame, Ind.: University of Notre Dame Press, 1994), 295.

3. On this point, see Julia Lamm's comments, in this volume, on the unfortunate misogyny of some earlier writers.

4. See Terry Pinkard's contribution to this volume, in which he follows the analyses of Weber and Strauss. In a parallel but somewhat different vein, compare the recent project of Alasdair MacIntyre.

5. For a discussion of this point, see Benedict M. Ashley, O.P., and Kevin D. O'Rourke, O.P., *Health Care Ethics: A Theological Analysis* (St. Louis: Catholic Health Association, 1989), 209–13.

Regarding the status of early human life, Wildes says that recent Vatican documents, including the present encyclical, make two "different assertions"—first, that the preimplantation embryo "is a person" and, second, that it "must be treated as a person." The two positions, he suggests, yield different moral constraints. This would be an odd result, because the second position is maintained, in the face of unresolved doubt about the time of ensoulment, precisely in order to assure the *same* moral constraints.

6. I note two places, however, in which ambiguous language obscures the precise point: a) Wildes says one will need an argument to draw conclusions "for all men and women;" b) later he says that "absent a commonly held view of human nature," one can not develop "content-full" moral constraints. A conclusion or constraint might be said by a moralist to *hold for* all persons, even if it is not *accepted by* all persons.

7. See *RH* 11–12, cited by Wildes. See also *EV* 80 on how the "Gospel . . . reveals the sublime heights to which the dignity of the human person is raised through grace."

8. Oliver O'Donovan, *Begotten or Made* (Oxford: Oxford University Press, 1984), 58.

9. On this matter, see, for example, Ashley and O'Rourke, *Health Care Ethics*, 256–67.

10. Richard A. McCormick, S.J., "The Gospel of Life," *America* 172, no. 15 (April 29, 1995): 17.

11. On this point, compare the somewhat divergent opinions expressed in this volume by Dr. Edmund Pellegrino and Father Kevin O'Rourke.

12. Ashley and O'Rourke, *Health Care Ethics*, 240–41.

13. English text: Congregation for the Doctrine of the Faith, *Instruction on Respect for Human Life in its Origin and on the Dignity of Procreation, Replies to Certain Questions of the Day*, with commentaries in Edmund D. Pellegrino et al., eds., *Gift of Life* (Washington: Georgetown University Press, 1990).

14. *Chronicle of Higher Education*, December 14, 1994, A32. President Clinton promptly overruled the advisory committee and directed the National Institutes of Health not to allocate any funds for this purpose.

15. Gina Kolata, "Gene Technique Can Shape Future Generations," *New York Times*, November 22, 1994, C–1.

16. LeRoy Walters, "Ethical Issues in Human Gene Therapy," *Journal of Clinical Ethics* 2 (1991): 267.

17. On this matter, see Ashley and O'Rourke, *Health Care Ethics*, 302–19.

18. As documented by John Conley, S.J., in his essay in this volume, John Paul II's own approach involves an intertwining of phenomenological and scholastic elements. In general, this fact has been underappreciated by English–speaking scholars.

Research and Experimentation:
A RESPONSE TO KEVIN WILDES'S ESSAY

LeRoy Walters

I have learned much from reading both *Evangelium Vitae* and Wildes's critique of the encyclical. On one issue I will be more positive toward the encyclical than Wildes is. In the end, however, I will agree with Wildes that some of the specific moral judgments in the encyclical are difficult to justify on secular grounds.

The perspective from which I comment is indebted primarily to moral philosophy and several Protestant theological traditions. Autobiographically, my roots are in the left wing of the Reformation, and especially the social and ethical thought of Quakers and Mennonites.

I will begin my response with three general comments on the encyclical. Two of these comments will be positive, and the third will raise a question. I will then turn to John Paul II's treatment of biomedical research, which is a subsidiary theme in *Evangelium Vitae*. Here I will note the encyclical's general attitude toward such research, then look at what is said about five specific types of research: human-embryo research, fetal research, fetal-tissue transplantation research, research on contraceptives and abortifacients, and research on methods of natural family planning.

My first general comment is that John Paul II warmly welcomes the establishment and flowering of the bioethics field: "The emergence and ever more widespread development of *bioethics* is promoting more reflection and dialogue—between believers and non-believers, as well as between followers of different religions—on ethical problems, including fundamental issues pertaining to human life" (*EV* 27). Later, John Paul expresses the hope that universities, especially Catholic universities, and "*Centers, Institutes and Committees of Bioethics*" will assist in building a new culture of life (*EV* 98). There must be numerous developments and writings in bioethics that John Paul II finds quite objectionable, but he graciously chooses to accentuate the positive.

Second, one of the central themes in *Evangelium Vitae* is "the value and dignity of every human being" (*EV* 31). Contrary to Wildes's critique, I find this emphasis to be quite helpful in the effort to find common ground with people of goodwill who have no religious presuppositions or commitments. Even though this general assertion will need to be specified, and even though we will need to decide exactly what sorts of beings it covers, it gives a starting point and a direction to ethical reflection. It can also help to provide a grounding or rationale for general ethical principles and particular moral rules.

My third general comment reflects a pacifist background. Part 3 of *Evangelium Vitae* is entitled "You Shall Not Kill." Six kinds of killing receive attention in this part. Murder, abortion, and euthanasia are condemned as being always morally wrong. Capital punishment is to be used sparingly and only as a last resort. But in the short space of two paragraphs, killing in self-defense or in a war fought on behalf of the common good is said to be morally justifiable (*EV* 55). On self-defense and warfare we seem to have fallen from the lofty heights of the Gospels to the pre-Christian ethics of Greece and Rome. There is, in addition, a question about relative emphasis. In a document that is concerned to counteract the culture of death, why is not more attention paid to worldwide military expenditures, to nuclear deterrence as a threat to the innocent, to vicious ethnic conflicts, and to the question of selective conscientious objection?

I turn now to the encyclical's discussion of biomedical research, a topic that intersects with the primary themes of the document at several points. John Paul's general approach to biomedical research is decisively positive. In fact, "medical science" is said to be one of the hopeful signs in contemporary culture. Here is his affirmation: "*Medical science*, thanks to the committed efforts of researchers and practitioners, continues in its efforts to discover ever more effective remedies: treatments which were once inconceivable but which now offer much promise for the future are today being developed for the unborn, the suffering and those in an acute or terminal stage of sickness" (*EV* 26). There are few parallels for this global affirmation in the entire bioethics literature. In writers such as Paul Ramsey, Leon Kass, and Hans Jonas, one finds a much stronger accent on the dangers of biomedical research and on the ever-present possibility of violating the covenantal relationship between researcher and subject.

John Paul II also strongly supports research aimed at benefiting human embryos. In the section entitled "You Shall Not Kill," he quotes the following passage from the 1987 document *Donum Vitae*: "One must uphold as licit procedures carried out on the human embryo which respect the life and integrity of the embryo and do not involve disproportionate risks for it, but rather are directed to its healing, the improvement of its condition of health, or its individual survival" (*EV* 63, quoting *DV* 1.3). This statement reiterates a point that John Paul II had made already in 1983 in an address, "The Ethics of Genetic Manipulation," to the World Medical Association. There, contrary to the more cautious view of many European bioethicists, he affirmed the ethical acceptability of gene therapy for early human embryos, which would surely pass on genetic changes to future generations.[1]

By implication, John Paul II also approves research on the fetus in utero when it is directed toward the benefit of the fetus. One of the two permissible reasons for prenatal diagnosis is "to make possible early therapy" (*EV* 63). The initial efforts to deliver in utero gene therapy or cell therapy would of necessity be experimental.

A third kind of biomedical research affirmed by John Paul II is research aimed toward developing "natural methods of regulating fertility" (*EV* 97). In John Paul's words, "The Church is grateful to those who, with personal sacrifice and often unacknowledged dedication, devote themselves to the study and spread of these methods, as well [as] to the promotion of education in the values which they presuppose" (*EV* 97).

John Paul II condemns research that consists in "the use of human embryos or fetuses as an object of experimentation." In his view, embryos and fetuses "have a right to the same respect owed to a child once born, just as to every person" (*EV* 63). It is not clear from this statement whether John Paul II would permit nonbeneficial research on children, fetuses, or embryos if that research involved only minimal risk.

The encyclical criticizes invasive or destructive research on human embryos under all circumstances, but it especially condemns the deliberate creation of embryos for research purposes (*EV* 14, 63). On a scale of relative evils, the creation of research embryos seems to be regarded as worse than the after-the-fact use of embryos left over from infertility clinics (*EV* 63). In John Paul II's view, the use of either kind of embryo for research "reduces human life to the level of simple 'biological material' to be freely disposed of" (*EV* 14).

The use of fetal organs or tissues for transplantation into patients with, for example, Parkinson's disease is also condemned. The reason John Paul II gives for this condemnation is that "the killing of innocent human creatures, even if carried out to help others, constitutes an absolutely unacceptable act" (*EV* 63). This description of the situation fails to capture an important nuance. In virtually all cases, fetuses are not killed in order to provide organs or tissues. Rather, following induced abortion, still-living cells from the remains of the dead fetus are selected, preserved alive, and transplanted. The issue of cooperation with the act of abortion is almost certainly the central question here.

It would be interesting to know how John Paul II would evaluate the transplantation of tissue from a spontaneously aborted fetus, or from an ectopic pregnancy, or from a fetus killed in an automobile accident. These cases would seem to me to be completely analogous to cadaver transplants from the bodies of children who are accidentally killed.

Finally, John Paul II finds morally unacceptable the development of abortifacient drugs (such as RU 486) and "intrauterine devices and vaccines which ... really act as abortifacients in the very early stages of the development of the life of the new human being" (*EV* 13). The encyclical does not discuss the possible development of, for example, a reversible vaccine that might suppress sperm production in males. I presume that such a vaccine would not be found acceptable by John Paul II; rather, it would probably fall into the same category as other artificial contraceptives.

There may be convincing pragmatic, secular arguments for opposing invasive research on the fetus in utero. Also, on expert panels in the United States and elsewhere, there has also been a well-documented hesitation to approve the deliberate creation of research embryos. In my view, however, it is much more difficult for John Paul II to convince non-Catholics to join in his condemnation of all nontherapeutic human-embryo research, most fetal-tissue transplantation research, and all research on abortifacients. The ontological and moral status of preimplantation embryos has been debated for millennia in the context of contraception and abortion; no clear end to the debate is in sight. If fetal-tissue transplantation is separated as sharply as possible from the decision about induced abortion and insulated from commercial considerations, many people in the United States find such transplantation to be a morally acceptable means to treat disease—at least until less ethically ambiguous alternatives are found. And the development of abortifacients that are less traumatic to a woman's body than current surgical techniques and that allow for earlier abortions may, on balance, seem morally justified to those who accept the moral necessity of abortion in some cases.

Thus, I agree with Wildes's judgment that some of the particular conclusions reached by John Paul II in his discussion of research ethics may find resonance only in those who accept his metaphysical and religious premises.

NOTE

1. John Paul II, "The Ethics of Genetic Manipulation," *Origins* 13, no. 23 (November 17, 1983): 386–89.

Situating the Teaching of John Paul II on Capital Punishment: REFLECTIONS ON *EVANGELIUM VITAE* 56

JOHN P. LANGAN, S.J.

Chapter 3 of *Evangelium Vitae* takes its title from the fifth commandment, a formulation that is both utterly stark and completely familiar. "You shall not kill," is, as John Paul II observes, "strongly negative" (*EV* 54). But he also wants the commandment against killing to be understood in positive terms, and he goes on to claim that "it encourages a positive attitude of absolute respect toward life; it leads to the promotion of life and to progress along the way of a love which gives, receives, and serves" (*EV* 54). He clearly desires the commandment not to be taken as a lapidary proscription to be contemplated in isolated austerity but as an element to be included in the great commandment of the love of neighbor and in a way of life expressive of that love.

The prohibition against killing has always been closely connected with the issue of capital punishment. A brief historical overview makes it obvious that capital punishment has been imposed for numerous crimes in addition to murder; treason, blasphemy, rape, kidnapping, robbery, counterfeiting, sabotage, adultery, and drug dealing have all been punished with death in different societies in comparatively recent times. But murder is the one crime that nearly all societies have until recently, that is, until 1945, regarded as calling for the death penalty. As John Paul II puts the matter, "To kill a human being, in whom the image of God is present, is a particularly serious sin" (*EV* 55). Murder is the paradigmatic offense mostly widely thought to justify imposing capital punishment. If capital punishment is not justifiable as a response to murder, then it is hard to see how it will be justifiable in response to other crimes, unless some very special story is told. Even in the case of terrorist activities, it seems that it is the killings that the terrorists either intend directly or welcome as a consequence of their deeds that are the central factor leading us to condemn terrorism so vigorously and to want to punish it so severely. The killings performed by terrorist organizations are not regarded merely as a way of inflicting casualties in an armed struggle but as murders, that is, as killings that are intended, premeditated, and carefully planned.

So in the first major section of this essay I will sketch four different approaches that are present in current American public debate on the question of justifying or rejecting capital punishment as society's response to murder. These four approaches are offered as ideal types that will illustrate what I take to be significant tendencies in current public arguments about capital punishment; they are not intended to capture the complexity of the views of individual thinkers on this problem. In the second section I will situate the teaching of John Paul II on this topic in *Evangelium Vitae* in relation to these four approaches.

FOUR APPROACHES

If one reflects on murder taken as a kind of action in itself, it is an action that is to be distinguished from killing. By definition it must meet the standard requirements of knowledge and consent appropriate to what St. Thomas speaks of as "human acts,"[1] and to what moral theologians have customarily called mortal sins. One can readily see that murder is an action that is destructive both of the life of the victim and of the moral order that ought to shape the life of the perpetrator. It is easy to conclude that such an appalling act can only be adequately punished or expiated by the death of the offender. Such a judgment is readily reinforced by an insistence on "the absolute sanctity of human life." In this line of thought, which I shall call approach A, capital punishment serves as both the means of establishing retributive justice and as the expression of society's disapproval of so heinous an act. If one thinks of punishments as forming a sort of pyramid, it seems that capital punishment, at least in our culture, serves as the ultimate step of the pyramid; it thus corresponds to murder or other capital offenses that occupy a similar position on the pyramid of crimes or offenses.

Approach A customarily includes a high view of human agency and responsibility, in which important actions are, at least under normal conditions, the result of deliberation and choice by those who perform them and in which cultural competence and the ability to foresee and evaluate consequences are taken for granted. Since these conditions are obviously not satisfied in the case of many violent and deadly crimes committed in our society, there has always been a good deal of room in this approach for recognizing the inappropriateness and unjustifiability of capital punishment in particular cases, even while one simultaneously continued to affirm its legitimacy as a matter of principle. The recognition that certain killings fail to meet the subjective or psychological conditions for murder can even obtain when the killings are shocking and grotesque in ways which manifest the psychic pathology and mental imbalance of the criminal, even while they also provoke public outrage and sympathy on behalf of the victims.

Now it is important to recognize that something like approach A has over the centuries been accepted by the great majority not merely of Christians but also of reflective persons from many different cultures and belief systems and that it includes some very important considerations (the sanctity of life, the moral necessity of punishment, the importance of treating the offender's action with the utmost seriousness, the common responsibility for protecting and affirming social order, the priority of the common good over the interests of individuals, the prevention of further offenses, the expression of solidarity with the victims) that any satisfactory position on capital punishment must honor and must incorporate in some form. We should also note that both the high view of human agency and the priority of the common good are considerations that figure prominently in the moral teaching of John Paul II, as we can see particularly in *Sollicitudo Rei Socialis* 36 and in *Veritatis Splendor* 65–83.[2]

We observe that when approach A is applied in a comprehensive and impartial fashion, it excludes many bad arguments against the use of capital punishment. For instance, arguing against capital punishment on the ground that the victim of the crime was female or black or Jewish or elderly or mentally retarded or homosexual or homeless or an enemy of the people and that the victim is therefore not within our circle of concern or responsibility and, alternatively, arguing that the victim did not have an interesting or pleasant life and was likely to die soon in any event exemplify approaches that fail to show appropriate regard for the values that justify capital punishment in approach A. In addition to the fact that they minimize the gravity of the deadly offense by derogating from the dignity of the victim, such arguments also present further moral problems of their own, since they spring from racism and intolerance and manifest a failure of human sympathy. The place where these considerations are most likely to come near the surface is a situation where someone is arguing for parity of treatment of victims and criminals in different cases and so wants to maintain that since the state has used capital punishment when the victim of the crime is white, it should also do so when the victim is black or is, for some other reason, likely to be devalued and discriminated against. My point is not that these arguments are very likely to be made in the course of a public-policy debate; I think that in fact it would be very difficult for anyone in contemporary society to stand up and advance such arguments openly. Rather, I want to underline the connections that exist between a fairly traditional approach to capital punishment and some important values that a good society needs to acknowledge, as well as the fact that sometimes the reluctance to inflict capital punishment in particular cases has been rooted in some very questionable attitudes. But these bad arguments manifest not so much a principled opposition to capital punishment as a prejudiced misuse of discretionary judgment and power. Of course, what is at stake in what are usually unvoiced and elliptical arguments is not the thesis that capital punishment is never legitimate but the judgment that in some cases we may find justifications (more or less satisfactory) for refraining from using it.

I have pointed to some of the unsatisfactory justifications; but there are also, we can readily acknowledge, many good and powerful reasons for not imposing the death penalty even on murderers. In fact, many of these reasons, particularly those that focus on the mental health and competence of the killers or on their status as juveniles, have over the years been incorporated within approach A. But it is important to recognize that these more acceptable reasons for not imposing the death penalty are understood within approach A as applying to particular cases and are not seen as general characteristics of the criminal population or as automatically applying whenever a murder is committed. For then we would be dealing with a systemic diminishment of human capacity, which is incompatible with the high view of human agency characteristic of approach A.

We can, in summary, regard approach A as the typical and historically dominant position, at least in Western societies in the post-Enlightenment period. It has legitimated the death penalty as society's response to the most grievous offenses against the law and against human dignity, murder being by general agreement preeminent in this category. It is the approach that we would expect moderate conservatives to hold, those who generally want to develop a humane jurisprudence without major departures from the traditional practices and beliefs that have molded our legal system.

Moderate conservatives should be distinguished from persons advocating approach B, whose main interest in the judicial system is simply in its effectiveness as an instrument for the repression of crime and criminals and who do not attach any great value to rules and procedures that are intended primarily to protect persons under suspicion from being unjustly tried and condemned. We might call these persons, who shape a good deal of the current American debate over capital punishment, warriors against crime or, perhaps better, militant conservatives. They come in two main varieties: the pragmatic and the symbolic. The pragmatic warriors against crime want results: they want crime levels reduced, they want to be sure that criminals are behind bars, they favor severe penalties for crime both as a means of deterrence and as an emotionally and even aesthetically satisfying form of retribution, satisfying both for the public at large and for the families of the victims. Their prime concern about capital punishment is that it is applied too rarely and only after long and expensive delays. Capital punishment is not for them a problematic practice or, at best, an inescapably ambiguous affirmation of the sanctity of life. It is what society rightly demands of those guilty of the most grievous offenses. In this view, a systemic reluctance to inflict capital punishment weakens the good of order in society; and the increasing urgency of the need to protect society and innocent potential victims should cause us to look with a critical eye at the complexities of the judicial process, to impose strict limits on the appeals process, and to facilitate the work of police and prosecutors by lowering evidentiary standards and perhaps by showing less concern for the diminished capacity of many criminal defendants.

This is a position that approves individual executions as steps toward the reestablishment of order in society but that is highly vulnerable, in both logical and political terms, to the possibility that a particular execution may be unjust or mistaken. From this standpoint, one can say about executions, "The more, the better," but also, "The more, the riskier." Insofar as executions are presented as a means to the larger social good of a society with significantly lower levels of violent crime, this approach also is vulnerable to counterarguments that show the ineffectiveness of capital punishment as a deterrent. Since it is an approach that stresses the importance of results in "the war against crime," it begs to be judged on the basis of effectiveness. Since approach B is not satisfied with the acceptance of capital punishment as legitimate in principle—which is central in approach A—but wants to press on to expedite executions, a mere reaffirmation of the legitimacy of capital punishment is not sufficient to rescue it if it runs into difficulties when it is put into practice.

The symbolic variant of approach B accords less weight to empirical considerations than does the pragmatic form of this approach. It affirms the legitimacy of the death penalty as a matter of general principle, but it is more interested in arguing for death as the uniquely appropriate punishment for exceptionally grievous crime. It is especially important in a period when the media are able to direct concentrated public attention toward a very small number of crimes, which then become crucial for working out the complex of emotional reactions and reasonable concerns that members of the ordinary public have about crime. Acts of violence directed against the police, against innocent minors, against persons who are simultaneously victims of sexual assault, against public figures and their families, against the wealthy, against religious leaders are all likely to draw the attention of the media and therefore of the general public. This concentration of attention is redoubled when the person accused of committing the crime also falls into one of these categories. Crimes may also draw special attention because of unusual or spectacular circumstances or because of the number of victims, because of gruesome details, or because of connections to the world of organized crime. But public awareness of the vast majority of crimes is uneven and transitory; even double and triple murders may rate no more than three or four inches on an inside page of a large metropolitan daily. Individual cases have to be taken up into the larger statistical picture, but it may be doubted whether statistical arguments ever touch the core of the widespread popular sentiment for the death penalty.

Pragmatist proponents of approach B should take statistics very seriously, since they provide the most reliable view of the general picture of what crime is doing to our society; but symbolists need not do so, since their version of approach B is more concerned with punishing the perpetrator of *this* particularly grievous crime. They are always able to point to the horrific aspects of the murder and to propose the inference that these details show the depraved state of mind of the murderer. The details of the crime may be especially repellent to particular groups in society, for instance, women or families of police members or Koreans or Colombians or residents of an affluent suburb. Instead of attempting to move the public in the direction of universality and impartiality, many of those who comment on such crimes focus the public's attention on the specifics of the case and use these details as the basis for determining the character of the accused and the appropriate punishment to be demanded. In relation to the larger trends of crime and violence in society, the accused and condemned person (usually but not always a man) serves as a scapegoat along the lines proposed in René Girard's account of violence.[3] The execution of the condemned serves as a fitting conclusion to a moral tale about crime and punishment and provides a kind of catharsis both for those who live with a significant level of fear about crime as an imminent possibility in their own lives and neighborhoods and for those who consume both fictional and factual stories of violence as a central part of the flow of information and entertainment that our society provides. I might add that I think that the symbolist approach, though not in a clearly or fully articulated form, dominates a great deal of the public perception and discussion of the issue of capital punishment.

In contrast to the endorsements of capital punishment in both principle and practice that are offered by moderate and militant conservatives, I would like to describe two approaches that argue for the rejection of capital punishment. The first of these, approach C, an approach that is present in the opposition of Amnesty International and other organizations to capital punishment, argues that it is a violation of human rights, most especially of the right to life but also of the whole range of rights that flow from that primordial and sacred right, for the state to execute even a person who has been convicted of the most grievous crimes in a trial conducted with meticulous care for the rights of the defendant. This is an approach that, despite the current unpopularity of its conclusion, has enormous appeal within the political and legal culture of the United States, for it relies in a crucial way on the notion of "rights," which are, in Ronald Dworkin's analogy, "trumps."[4] The affirmation of an absolute right to life even for those guilty of murder has the further advantage of offering a close parallel to the affirmation of the right to life of the unborn, which has played a central part in the opposition of Catholics and others to legalized abortion. It also implies as a corollary the denial of the state's right to take life, even for the sake of the common good and perhaps even in the defense of the innocent and their rights. It is possible to construct an ethical position that would emphatically condemn the death-inflicting and death-authorizing activities of the state and that would bring together opponents of war, abortion, and capital punishment. One promising way to develop such a view in our culture would be to rely on an array of concepts taken from liberal and individualistic theories of society, in which the concept of rights has primacy of place and in which there is usually a strong emphasis on restraining the powers of the government so that it does not assert itself in ways that are beyond the consent of the governed. This could be supplemented with a vigorous use of antigovernment and countercultural rhetoric that would be designed to cast doubt on the connections mentioned earlier in approach A between capital punishment and the affirmation of a series of socially and religiously important values, such as the common good, the good of order in society, and the lives of innocent potential victims.

In this view, the action of inflicting capital punishment is fundamentally wrong, and no reinforcing or protecting effects that it may have on other values will save it. Approach C can often be accompanied by an anti-institutional radicalism, but this need not always be the case. It may well be that, quite independently of larger social and political attitudes, the person who reflectively contemplates the infliction of capital punishment concludes that it is an inherently unacceptable violation of human dignity and that, instead of protecting other important values, it taints them. The action, in this form of approach C, is *malum ex objecto*, bad simply by reason of the kind of action that it is. But this manner of making the argument also implies the denial of the state's right to take life, and we shall see that this is an important sticking point for John Paul II and for most Catholic moral teachers.

Approach D also involves a rejection of the use of capital punishment, but it does not rely on a complete condemnation of the death penalty in principle. Rather, it allows that capital punishment may be legitimate in principle, precisely because there are or can be situations in which the common good or the order of society or the lives of innocent persons require that a person guilty of murder or some other crime that strikes at the continuity and security of society be put to death. But this approach looks in a more complex and nuanced and sceptical way at the social context and the outcomes of capital punishment and arrives at a negative judgment about the practice of capital punishment in contemporary developed societies. Its condemnation of capital punishment is not total, and it relies on premises that may well be subject to change in the course of history and that may be at any given moment false. The crucial elements supporting the negative assessment of capital punishment will be 1) judgments that the practice of capital punishment as it is actually carried out fails to protect the values mentioned in approach A and may even have negative effects on some of these values; 2) judgments that the practice brings with it many undesirable and unacceptable consequences; and, finally, 3) judgments that alternative, less harmful practices can be or have been developed that attain or at least do not unnecessarily jeopardize the purported objectives of capital punishment.[5]

These are judgments that involve an assessment of the course of social and historical development and that cannot attain the status of eternal or necessary truths. But the argument in which they figure is not simply a claim that capital punishment is a bad thing in some particular cases, as, for instance, when there is serious likelihood of error or when the accused person is mentally retarded or insane. Rather, it is an affirmation that the practice is, all things considered, a harmful, ineffective, unnecessary practice that therefore ought to be curtailed or abolished or replaced by a less harmful alternative. Even if the practice is in general something to be rejected, there might still be overwhelming reasons in some cases to allow action in accordance with it. This is an approach that is essentially the same as that taken by those moral philosophers who interpret moral rules derived from social institutions and practices as prima facie rules that are revisable over time and that admit of exceptions and overrides when more important values would be damaged if the rules were taken as inflexible or absolute norms.[6] On our topic, such an approach affirms that capital punishment is a bad practice, but leaves room for the possibility that this judgment could be overridden in exceptional circumstances. It thus does not constitute an explicit contradiction of the view that capital punishment can be morally acceptable, at least under some circumstances.

JOHN PAUL II

After this typological review of the main approaches to the justifiability of capital punishment in contemporary American society, we are now, I hope, in a position to examine how we are to situate the teaching of John Paul II in relation to these four approaches, which are at variance with each other in so many respects, ranging from substantive conclusions to the spectrum of admissible considerations, from moral sensibility to moral methodology, from likely audiences to possible ideological allies. I maintain that John Paul II indeed exhibits affinities with all four approaches, which accounts for the puzzling but still enriching character of his treatment of the subject of capital punishment in *Evangelium Vitae*. Here it will be helpful to look more closely at the text of the document itself and at the immediate context of *Evangelium Vitae* 56, which is found in the earlier paragraphs of chapter 3, "You Shall Not Kill: God's Holy Law."

John Paul II begins the chapter with a reference to the story of the rich young man in Matthew 19, a story that he took as the starting point for his general presentation of Catholic moral teaching in *Veritatis Splendor*. He insists on the necessity of interpreting the commandments as an expression of God's love and as both gift and task. In *Evangelium Vitae* 52, he quotes St. Gregory of Nyssa on man's likeness to God precisely in his task of ruling the universe; and John Paul himself characterizes man as a being called on to exercise a ministerial lordship over things and over life, a lordship that does not imply absolute mastery but is a ministry to be exercised with wisdom and love in obedience to God's law and with accountability to God's judgment. This general perspective should be seen as preparing us for the fact that human beings do have to make decisions about matters of life and death, even while John Paul himself later affirms that "only God is the master of life" (*EV* 55).

In *Evangelium Vitae* 53, John Paul II makes two key moves. The first is his citation of *Donum Vitae* 5 in its affirmation that "no one can, in any circumstance, claim for himself the right to destroy directly an innocent human life." This, of course, does not break any new ground, but it is a point that fits well both with approach A, where the gravity of killing the innocent is a reason for capital punishment, and with approach C, when we think of those cases where the legal justice system has erred in condemning the innocent. The second move is his insistence on the social dimension of the commandment. For the killing of the innocent is not merely a violation of the individual victim who is the possessor of human rights; it is also at the same time a serious blow against society, as any observer of the effects of crime on American urban life can attest. So John Paul II describes the prohibition of killing as "the commandment which is at the basis of all life together in society."

In *Evangelium Vitae* 54, the Pope moves from the negative formulation of the commandment itself to its implicit encouragement of "a positive attitude of absolute respect for life." It is particularly significant that he explicates this positive attitude as leading "to the promotion of life and to progress along the way of a love which gives, receives, and serves." This is, I would argue, a step toward a more holistic conception of the place of murder and its punishment within the Christian moral universe so that the issue of violent crime and its punishment is not treated in isolation from broader issues of social justice and moral development.

But it is in *Evangelium Vitae* 55 that the picture becomes considerably more complex as a result of "the many and often tragic cases which occur in the life of individuals and society." John Paul II grants that "there are in fact situations in which values proposed by God's Law seem to involve a genuine paradox." The first case of this type that he considers is the case of legitimate defense, "in which the right to protect one's own life and the duty not to harm someone else's life are difficult to reconcile in practice." In this case of conflicting moral claims, the Pope gives effective priority to the right to protect one's own life, since he holds that "there is a true right of self-defence," which is based on "the intrinsic value of life and the duty to love oneself no less than others." Renunciation of this right because of a lack of love for life or for oneself is condemned; only "heroic love" in the spirit of the gospel can make such renunciation legitimate. When we move from the level of the individual defending himself or herself to the level of society, even at that minimal level where there are third parties who may be grievously harmed by the violence of the aggressor, defense becomes a duty. When those who are striving to disable the aggressor take his life out of necessity, "then the fatal outcome is attributable to the aggressor whose action brought it about."

This section makes it clear that the Pope is willing both to endorse killing in self-defense and to reaffirm the general principles of just-war theory. He is not ready to contemplate a general and absolute prohibition against the taking of life of the sort that would follow from accepting the absolute view of the right to life that is at the heart of approach C. John Paul II here and elsewhere is quite willing to use the language of rights and to allow for the paradoxes that result from allowing rights to be overridden. It is immediately after affirming the right and duty of legitimate defense that John Paul II observes, "This is the context in which to place the problem of the death penalty" (*EV* 56). This, I submit, in effect places the discussion of the death penalty under the signs of tragedy and paradox in the realm of values in conflict, that is, in a territory that the Pope has already seen as unavoidable in the forward development both of Christian reflection and of Christian responsibility for others. This is territory for which the restricted justification of capital punishment in approach A and the considered rejection of capital punishment in approach D can provide guidance, but it is clearly not congenial territory for either the unqualified rejection in approach C or the enthusiastic endorsement found in approach B.

John Paul II then goes on to observe that "there is a growing tendency, both in the Church and in civil society, to demand that it [the death penalty] be applied in a very limited way or even that it be abolished completely." Clearly, the Pope is not focusing here on the course of events in the United

States since the end of the moratorium on capital punishment in 1976 but on the many other countries, many of them in the affluent West but many also in troubled areas of the world, which have moved to abolish the death penalty. The Pope then alters the terms of the discussion in a very significant way, that is, by turning to the task of the system of penal justice, which he thinks should be "ever more in line with human dignity."

The proper treatment of the offender is to be determined not simply by reflecting on the gravity of the crime or on the proportion between the gravity of the crime and the severity of the punishment but by determining the form and level of punishment that accomplishes the goals of punishment. This counts as a prime example of the Pope's tendency to view the issue in holistic rather than in discrete terms. So long as the purposes of punishment are achieved, the death penalty, which the Pope characterizes as "the extreme of executing the offender," is not to be employed. Among the purposes of punishment that the Pope proposes in *Evangelium Vitae* 56 are: redressing the violation of rights by restricting the freedom of the offender, defending public order, ensuring people's safety, and providing incentives for the offender to be rehabilitated. The execution of the offender is only justifiable "in cases of absolute necessity: in other words, when it would not be possible otherwise to defend society."

The Pope, unlike most moral philosophers of the analytic tradition and unlike traditional Catholic casuists, is not eager to offer examples to illustrate his point, and so it is not clear just what scenario he would regard as confronting a modern society with a case of absolute necessity. It is possible that certain forms of terrorist activity might present such a continuing threat to public order and to innocent lives that they could count as instances of absolute necessity. Perhaps, in earlier times, a person who misrepresented himself as the heir to a royal throne would pose such a continuing threat to public order and such a focus of attraction for malcontents that mere imprisonment would not be enough of a protection for society. But these are also the sorts of cases that serve to remind us of the dangers of political justice, of the difficulty of treating fairly those who challenge the legitimacy of the political and legal processes in a society.

But it is not the Pope's intention that we should focus our attention on such cases; for he assures that "today however, as a result of steady improvements in the organization of the penal system, such cases are very rare, if not practically non-existent." Again, it is less than clear just what improvements the Pope has in mind. At least in the United States, it would be difficult to establish a consensus that such great progress has been made in shaping the penal system that it successfully rehabilitates criminals or that the administrators of the system have achieved a significantly higher rate in successfully predicting the future behavior of criminals who are considered for parole or for gradual release into the larger society. It may be that the Pope has primarily in mind the development of new security systems that enable fewer guards to maintain control over the most dangerous prisoners and that make escapes less likely and less frequent.

It is also unclear, and this is a more serious matter, whether the Pope, when he speaks of "cases of absolute necessity . . . when it would not be possible otherwise to defend society," has in mind the defense of individual members of society or the defense of the core institutions of society. In the United States (unlike Mexico or Colombia or Italy), crime does not pose any significant threat to the stability of the political order or to the working of democratic processes, though there may be local instances where crime seriously taints the political order; but it is virtually impossible to protect all the individual members of a modern society from the possibility of meeting a violent end. (This, one might add, is especially true in the United States because of the ready access that people have to handguns and other weapons.) Perhaps one should surmise that John Paul II is concerned with some intermediate level between these two, where the task would be to protect society in general from the rising tide of crime. But since he affirms that the cases are rare, then one should probably interpret him as thinking of the cases where crime threatens the continuity of the political order as a whole. But this focus, while it is important, does very little in a country such as the United States to reassure ordinary citizens, who are not worried that the Mafia will seize control of the federal government but that their neighborhoods may become virtually unhabitable as a result of drive-by shootings and gang warfare, cases that are anything but rare in urban America.

The argument of this section of *Evangelium Vitae* 56 is quite elliptical, but it seems clear that its character is empirical and historical rather than theological or philosophical. It would be quite possible for conscientious Catholics to disagree strongly with the Pope in his view of the progress made by modern systems of penal justice without challenging any significant part of his religious teaching. One might also, since the Pope is speaking about the situation in general without referring to particular countries, accept his argument in general but hold that the situation in the United States is exceptional. This would not be an unreasonable claim, given the remarkable disparity between the United States and other economically advanced societies both in the levels of violent crime and in the easy availability of weapons. But it is clear that, both for the Pope and for those who would disagree with his teaching on this point, the argument has to be conducted along the lines of approach D, where many diverse considerations are weighed before reaching a moral conclusion and where the conclusion is held provisionally, depending on changes in the circumstances and likely outcomes and on our progress in understanding the situation. Affirming this point does not trivialize the Pope's teaching in

Evangelium Vitae 56, for even if exceptions were to be allowed on a wider basis than he seems ready to contemplate, he would have made the important contribution of putting the burden of proof on those who would argue that capital punishment is necessary in a particular situation, since he effectively rules out the view that it is legitimate in some routine fashion, so that its rightness could be presumed unless there were serious arguments to the contrary. His line of thought only makes sense if capital punishment is seen as a deeply problematic practice, something we should be striving to put behind us though it may once have been necessary. At the same time, his view also requires us to give up the quick and easy condemnation of capital punishment that follows from the claim that the taking of any human life is intrinsically immoral.

Some further support for this reading of *Evangelium Vitae* 56 can be drawn from a contrast that the Pope makes at the beginning of number 57: "If such great care must be taken to respect every life, even that of criminals and unjust aggressors, the commandment 'You shall not kill' has absolute value when it refers to the *innocent person.*"

In summary, then, we can see that in assessing the practice of capital punishment, John Paul II combines the affirmation of the gravity of the offense and the high view of human agency that are at the heart of approach A. He sets the issue of punishment in the context of the defense of self and society, which is a central point in approach B. He relies heavily on the concept of rights, which is fundamental to approach C. He resolves the issue by appealing to empirical and historical considerations in such a way that he resorts to the modes of argument characteristic of approach D and of the proportionalist moral theology that he rejected in *Veritatis Splendor*. His compressed treatment of this very contentious issue can be regarded as moving toward a masterly synthesis, but it can also be regarded as evidence of serious tensions in his own moral methodology.

NOTES

1. *ST* I–II, 99. 6–17.

2. John Paul II, *Sollicitudo Rei Socialis* (Washington: U.S. Catholic Conference, 1988); *Veritatis Splendor* (Vatican City: Libreria Editrice Vaticana, 1993).

3. See, for instance, René Girard, *Violence and the Sacred*, trans. Patrick Gregory (Baltimore: Johns Hopkins University Press, 1977).

4. Ronald Dworkin, *Taking Rights Seriously* (New York: Basic Books, 1981).

5. This is the general approach taken in the 1980 statement of the U.S. Catholic Bishops on capital punishment, which can be found in *Origins* 10, 373–77.

6. The prototype of this treatment of moral rules as prima facie binding is found in W. D. Ross, *The Right and the Good* (Oxford: Oxford University Press, 1930).

Evangelium Vitae *on Capital Punishment:* A Response to John Langan

George Weigel

Persistent journalistic confusions notwithstanding, the papal magisterium in Roman Catholicism is *authoritative* rather than *authoritarian*. That is, when the bishop of Rome speaks as the first among the Church's teachers, he does so in order to give contemporary expression to the abiding tradition of the Church, rather than to impose his own personal philosophical or theological opinions on the consciences of the faithful. When Pope John Paul II, in *Evangelium Vitae*, confirmed that the "direct and voluntary killing of an innocent human being" (*EV* 57), abortion (*EV* 62), and euthanasia (*EV* 65) are always gravely immoral acts, he appealed to the natural law "which man, in the light of reason, finds in his own heart (cf. *Romans* 2.14–15)," to "the written word of God," to the "Church's Tradition," to the "ordinary and universal magisterium," and to the consensus of the college of bishops.[1] These condemnations are not, in other words, the private judgments of Karol Jozef Wojtyla, who happens to be the incumbent in the See of Peter. Rather, they are the common judgments of those charged dominically with the authority and responsibility to transmit faithfully the Church's tradition over time. To borrow a phrase from another ecclesial context, the magisterium of the Church as exercised in teachings such as those found in *Evangelium Vitae* 57, 62, and 65 is saying, on behalf of the entire Church, "Here we stand. We can do no other."

That being noted, however, the personal experience and distinctive discernments of a given pope will, necessarily, bear upon his articulation of the Church's tradition. This will be especially true when, as is the case today, the pope is a man of considerable intellectual energy and creativity. Those who have carefully followed the teaching of John Paul II can thus detect within that papal magisterium echoes of Karol Wojtyla's personal life experience and intellectual project. Previews of the christological humanism that has suffused this pontificate from *Redemptor Hominis* to *Tertio Millennio Adveniente* may be found, for example, in retreats the archbishop of Kraków preached for college students in the 1960s.[2] *Dives in Misericordia* picks up and extends some of the dramatist Wojtyla's reflections on the nature of paternity in plays such as

Radiation of Fatherhood.[3] In *Centesimus Annus* and in his recent address to the U.N. General Assembly, John Paul II takes the experience of the revolution of 1989 in east-central Europe—a revolution in which he played a determinative role—as a kind of paradigm for understanding the morally driven character of politics in late modernity.[4]

JOHN PAUL II AND THE RECONSTRUCTION OF HUMANISM

I believe that we cannot adequately understand the Holy Father's teaching on capital punishment in *Evangelium Vitae* 56 unless we reflect upon John Paul II's vision of the human condition at the end of the twentieth century: a vision that has been shaped by the singular biography of Karol Wojtyla.

Like Aleksandr Solzhenitsyn, another prophetic Slav who views the history of this century primarily through a moral prism, John Paul II believes that the catastrophes of the twentieth century—two world wars, a cold war, the Holocaust, the threat of nuclear annihilation, post–cold war ethnic and racial conflict of an exceptionally murderous variety—are due to modernity's having forgotten God and thus having forgotten the unique dignity and value of the human person, made in the image and likeness of God. The instrumentalization of human life, which the Pope frequently deplores under the rubric of "utilitarianism," degrades both the individual and society. And that instrumentalization has taken place because false humanisms have displaced the truth about the human person that, the Pope argues, can be known by both reason and revelation.

Unlike Solzhenitsyn, however, the Holy Father does not seem to attribute the pathologies of late modernity to an insuperable flaw in the modern social-political-economic project, which would require us to reconstruct essentially premodern forms of public authority in order to reconstitute the good society. In the Pope's view, the institutions of modernity—by which I mean, chiefly, democratic politics and the free economy—are not, in and of themselves, the problem. The problem is that the (essentially "utilitarian" and/ or liberal-individualist) accounts being given of those institutions in advanced societies today are inadequate to shaping the kind of public moral culture that is capable of channeling the explosive energies of a free people into activities that lead to genuine human flourishing. Thus, in a triptych of encyclicals that includes *Centesimus Annus*, *Veritatis Splendor*, and *Evangelium Vitae*, John Paul argues that the path to social, political, and economic renewal on the edge of the third millennium involves building the "culture of freedom" on the basis of those fundamental "truths about man" that provide a more secure moral foundation for the free and virtuous society than that provided by liberal individualism (worshipping at the totem of the imperial autonomous

Self) or "utilitarianism" (which, by confusing what is good with what is advantageous, erodes the moral horizon against which individual rights and common responsibilities are discerned).[5]

As both philosopher-theologian and pastor, John Paul II seems deeply concerned about the coarsening of human life and human moral sensibilities that has been caused by a century of unprecedented slaughter. He saw that coarsening as a young man, in Nazi-occupied Kraków; he fought it, as a young bishop, in Communist-dominated Poland; he has, as pope, continued to resist whatever "shortens the horizon of man's aspiration to goodness."[6] The crucial point, however, is that Wojtyla's resistance to dehumanization has been based not on an otherworldly asceticism that gives short shrift to social and political struggles *in hac lacrimarum valle* but on an alternative, christologically conceived humanism that lifts up and exalts the redeemed human person as a creature capable of living freely and virtuously. That distinctive form of "resistance" to the degradation of humanity, in which fear and violence are challenged by faith-grounded hope, has been perhaps the central leitmotif of the Holy Father's "public" ministry; it was forcefully displayed at the U.N. General Assembly on October 5, 1995, when the Pope told the nations that, because of the Incarnation, in which God was "made man and made a part of the history of humanity," Christian hope for the world "extends to every human person."[7]

This distinctive angle of vision on contemporary history and on our present circumstances had, I believe, a decisive impact on the drafting of *Evangelium Vitae* 56. This section of the encyclical struck me, as I expect it struck many, as rather more personal in tone than other sections of the document. I heard here echoes of the life experience of a man who had seen the trucks rounding up political prisoners and Jews for wanton slaughter during World War II; between the lines, so to speak, I read the experiences of a local bishop defending his people against a regime that did not hesitate to use lethal force for political ends, and of a pope who is keenly aware of the murderous assaults being mounted on Catholics out of *odium fidei* today.

In sum, the Holy Father was, it seems to me, trying to extend the boundaries of the argument about capital punishment—an issue about which he has deep personal feelings—without prematurely closing a question on which, it hardly needs saying, there is considerable disagreement within the Church today and on which there is a traditional position of no small weight. As Father Langan's paper indicates, John Paul did not fundamentally "change" the magisterium's position on capital punishment at the level of moral principle (although some might argue that the Pope's location of capital punishment solely in terms of society's self-defense constitutes a narrowing of the grounds on which the practice might be deemed morally acceptable). Rather, he seems to be asking the nations to consider whether there are not ways to address the gross and violent violation of rights and of the social order without resort to the juridical use of lethal force. And he is asking whether those alternatives are not preferable not only in themselves but given the necessity of confronting those false humanisms and that coarsening of public moral sensibility to which I referred a moment ago.

Put even more briefly, the Holy Father's pressing of the question of capital punishment, such that the burden of proof would now seem to rest on those who would argue for its social necessity in terms of society's self-defense, ought to be understood in terms of John Paul's more comprehensive project of securing the moral-cultural foundations of the free society for the twenty-first century. And that "public" project is one specification of his effort to revivify Western humanism by reference to the abiding "truth about man."

THE STATUS OF EVANGELIUM VITAE 56

The discussion of this section of the encyclical was somewhat confused in the early going by press reports that indicated that, in presenting *Evangelium Vitae* publicly, Cardinal Joseph Ratzinger, the prefect of the Congregation for the Doctrine of the Faith, had described *Evangelium Vitae* 56 as constituting a genuine development of doctrine that would require a revision in the *Catechism of the Catholic Church* during the preparation of its definitive Latin text. This seemed odd both in itself (the encyclical asserts no development of doctrine) and in terms of the *Catechism*—could a text subject to a manufacturer's recall be considered a sure guide to the Church's teaching?

Father Richard John Neuhaus, the editor of *First Things*, asked Cardinal Ratzinger for a clarification on this point, and the following letter from the cardinal prefect was published, with Ratzinger's permission:

> You ask about the correct interpretation of the teaching of the encyclical on the death penalty. Clearly, the Holy Father has not altered the doctrinal principles which pertain to this issue as they are presented in the Catechism, but has simply deepened the application of such principles in the context of present-day historical circumstances. Thus, where other means for the self-defense of society are possible and adequate, the death penalty may be permitted to disappear. Such a development, occurring within society and leading to the foregoing of this type of punishment, is something good and ought to be hoped for.
>
> In my statements during the presentation of the encyclical to the press, I sought to elucidate these elements, and noted the importance of taking such circumstantial considerations into account. It is in this sense

that the Catechism may be rewritten, naturally without any modification of the relevant doctrinal principles.

Of course it must be remembered that the substance of the [Catechism's] text as approved by the Apostolic Constitution *Fidei Depositum* is to remain unchanged; at the same time, however, the preparation of the *editio typica*, the official Latin text, affords the Church, as was explained when the vernacular versions were published, the opportunity to introduce small clarifications and minor improvements. While there is certainly no intention of including references to every document issued since the appearance of the Catechism, in the specific case of the Church's teaching on capital punishment many opinions have been expressed in favor of an *aggiornamento* of the text in the light of the papal teaching in *Evangelium Vitae*. Such suggestions appear to be well-founded, consonant as they are with the substance of the text as it presently stands in the Catechism.[8]

That clarification refutes the claims of some that *Evangelium Vitae* flatly rejected capital punishment or somehow equated the death penalty with abortion and euthanasia, two practices that are indisputably condemned by the encyclical. Rather, according to Cardinal Ratzinger, the Holy Father intended to urge Catholics and indeed all people of goodwill to a more careful exercise of prudential judgment in the matter of society's self-defense. The argument about the "necessity" of capital punishment will thus continue, within the Church and within the boundaries set by *Evangelium Vitae*.

WHAT TO DO WITH EICHMANN

As that debate proceeds, we shall have to think through the question of whether the "self-defense of society" is to be understood in merely physical terms or whether "social self-defense" has a moral-cultural component. On this point, it would be useful to revisit Peter Berger's discussion of heinous crime or "monstrous evil" in *A Rumor of Angels*.[9]

Here Berger drew our attention to "experiences in which our sense of what is humanly permissible is so fundamentally outraged that the only adequate response to the offense as well as to the offender seems to be a curse of supernatural dimensions."[10] The paradigmatic instance of this phenomenon in our times was the case of the Nazi war criminals who contrived and carried out the Holocaust. There were, of course, lots of questions about the authority of the Nuremberg tribunal and its indictments charging "crimes against humanity" that had never been previously defined legally, and we can recognize, perhaps more clearly today, the obscenity of Soviet prosecutors and judges—who had themselves practiced judicial murder—sitting in judgment at Nuremberg. Different questions, some no less pressing, could be raised from a strictly legal point of view about the abduction and trial of Adolf Eichmann and his subsequent execution by the state of Israel. Yet at the end of the day, these legal arguments, however important, seem wholly, even grotesquely, inadequate to the imperative of framing an appropriate moral response to the Holocaust. And that sense of inadequacy tells us something important about evil and the world.

Thus, Berger asks us to focus not on the question of how Eichmann should have been dealt with but, rather, on "the character and intention of our condemnation of Eichmann." Here, Berger argues, we find a case in which "a refusal to condemn in absolute terms would appear to offer prima facie evidence not only of a profound failure in the understanding of justice, but more profoundly of a fatal impairment of *humanitas*."[11] The failure to condemn Eichmann and his deeds absolutely and without cavil would have disclosed a debased humanity in which relativism had made a mockery of common moral decency. The Holocaust is, in this sense, *the* ikon of evil in the contemporary world, and to trifle with that ikon is to risk damaging both history and our capacities to discern evil in the future.

According to Berger, our reaction to instances of the "monstrously evil" becomes a "signal of transcendence" because of the *absolute* quality of our condemnation of these deeds (i.e., this is a condemnation that permits no exceptions or qualifications and thus discloses a transcendent moral horizon) and because our condemnation "does not seem to exhaust its intrinsic intention in terms of this world alone." Nothing that could have been done to the perpetrators of the Holocaust would have seemed a sufficient punishment for crimes of such viciousness and magnitude. If, for example, Eichmann had been slowly tortured to death rather than hanged, would that have been "enough"? No. Indeed, it is precisely a characteristic of the "monstrously evil" that such deeds cry out not simply for condemnation but for damnation. "No human punishment is 'enough' in the case of deeds as monstrous as these."[12] We instinctively look to a justice beyond this world when we reflect on our inability to condemn and punish adequately cases of monstrous evil.

Berger's analysis of these cases settles nothing about the morality of capital punishment (which Berger himself opposes). But it does, I think, have interesting implications for our reflection on what I have called elsewhere the "moral ecology" of the free society. If our freedom is not merely instrumental but is meant to be fulfilled in goodness, then it is important that the free society understand, and be able to give expression to, its understanding that some things are off the board definitively. If our public morality becomes so riddled with relativism (cultural, racial, philosophical, whatever) that we cannot condemn, flatly and passionately, the monstrously evil, then we have lost a crucial set of reference points for the dialogue about how we *ought* to live together—which is *the* basic question for the free society, as John Paul II said in Baltimore on October 8, 1995.[13]

As Father Langan's essay notes, the traditional response of Western societies to the monstrous evil of willful murder has been capital punishment. For a variety of reasons, many of those societies have now abandoned this practice. Abolition, according to *Evangelium Vitae*, is the morally preferred course if it can be accomplished in ways that do not amount to an abrogation of society's right of self-defense. But abolitionists have not completed the necessary public moral argument when they make a strong case, on prudential grounds, for eschewing the death penalty. For if a public moral recognition of the reality of monstrous evil is a necessity in a free society, then abolitionists have to tell us how society is to give expression to its unambiguous condemnation of monstrous evil if it lays aside the death penalty.

This is not to suggest that the current practice of capital punishment in the United States is essentially a matter of bearing witness to the reality of monstrous evil. Insofar as one can tell, it is a sense of retributive justice, combined with fears for public safety, that motivates most supporters of the death penalty today. Moreover, supporters of the traditional position (Father Langan's "approach A") ought to be deeply concerned that the trivialization of the death penalty through ubiquity or frivolous sentencing (which might happen were "approach B" to prevail in either its pragmatic or its symbolic forms) could have deleterious coarsening effects on the public moral order.

Still, the free society must attend seriously to its definition of the boundaries of the morally acceptable. And it must be able to give public expression to its absolute condemnation of certain monstrously evil acts. If that is not to be done through the instrument of capital punishment, then other instruments will have to be devised.

NOTES

1. Each of these three statements contains a footnote reference to LG 25, in which the infallibility of the ordinary and universal magisterium is discussed.

2. See Karol Wojtyla, *The Way to Christ: Spiritual Exercises* (San Francisco: Harper, 1994).

3. See Karol Wojtyla, *The Collected Plays and Writings on Theater* (Berkeley: University of California Press, 1987), 323–68.

4. See *CA* 22–29; John Paul II, "Address to the U.N. General Assembly," October 10, 1995, no. 4, *Origins* 25, no. 18 (October 19, 1995): 295.

5. A highly condensed version of this argument may be found in John Paul, "Address," 12–13 (*Origins*, 297–98). See also *CA* 44–47 and *EV* 96, 97, 101, 103–4. The teachings of *Centesimus Annus* and *Veritatis Splendor* on moral truth and its relationship to the democratic project are discussed at much greater length in my forthcoming book, *Soul of the World: Notes on the Future of Public Catholicism* (Grand Rapids, Mich.: Eerdmans, 1996).

6. See John Paul, "Address," 16 (*Origins*, 299).

7. Ibid., 17 (*Origins*, 299).

8. See Richard John Neuhaus, "A Clarification on Capital Punishment, *First Things* 56 (October 1995): 83–84.

9. Peter L. Berger, *A Rumor of Angels: Modern Society and the Rediscovery of the Supernatural* (New York: Doubleday Anchor Books, 1970).

10. Ibid., 65.

11. Ibid., 66.

12. Ibid., 67.

13. See John Paul II, "Homily at Camden Yards," 7, *Origins* 25, no. 18 (October 19, 1995): 314.

A Response to John Langan's Essay

HELEN PREJEAN, C.S.J.

John Langan has done an excellent job of clarifying four basic moral positions on the death penalty and situating Pope John Paul II's stance in relationship to these positions.

I write having accompanied three men to the electric chair in Louisiana and watched as they were killed in front of my eyes. I told them, "Look at me. Look at my face. I will be the face of Christ for you. Look at me." And mine was the last face they saw on this earth, and I know I was grace for them, I know that I was the face of Christ for them and for some murder victims' families as well. I write with fire in my heart, for I can never forget what I have seen and heard and felt as I have watched U.S. Supreme Court decisions and state statutes translated into flesh-and-blood torture and execution.

When I read Pope John Paul's discourse on capital punishment in *Evangelium Vitae*, I was heartened and inspired and challenged by much that he said, but when he stated that he upheld the state's right to execute in cases of "absolute necessity" (*EV* 56), I felt as if I had been hit in the stomach. I had so hoped that when he did address the death penalty, he would take a strong, unequivocal position in opposition to government-sanctioned executions. Now, after thirteen years of association with people on death row and the lawyers who try so hard to save their lives, I know the effect that words in laws and court decisions and encyclicals can have when applied to real human lives— especially words rendered in a religious context and claiming to represent the mind and heart of Christ. In working closely with those condemned to death by state governments, I have watched again and again as religious arguments—Christian arguments—are used to uphold the state's right to take life. The Pope's loophole, "except in cases of absolute necessity," will be used against those who stand trial for their lives before governments. Already the Catholic district attorney of New Orleans, Harry Connick, Sr., who seeks the death penalty every time he has a chance, has already seized on the Pope's words to justify his pro–death penalty position. As the death penalty is practiced now, Connick said in a recent interview with the BBC, it is "all too rare, practically nonexistent," and so he feels that every hard-fought death penalty that he gets is an "absolute necessity." The Pope gave no examples of "absolute necessity," so district attorneys like Harry Connick and judges and government officials are left to interpret the principle as they will; and as Amnesty International has amply documented, when governments around the world punish criminals by killing them, they always claim to act out of "absolute necessity." In contrast, recently the constitutional court of South Africa unconditionally forbade state executions. The black people of South Africa—and wise Afrikaners as well—know all too well that when state governments are given the right to execute their citizens, invariably the deepest prejudices and biases of the society exert full sway in the punishment of those considered the "dangerous criminal element." The U.S. Catholic bishops in their 1980 statement *Capital Punishment*, also allude to the racial and class bias that riddles the practice of the death penalty in this country.

What is so anguishing about the Pope's statement on capital punishment is that—apart from the gaping moral loophole—he upholds so many other life-affirming, gospel-rooted values, which, if followed, would transform the practice of criminal justice. He strongly upholds the dignity of the human person made in the image of God. He states that human life—all human life—is given "a sacred and inviolable character" (*EV* 52), and here he does not specify that only innocent human life is sacred and inviolable. He takes "Thou shalt not kill" beyond its negative prescription to the positive commandment of Jesus to love, a love that "gives, receives, and serves" (*EV* 54), and emphasizes, as Jesus did, that our love of neighbor mirrors our love of God. (Interestingly, in the context of the Gospel that he sets forth, he does not speak of Jesus' call to love our enemies, nor does he mention the call to forgiveness that Jesus made again and again, nor does he call attention to Jesus' identification with the "least of these"—those aspects of love that Jesus urged that most challenge the use of the death penalty.) When the Pope speaks of the goals of punishment, there is no hint in his words of a punitive, "eye-for-eye," "make-them-suffer" spirit so prevalent in our country today. Instead, he speaks of redressing the violation of personal and social rights by restricting offenders' freedom, thus ensuring public order and safety, and—almost unheard in public discussion today—he speaks of punishment as an "incentive and help" to the offender to "change his or her behaviour and be rehabilitated" (*EV* 56). These goals of penal justice, he maintains, uphold human dignity and God's plan for people in society. And he reaffirms the principle set forth in the *Catechism*—a very important principle that the U.S. Supreme Court was not willing to grant: "If bloodless means are sufficient to defend human lives against an aggressor . . . public authority must limit itself to such means, because they better correspond to the concrete conditions of the common good and are more in conformity to the dignity of the human person" (*EV* 56). In *Furman v. Georgia* as well as in *Gregg v. Georgia* the Supreme Court took the opposite view: "We cannot invalidate a category of penalties [death] because we deem *less severe penalties* [life imprisonment] [emphasis mine] adequate to serve the ends of penology." And while the Pope upholds such "bloodless" punishment as being more in conformity with the dignity of the human person, the Court in *Furman* and in *Gregg* upheld that retribution, even in its most extreme form, execution, is not "inconsistent with our respect for the dignity of men."

Placing penal justice in such a life-affirming context and recognizing "steady improvements" of penal systems, the Pope endorses the "growing tendency, both in the church and in civil society, to demand that [the death penalty] be applied in a very limited way or even that it be abolished completely" (*EV* 56).

If only the Pope had followed through to their conclusion these principles: the dignity of the human person made in the image of God, the example of Jesus' love and his challenge to love our enemies, the goal of punishment that seeks "bloodless" alternatives. These principles, when followed, lead us inexorably, I believe, to principled opposition to the death penalty. For how can we uphold the dignity of a human person even as we put him or her to death? "I just pray that God holds up my legs." That is what each of the men who were executed said to me in the weeks and days preceding their death. And by the time they died, after the years and months and weeks of preparing to die—sometimes being brought within hours of death, getting a stay of execution, and starting the process all over again—they each said, "I am so tired." Who among us—conscious beings that we are—once condemned to death, would not anticipate our fate and die a thousand times before we die? Who among us could withstand such an ordeal? Who of us could be sure that our legs would hold us up as we walked to our deaths? And who with a "pure heart and clean hands" can assert that such treatment of human beings is in accord with their dignity? To permit the execution of human beings is per se to permit torture, and at this point in our history we must look not to the Catholic Church but to the U.N. Universal Declaration of Human Rights for the clearest, unequivocal endorsement of every human being's inalienable right not to be killed (article 3) or "subjected to torture or to cruel and degrading punishment" (article 5).

When the Pope gets to the crunch—when he has the chance to stand unequivocally against state executions—he turns, for his context, not to the principles of the love of Christ and the dignity of each human person but to the traditional teaching of the Church on self-defense. But given the alternative of imprisonment, which societies today have as a way of incapacitating violent criminals, is it really valid to argue that for "the common good of the family or of the State," self-defense justifies executions? The Pope comes so close. He marches up to the breach. He talks about how today, because of improvements in the organization of the penal system, the extreme act of executing offenders is indeed "rare, if not practically non-existent." And then he retreats and holds out the tragic loophole: in cases of absolute necessity we still must allow for the state to carry out executions.

I have noticed—I can't help but notice—that in his visits to the United States or to any country for that matter, the Pope never speaks out against capital punishment. He also, to my knowledge, has never visited people on death row. It would be difficult for him, I suspect, to look into the eyes of the flesh-and-blood people condemned to death, even those guilty of the most horrid crimes. He is a man of such compassion and such felt love for human beings that I wonder what would happen to him if he ever personally encountered people condemned to death. He even has forgiven the man who tried to kill him.

This reminds me of my experience with New Orleans archbishop Philip Hannan on the issue of the death penalty. He was one of the few dissenting U.S. bishops when the bishops wrote their pastoral letter in 1980 in opposition to the death penalty. His experience in the military made Archbishop Hannan a hard-liner on the death penalty. We must uphold the state's right to take life, he said, and we must keep the death penalty to protect ourselves against terrorists. But as I got involved with men on death row and was doing all I could to keep them from execution, I called Archbishop Hannan to ask him to appeal on their behalf to the governor and the pardon board for clemency. Sure, he said. The truth was that he was for the death penalty in principle but he wasn't for real people being executed. He wanted, to be sure, to keep his "absolute necessity" principle intact, but he really didn't want to see a human being die, and he raised his voice on behalf of clemency every time I asked him. He didn't even ask for particulars about the case. Even guilt or innocence was irrelevant.

I believe this is also true of the Pope. I think his heart would dissolve in grief if he came anywhere near the real execution of human beings. What would he say to the mother or the younger brother of the one about to be executed? What would he say to the guards on the strap-down team whose job it is to strap the man onto the gurney or into the electric chair or gas chamber? What would he say to the executioner? Could he bless the executioner's work? Could he offer to take the executioner's place? Because if he truly believes in the moral rightness of the death penalty, even in those rare instances of "absolute necessity," then it is an action that he should be willing to carry out himself. Certainly he shouldn't ask others to carry the moral burden of doing what he is not willing to do himself. The very thought is preposterous. We all know the Pope could never participate in such a deed. Perhaps that is the clearest reason why he should not ask it of anyone else.

Maybe the Pope retreated to the traditional argument of self-defense because he didn't want to give the impression that Church teachings can change too radically. Commenting on the encyclical at a press conference, Cardinal Joseph Ratzinger was quick to point out that the Pope has made so much "important doctrinal progress" in his discussion of the death penalty that the *Catechism* would need to be revised to reflect the Pope's "stronger reservations" about the death penalty. And then Ratzinger added: "Catholic teaching develops by building on past affirmations rather than on overturning them."

From the time of Augustine of Hippo, one of the first to argue that the "wicked" might be "coerced by the sword," the Church has upheld the state's right to take life. Perhaps the Pope and his advisors intend a gradualist approach. First, the bishops of various countries write pastorals voicing concern and opposition to the death penalty (this has been going on for the last twenty years), then the Pope voices strong reservations about the use of the death penalty but still upholds the state's right to execute in cases of "absolute necessity." That way the teaching authority of the Church is safeguarded. No doctrinal boat is rocked too badly. Later—in a few years, in a decade, perhaps in a hundred years or so—more radical doctrinal change can come.

Please God, may this not be true. For while the Church seeks to maintain the "consistency" of its doctrinal position before the world, human beings will continue to be executed.

Willie Watson's mama said it best. Her son Willie, an indigent black man, was executed by the state of Louisiana in the electric chair in the summer of 1987 after a jury sentenced him to death, a jury before whom Archbishop Hannan sent two priests to testify that Catholics could vote for the death penalty "in good conscience." After the trial Willie's Mama said, "Ain't anybody who's of God want anybody killed."

Evangelium Vitae, *Euthanasia, and Physician-Assisted Suicide: John Paul II's Dialogue with the Culture and Ethics of Contemporary Medicine*

EDMUND D. PELLEGRINO

> *The whole notion of euthanasia and abortion is very reasonable without the Christian Ethic.*
> — Walker Percy, *The Thanatos Syndrome*[1]

This essay examines the meanings and implications of *Evangelium Vitae* with respect to the issues of assisted suicide and euthanasia for those who are to be exemplars of the Gospel of life, that is, Catholic health care professionals and institutions.[2] This delimitation is necessary, but a little artificial. *Evangelium Vitae* discusses euthanasia and assisted suicide within the larger context of the other human-life issues such as abortion, infanticide, techniques of reproductive biology, human-embryo experimentation, and the wider perspective of the sociocultural matrix of values that generate the "culture of death" the Pope opposes to the Gospel of life. But hastening the death of the sick is so central to the message of *Evangelium Vitae* that much of what John Paul II says about it applies by analogy to the other human-life issues.

I have chosen three aspects of *Evangelium Vitae* that I think important for Catholic health professionals and health care institutions and that should guide their thought and actions in response to the encyclical.

The first is to schematize how the Pope "does" medical ethics in this encyclical, since those who would be exemplars of the Gospel of life need to understand its mode of argumentation and the line of argument that mode advances. One cannot be an exemplar of *Evangelium Vitae* in the world of medicine and bioethics, or be able to explicate it for others, without understanding how the Pope arrives at his unequivocal opposition to both euthanasia and assisted suicide.

The second aspect is to outline the responses, implicit as well as explicit, of *Evangelium Vitae* to four of the major arguments used by sincere and conscientious proponents of euthanasia and assisted suicide: the arguments from autonomy and freedom, from compassion, from the meaninglessness of human suffering, and from the preservation of human dignity. To each of these appeals for relaxation of the proscriptions against the intentional hastening of death there is a Catholic Christian response based in the Gospel of life, in love and charity. Freedom, compassion, suffering, and dignity are construed differently by secular and Catholic Christian belief systems.

The third aspect I have chosen is a practical one: how *Evangelium Vitae* should shape the daily decision making and action of those who are expected to be exemplars of the Gospel of life—first, in their bedside decisions, that is, in the way they confront death and dying and the requests to hasten death, and the moral obligation to practice comprehensive palliative care as a form of the Christian apostolate; and second, how those exemplars fulfill their obligations to the Gospel of life in the "public square," that is, in the public debate and social-policy formation in a democratic society.

Evangelium Vitae undertakes to engage what is arguably the most parlous divergence between the Catholic Church and contemporary culture—the growing trend to regard human life as a utilitarian, statistical, relative good disposable at the will of individuals and societies when circumstances or personal choice dictate. There is no more challenging, fundamental, or timely issue for the contemporary dialogue between the Church and the world in which it resides.

Ours is the bloodiest of centuries in the sheer number of lives taken by wars, totalitarian oppression, ethnic cleansing, the Holocaust, and abortion. No century has had greater control over the genesis, duration, and ending of life. In none has there been so energetic an effort to challenge, philosophically and even theologically, the sovereignty of humanity over God in assigning meaning, purpose, and value to human existence.

Nowhere is John Paul's Gospel of life at more divergence with our culture than in the growing trend to public and professional acceptance of euthanasia and assisted suicide (*EV* 3–6). Here the questions of the dominion, quality, and purposes of human life and of suffering become concrete and specific choices we shall all face for ourselves and for our friends and family members. Here, as with abortion, some Catholics and other Christians are, with varying convictions, taking positions of acceptance, or at least tolerance, at variance with traditional and official teachings. Here health professionals daily face the moment of truth in decisions at the end of life when they must deal with their patients' requests, with their own feelings about suffering, and soon with what may become a legal right (*EV* 14). All of this, paradoxically, is occurring just when human rights are being widely acclaimed (*EV* 18).

THE MODE AND CONTENT OF THE ARGUMENT

The Mode of Dialogue

From its earliest beginnings, a recurrent and major theme of the pontificate of John Paul II has been the "dialogue" with culture—the necessity to engage every major facet of contemporary culture from the perspective of Christian and Catholic faith and reason. The Pope speaks of "the need to bring the Gospel of Life into the heart of every man and woman and to make it penetrate every part of society" (*EV* 80). Through such a "dialogue," the Pope has consistently pursued his mission to evangelize the whole culture by bringing the message of the Gospels to bear on the crucial moral questions of the times—for all people, believers as well as nonbelievers. The Church, he says, "exists to evangelize" (*EV* 78).

Some may be put off by being asked to see *Evangelium Vitae* as a dialogue. This word has come to mean seeking compromise by an exchange of ideas in an irenic and comfortable conversation where the emphasis is often more on the process than the content. *Evangelium Vitae* instead follows Paul's exhortation to "preach the word, be urgent in season and out of season, convince, rebuke, and exhort being unfailing in patience and in teaching" (2 Tim 4:2; *EV* 82).

Certainly, we do not have dialogue here in the literary sense, nor a back-and-forth discussion between opposing views like Plato's or Galileo's.[3] Rather, *Evangelium Vitae* uses dialogue in a more strictly etymological sense, to mean "speaking through" the word—*dia* plus *logos*—making the truth, as Pope John Paul II sees it, known through a conversation with the dominant countervailing ideas of our culture. In this sense, the Pope's method is more in the nature of a dialectic, a logical and rhetorical inquiry into the truth of an opposing position—in this case, what the Holy Father apocalyptically construes as the "culture of death."

John Paul II's personal construal of dialogue is important in any interpretation of the tone of *Evangelium Vitae*. He recognizes that dialogue may "induce strife," but despite this, dialogue must "take up what is right and true. . . . In a constructive communal life, the principle of dialogue has to be adopted regardless of the obstacles and difficulties that it may bring with it along the way."[4] This is the spirit in which the argumentation of *Evangelium Vitae* is presented. This is dialogue taken in a prophetic, as well as a dialectic, sense. In his role as Vicar of Christ, the Pope speaks out the truth to warn the people of evil; as philosopher, he appeals to human reason to see the truth in his position.

Compromise is, therefore, not the intent of the encyclical. The conversation is already assumed to have been started by those who now challenge the

Catholic Christian tradition against assisting in, or bringing about intentionally and directly, the death of a sick and dying person for any reason (*EV* 4). *Evangelium Vitae* is a response to a set of propositions about human life, and I shall treat it as such. The logic of its conclusions is not vitiated by its impassioned language. While some might wish a more conciliatory tone, the line of argument set forth in *Evangelium Vitae* must be judged on its own terms. Clearly, the Pope takes the matter to be too important to risk the possibility of indifference or misunderstanding. Those who reject, those who favor, and those who take a lenient view of euthanasia and assisted suicide have an obligation to take the arguments of *Evangelium Vitae* seriously and on their merits.

The Lines of Argument: Evangelium Vitae *and Bioethics*

Evangelium Vitae sees the current growth of critical reflection on ethical issues reflecting life as a sign of hope (*EV* 27). But at the same time, it recognizes the danger of erroneous or distorted ethical arguments when they justify practices that run counter to the scriptural and natural law foundations of morality.

    Evangelium Vitae is a vigorous, negative response to the growing assertion that, under certain circumstances, the lives of seriously ill persons may be taken directly in response to a voluntary request or that patients may be "assisted" by providing the means whereby they may bring about their own deaths. To these assertions, *Evangelium Vitae* 65–77 responds that euthanasia and assisted suicide (no distinction is made between them) are unequivocally, intrinsically, and without exception always morally wrong. John Paul defines euthanasia as "an action or omission which, of itself and by intention, cause death with the purpose of eliminating all suffering" (*EV* 65). This condemnation, "based in natural law and the written word of God is (*sic*) transmitted by the Church's tradition and taught by the ordinary and universal Magisterium" (*EV* 66). It applies as well to suicide (*EV* 66). This condemnation is exceptionless (*EV* 57). No intention, motive, circumstance, or presumed benefit can justify what is an intrinsically evil act.

    The argumentation in *Evangelium Vitae* is grounded in an appeal to the Hebrew and Christian Bibles and the natural law (*EV* 29). This is the same mode of argumentation used in *Veritatis Splendor*, which lays the theological and philosophical groundwork for the argumentation in *Evangelium Vitae*. In addition, both Scripture and natural law are also interpreted in a philosophical context special to John Paul II himself. He is a philosopher of standing, influenced by the phenomenology and personalism of Max Scheler.[5] He therefore sees the moral and existential questions pertaining to euthanasia and assisted suicide in terms of the human and personal experience of those who suffer and those who share that suffering with them.[6] His thinking proceeds by meditative analysis on levels of human experience peculiar to the acting person.[7] This added dimension will be touched upon more specifically in the next section of this essay.

The scriptural sources of *Evangelium Vitae* are in Genesis, especially the story of Cain and Abel. *Evangelium Vitae* argues that the act of taking human life is intrinsically evil because it flies in the face of the sovereignty of God. God is the author of human life, over which he has given humans stewardship but not absolute dominion. Human life has a special dignity because humans are created in the image of God, *imago Dei*. Thus, humans receive something of God's own uniqueness. The human being thereby possesses an inviolable dignity. To take a life by intent affronts God's creative act. This is a violation of divine will and law. According to natural law doctrine, this will and law can be known by the human mind by reason as well as faith.

Others in this volume are charged with a more explicit analysis of John Paul II's mode of argumentation. For my purpose, it is sufficient to comment upon its status as a response to the cultural drift away from ascribing special dignity and sacredness to human life. For Catholics and other Christians, and in large measure for Jews and Muslims, this argument should carry great weight and persuasion. For atheists or agnostics, this argument would not be at all persuasive. Indeed, its origin in divine law would be considered inadmissible. Such persons would want to know why taking a life with the intention of relieving suffering would be a wrongful act in the first place. I have tried to show elsewhere, on philosophical grounds alone, that for reasons other than those advanced in *Evangelium Vitae*, the beneficence of euthanasia and assisted suicide is illusory.[8]

The reasoning of *Evangelium Vitae* is act-centered. It takes intentional killing as intrinsically wrong and thus rejects the doctrine of proportionalism, as did *Veritatis Splendor*. Proportionalists here would argue that the moral character of the act of killing would be altered by circumstances and consequences. For *Evangelium Vitae*, good intentions and the good end of relieving suffering reached by the intentional death of the sufferer simply cannot change the inherent immorality of the act.

This contrasts with the concept of proportionality, which, in the case of foregoing aggressive medical treatment, may be invoked licitly (*EV* 65). Here the duty to take care of oneself and to be cared for can be modified in terms of concrete circumstances if the means of treatment "are objectively proportional to the prospects of improvement. . . . To forego extraordinary or disproportionate means is not the equivalent of suicide or euthanasia" (*EV* 65). Whether this amounts to a nod in the direction of proportionalism, as McCormick suggests, is dubious.[9] There is a real difference between taking an act to be morally neutral until it is set within the context of intention, motive, consequence, amount of good and harm, and so forth, and the principle of proportionality, which takes an act to be wrong by its nature but permits exception under carefully specified conditions. In terms of practical decision and action, the conclusions of proportionalists and of those who follow the principle of proportionality are sufficiently different to point to a real difference in their operating presuppositions.

The mode of argumentation used in this encyclical is at odds with many of the current trends in moral reasoning in biomedical ethics and in ethics generally. In a discussion such as that of *Evangelium Vitae*, directed to Catholic Christians as well as those who do not share their beliefs, the differences are critical. For Catholics, *Evangelium Vitae* implicitly and explicitly sets out a particular way of "doing" medical ethics in the domain of human-life issues, much in the same way *Veritatis Splendor* did in a more formal manner for ethics generally.

There is little room in *Evangelium Vitae*, for example, for the moral skepticism (*EV* 11), antifoundationalism,[10] and relativism that doubts or denies the objective reality of ethics or even the possibility of arriving at any stable version of moral truth. Extremes of intuitionism, contextualism, or consensus-based ethics find no support in the Holy Father's stance on euthanasia and assisted suicide. Moral truths transcend time, culture, and history. They are not determined by public opinion, even in democratic societies. Democratic opinion does not substitute for morality (*EV* 70). The aims and purposes of moral and civil law must be distinguished and related properly to each other (*EV* 71). Without the restraint of moral law, democracy can itself become totalitarianism (*EV* 20), especially when the right to freedom includes an absolute right to abortion or euthanasia.

For *Evangelium Vitae*, principles, virtues, intentions, and circumstances are important, but they do not per se constitute the whole of moral justification.(*EV* 75). The way these facets of the moral life are related to each other, and in what order of priority, is important for making moral judgments. Alternatives to traditional ethics, such as the ethics of care, of narrative, and of particular experience, can contribute to, but can never be the sole source of, normative justification for the morality of the acts of individuals or societies. *Evangelium Vitae* thus stands in contrast with the direction of movement in secular and even theological ethics.

While its arguments can be defended on the basis of natural law, the ethics of *Evangelium Vitae* is most firmly grounded in an ultimate source of morality—Scripture, divine law, and revelation. Moreover, these sources of morality are given weight in moral discourse and may be the determining criterion of what is right and good. This is very different from the overtly secular and even antireligious temper of much of contemporary bioethics. For many of the most influential bioethicists of our time, there is no ultimate source for morality except human reason, will, consensus, or sentiment. Religious arguments are discounted, and those who hold them, discredited. Even if one argues philosophically—that is, does not introduce Scripture, Church teaching, or theological reflection—a conclusion may be disallowed if one is a believer and arrives at a position congruent with Church teaching. The message of *Evangelium Vitae* is as clear, unequivocal, and uncompromising as its method of reasoning. Human life is sacred; it is a gift of God; we are its stewards, not its masters. We may not take life, even for ostensibly good reasons, by abortion, euthanasia, assisted suicide, to relieve suffering or to obtain organs for transplantation. We must respect human life from the stage of its earliest development until its natural end, which we are not intentionally to accelerate—even in the name of compassion. We may not create or use human embryos for experimental purposes, no matter how promising or utilitarian they might be. We may not bypass the normal processes of reproduction by in vitro fertilization, barrier contraception, surrogate motherhood, and so on.

On these central ethical questions, *Evangelium Vitae* does not make new doctrine. It iterates teachings of the Holy Father's predecessors, Pius XII, John XXIII, and Paul VI, of the Second Vatican Council on euthanasia, of *Donum Vitae* and *Humanae Vitae*, and of Pope John Paul II's own allocutions on the sacredness of human life. In *Evangelium Vitae*, John Paul restates these teachings with renewed vigor and deepening concern, since he sees the growing power and attraction of those who teach to the contrary.

CHRISTIAN RESPONSES TO PRO-EUTHANASIA ARGUMENTS

In addition to the formal argumentation demonstrating that assisted suicide and euthanasia are intrinsically immoral acts, *Evangelium Vitae* contains explicit as well as implicit responses to the arguments of conscientious persons who regard these acts as beneficent and even charitable. I will examine just four of these arguments, the ones from autonomy, compassion, human dignity, and the evil of suffering. To each of these arguments, there is a Christian response that, in some ways, may be more effective than the more formal line of positive argumentation summarized in the previous section.

The Argument from Autonomy

If there is one principle that has had the widest acceptance in biomedical ethics in our time, it is the principle of self-government, the moral claim to self-determination in matters that are presumed to be private. Indeed, increasingly autonomy is assuming the status of an absolute principle. In this vein, freedom should extend to the right to ask to be killed by someone else, provided the request is truly voluntary. This should be protected by law. Physicians should satisfy the patient's request.

For *Evangelium Vitae*, this is a distorted notion of freedom, one that negates and destroys itself, since it severs the connection with truth and destroys, at the same time, our solidarity with other human beings. This kind of freedom also exalts the subject and accords rights only to those who are capable of full autonomy, imperiling those who are retarded, demented, or in a permanent vegetative state (*EV* 18–19). The Christian concept of freedom is the freedom to be and do what one discerns God wants one to be and do. It includes the freedom to accept illness and suffering, which may not be entirely relieved by treatment. The patient may make an autonomous choice to accept or reject the sufferings and indignities of illness, even to abandon oneself to God's will.

A central feature of John Paul II's phenomenology is to see freedom in relational terms, in the freedom to act and to give oneself to others and thus to "act" fully as a person. The way a dying person dies may be the last gift of self as an example to those who survive. In the long run, claims to absolute autonomy and freedom are claims against any universal truth that might put constraints on that autonomy (*EV* 19). In John Paul II's view, there are absolute moral truths that we are not free to violate. To violate these truths is an act of radical ethical solipsism and, thus, of moral relativism. This applies to the freedom of individuals as well as to the "freedom" of the popular will in moral matters (see the next section, "*Evangelium Vitae* at the Bedside").

The Argument from Compassion

This is perhaps the most difficult argument for Christians to confront when put forth by sincere and caring protagonists of euthanasia. Christians, after all, are committed to a Gospel of love and to the Beatitudes. Jesus reached out in love to all who were burdened. Compassion for the sick and dying is woven into the fabric of Christian solicitude. John Paul II's apostolic letter on the meaning of Christian suffering, *Salvifici Doloris*, began with the parable of the Good Samaritan, the exemplar par excellence of disinterested love for the suffering of others.[11]

Compassion for the suffering of others is an experience shared by Christians and secular humanists. Christians and euthanasia advocates, therefore, begin at the same place—with a common human emotion, with the affective state in which they feel and suffer along with the suffering of another, as the

Latin roots of the word "compassion" suggest. Compassion, in this sense, is a human experience shared by all but the most emotionally blunted among us.[12]

There is, however, a vast difference between Christians and euthanasia proponents in the moral weight they give to compassion (*EV* 9). For a Christian, compassion, laudable as it may be, cannot by itself be a justification for moral action. It should accompany moral action, but in the case of euthanasia and assisted suicide, compassion that leads to taking the life of the sufferer is a distorted compassion. The modern origin of this distorted compassion is the sentimentalist philosophy of the eighteenth century. Thinkers such as Rousseau (1712–78) and Hume (1711–76) thought compassion was a better guide to morality than Christian teaching. Their view spawned a natural religion whose tenets include life without suffering and relief of suffering by any means, even if it means bringing about the death of the sufferer. Compassion becomes a first and self-justifying principle.[13]

Suffering is meaningless according to the canons of this natural religion, and not to relieve it, even at the sacrifice of life, is immoral and maleficent. Relief of suffering has even been cast as the end and moral definition of all of medical ethics.[14] For the Christian, compassion is just as moving as it is for the euthanasia proponent and the sentimentalist philosopher. But compassion must itself be judged for its moral quality, which derives not simply from experiencing the emotion of compassion but from the way we choose to act with reference to that emotion.[15] The Christian concept of compassion, like the secular concept of compassion, calls upon us to relieve pain and suffering, but within the constraints of respect for human life as it is developed in *Evangelium Vitae*.

Christian compassion, for example, can and should be felt and directed to the woman who has, for whatever complex circumstances in her life, had an abortion (*EV* 59). But the act of abortion itself is still morally wrong. Feeling compassion for the woman's plight does not eradicate the evil. Nor can it be a justification for aborting the fetus even if we sympathize with the predicament of the pregnant woman driven to this desperate measure (*EV* 99). In the Catholic theological tradition, we are impelled to extend charity and love to the sinner but not to her sin. This is charitable compassion, the capacity to see Christ in our suffering neighbor, to be moved by and feel his predicament, to relieve his suffering, but always with the understanding that suffering, too, has meaning and that the true dignity of humans is not destroyed by suffering.

Christians must be particularly compassionate and non-self-righteous with the patient who feels so desperate as to request death be hastened. Even so Christ-centered a person as St. Thérèse of Lisieux admits how easy it is to contemplate suicide when suffering is intense: "If I had not any Faith, I would have committed suicide without an instant's hesitation;"[16] "I assure you it needs only a second when one suffers intensely to lose one's reason. Then one would easily poison oneself." [17] If St. Thérèse could come to such thoughts, how much more understandable it must be for those of us who have not her strength of faith, or no faith at all.

The Argument from the Evil of Suffering

This argument is that suffering cannot possibly have meaning and that it is an unmitigated evil that justifies relief, even if it means accelerating death. This is the argument of "natural" religion and of sentiment theorists. In this view, the only life worth living is one with "quality"—an attribute defined solely by the individual or those around her. When life falls below a certain level of quality, it is disposable. The Christian response in *Evangelium Vitae* is to the contrary: Suffering is not meaningless. It is an inevitable part of living and dying. Like Job, we will not know why we suffer. But in Christ's life we know suffering was not meaningless. His death gained salvation for us. In suffering we follow in his way. Through suffering we may grow spiritually. It may be our means of atonement and redemption. It may have unforeseen impact spiritually on those who attend us when we suffer and die. We cannot know any of this with certainty. Through suffering each of us in our own way enters into Christ's suffering and dying. This is the "intangible mystery" of suffering. [18]

This does not mean that unrelieved suffering is per se redemptive or better than relieved suffering. Nor should we seek out suffering or avoid relieving it to the fullest extent. For Christians, suffering is a mystery to be accepted as we accept and confront our finitude when the time comes to die. In *Evangelium Vitae*, John Paul II meditates on Christ's suffering and dying, emphasizing how Jesus' life "finds its center, its meaningful fulfillment, when it is given up" (*EV* 51). This is "the scandal of the cross." [19]

Suffering is separable from pain, and it often persists even when pain is mitigated or relieved. Suffering is the key to the dying person's spiritual response to alienation or anger with, and hostility toward, God for what the sick person perceives to be the injustice of his affliction. Suffering rises from guilt, fear of the unknown, and fear of abandonment by those around us. For Christians, often the true relief of suffering comes only when they abandon themselves to God and accept finitude, suffering, and death as mysteries that cannot be fathomed. [20] In the end the spiritual and emotional crises of suffering, dying, and death are best relieved by a supreme act of obedience to God's sovereignty over the world and us (*EV* 67; Phil 2:8). Or as John Paul II puts it elsewhere, "In order to hope for salvation, man must stop beneath Christ's cross." [21]

The Argument from Loss of Dignity

Finally, *Evangelium Vitae* responds, again counterculturally, to the argument of many sincere proponents of euthanasia and assisted suicide for a "death with dignity." In the view of *Evangelium Vitae* and the Catholic moral tradition, this is a distorted notion of human dignity. When people speak of the loss of "dignity," it is something they perceive as subjects or observers of human suffering. They are speaking of *imputed* dignity, not true dignity. Imputed dignity is in the eyes of the beholder, in the ways she reacts to the results of the ravages of serious illness and dying—pain, wasting, incontinence of urine or feces, weakness, depression, anxiety, being an object of pity, or no longer looking like oneself.

These are undeniable realities. They make the sufferer feel less than a person. This is a human and natural response, often exaggerated and even caused by how those around the dying person behave—in the way they shun him, are discomforted by his appearance and plight, and treat him like a child or alien being, sometimes only thinly and unsuccessfully veiling their unconscious wish for his demise. None of these realities, which lessen the dignity imputed to us by ourselves and others, can lessen to the slightest degree our true dignity, which has other origins.

As *Evangelium Vitae* and *Dignitatis Humanae* insist, humans have dignity because they are created in the image of God, they are unique, "the only creature on Earth God wanted for its own sake."[22] Kant's attribution of dignity to persons is a negative one. It prohibits the use of humans as means. But in the personalist philosophy of John Paul II, which *Evangelium Vitae* reflects, "a person has value by the simple fact that he is a person."[23] This positive affirmation of the dignity of the person transcends completely our human assessments of that dignity. It is the concept of dignity John Paul II underscored in his first encyclical, *Redemptor Hominis*, and reiterated in *Christifideles Laici* 38 and *Centesimus Annus* 39.

A dignified death on Christian terms is a death in which the person gives of himself to the mystery of suffering and thus affirms himself most completely as a person. This kind of dignity has nothing to do with the dignity we or others impute to ourselves in the midst of the ravages of illness. We must be compassionate and understanding of those whose sufferings drive them to the desperate act of suicide or to asking for deliverance from euthanasia, but we cannot shy away from the conclusion that this is the dignified death of a Stoic, of Marcus Aurelius, or Seneca. With the Jewish and Christian Bibles, the attribution of dignity moved from the philosopher and sage to a personal God. The Stoic or naturalist concepts of dignity were forever radically altered as a result.

EVANGELIUM VITAE *AT THE BEDSIDE*

Clearly in his line of argument and in the implicit responses of *Evangelium Vitae* to the moral claims of those who favor euthanasia, John Paul II has taken a stand against the major forces at work within medical practice and bioethics today. In this section I will attempt to flesh out briefly some of the obligations *Evangelium Vitae* places on Catholic health professionals specifically.

The Pope recognizes the crucial central role of medicine and physicians, who today may move either way—toward the Gospel of life or the culture of death (*EV* 88–89). For physicians, the moral onus of the choice cannot be escaped. Medicine and physicians are inevitably moral accomplices if they cooperate directly or formally in any way with the culture of death (*EV* 74). They write the orders for what happens, they have the power to agree with or refuse a request for euthanasia, they provide the means for assisted suicide, they discover and apply the new technologies that can be used for good or evil (*EV* 13–17). *Evangelium Vitae* praises medicine for its progress (*EV* 26), but at the same time it warns about the ethical abuses that may result from technology without ethical constraint.

Clearly, Catholic physicians, and health professionals generally, are obliged to take *Evangelium Vitae* as their guide to a whole series of procedures and treatments involving human life (*EV* 14–16, 58–66).[24] This essay will consider only those responsibilities relating to euthanasia, assisted suicide, and withholding and withdrawing life support. I have discussed these issues in greater detail elsewhere and will confine myself only to selected topics here.[25]

Avery Dulles, commenting on the obligatory force of *Evangelium Vitae*, says, "It is difficult to pin down."[26] In his opinion, *Evangelium Vitae* does not "define any irreformable dogma." But in part 4 the Pope is very clear in his instruction that the encyclical be accepted in seminaries and Catholic institutions. Dulles takes it that serious discussion of some of the technical and detailed teachings is not excluded, and this is certain to occur.

Richard McCormick, although he raises some issues and questions about the document, agrees that its proscriptions against euthanasia, assisted suicide, and abortion are "as solemn as can be short of infallibility."[27] McCormick is in agreement with the Pope's position on euthanasia, particularly with his deep concern with the contemporary trend to the absolutization of autonomy as a moral warrant for euthanasia (*EV* 20).

For the health professional and for Catholic health care institutions, with respect to abortion, euthanasia, and assisted suicide in the realm of daily practice, the prohibitions are unequivocal and exceptionless (*EV* 88–89). They are argued with unusual vigor and at length. The condemnation of euthanasia is phrased in the most forceful and authoritative language short of infallibility:

"By the authority which Christ conferred on Peter and his Successors in Communion with the Bishops of the Catholic Church, I confirm that euthanasia is a grave violation of the law of God" (*EV* 65).

In keeping with well-established teaching on the morality of cooperation, the Pope's enunciation would also preclude any formal cooperation or consultation with respect to euthanasia or assisted suicide (*EV* 74). The recent argument by Miller and Brody that refusing to assist in the death of a suffering patient violates the integrity of medical ethics would have to be rejected out of hand by Catholics.[28] So, too, would Quill and Cassell's allegation that failing to satisfy the patient's wish is tantamount to ethical abandonment.[29] These are distortions of philosophical ethics refutable on philosophical grounds, to say nothing of their theological implications.[30] Catholic physicians would clearly be obliged also to refuse to participate if euthanasia or assisted suicide were made legal or part of an insurance benefits package. *Evangelium Vitae* asserts that the right to refuse is a legal right of Catholic physicians, health professionals, and institutions and should be guaranteed (*EV* 74).

Some, such as Blustein and Fleischman, have argued that those who hold a pro-life position like the one promulgated in *Evangelium Vitae* are by that fact disqualified from practicing medicine, at least in those specialties that deal with the so-called human-life issues. This is an outrageous assertion based on the absolutization of the autonomy of the patient. In this view, the patient's moral autonomy may be imposed on the doctor, but the doctor may not exercise her moral autonomy. As euthanasia and assisted suicide become legalized or, if not legalized, socially tolerated as in the Netherlands, we can anticipate pressure to deny Catholic physicians even their rights of conscience.[31]

When this occurs, Catholic physicians will have to enter the "public square" and defend their beliefs and take legal action if necessary to protect against the loss of their rights of conscience. This is part and parcel of the obligation of physicians and the health community to give witness to the faith in the way they live their lives, and thus to fulfill the obligation to evangelize.[32]

This is not the place to enter into greater detail with respect to the implications of *Evangelium Vitae* for practical ethical decision making. The general guidelines are very clear and summarized succinctly in the document itself (*EV* 81). Any direct, voluntary, intentional act leading to the death of a sick person, terminal or not, is morally condemnable. Any form of cooperation with such acts is inadmissible. The claim that Catholics are free not to participate but, because they are physicians, have an ethical responsibility to refer patients to those who will practice euthanasia is a contradiction of the whole thrust of *Evangelium Vitae*.

Evangelium Vitae makes a special point of rejecting the idea that good intentions or weighing consequences, that is, the amount of harm versus good, can redeem euthanasia or assisted suicide (*EV* 75). In their daily care for the sick, suffering, and dying, every compassionate physician or nurse has at some time hoped and prayed that death might come. This is not the same, however, as intentionally hastening that death. As Pius XII taught, pain should be relieved even if *per accidens* it accelerates death.[33] Catholic physicians should titrate the dose of narcotics as best they can, realizing the pharmacological realities. Absolute precision of dosage is not possible. Intention is what can be controlled, and it is here that attention must be focused if death does in fact ensue (*EV* 65). Similarly, care must be exercised not to depress consciousness without good reason (*EV* 65). Here, too, the uncertainties and individualization of responses to narcotics may make precise control difficult or impossible.

Catholic physicians therefore should not fear using narcotics or other measures to relieve pain maximally, so long as the intention is not to hasten death no matter how moved they may be by compassion. Clearly, fears of making a terminal and suffering patient an "addict" and withholding pain medication because of uncertainties of dosage are a species of scrupulosity without moral justification.

Evangelium Vitae does not specifically address the issue of intent in those situations where it may be a morally licit act to discontinue or withhold treatment, that is, with "medical procedures which no longer correspond to the real situation of the patient either because they are now disproportionate to any expected results or because they impose an excessive burden on the patient and his family" (*EV* 65). Patients have a duty to take care of themselves and to be taken care of. But this duty is lessened when treatment is "extraordinary or disproportionate." To reject treatment then is not to be equated with suicide (*EV* 65).

Letting the patient die by withholding or withdrawing "aggressive treatments" under the circumstances described must also take intention into account. Patients may licitly refuse treatment, but if the expressed intent is to "get it over with," a question of disordered intention and moral validity may arise for the patient and the doctor who complies. Similarly, removing a respirator under conditions that might be morally licit but with the intent of bringing about death raises some difficult questions on the way the relationships between act, intention, circumstance, and outcome are to be properly nuanced in moral judgements.

The encyclical does not directly address the debate still current among some Catholics about the moral status of withholding or withdrawing food and hydration, particularly from patients in the persistent vegetative state. We may anticipate continued discussion among Catholic moralists on these questions with *Evangelium Vitae* now as the reference point. On balance, a presumption to treat should be the guide, unless there is compelling evidence of excessive burden in maintaining nutrition and hydration.

In *Evangelium Vitae* organ donation is deemed "praiseworthy" (*EV* 86). Presumably, however, the general interdiction against directly and intentionally taking human life applies here. The encyclical would therefore forbid taking organs from anyone, anencephalic infants included, until they were dead by standard medical criteria. *Evangelium Vitae* would therefore directly oppose the recent recommendation of the AMA Council on Ethical and Judicial Affairs approving the practice of removing organs from anencephalics before death is pronounced.[34]

Evangelium Vitae is unequivocal in its recognition that those who reject euthanasia and assisted suicide have special responsibilities of charity to provide loving and compassionate care to suffering and dying patients. At the bedside it means that Catholic professionals and institutions are morally obliged to master and offer all the resources encompassed under the rubric of comprehensive palliative care—optimum relief not only of pain but also of suffering, which is a far more complex human response to illness and death (*EV* 65, 67). Attention to diagnosis and specific treatment of the reasons for suffering is therefore mandatory. We must understand and respond to the desperate plea for death, and this means giving ourselves as individual health professionals and institutions to relieve the causes of suffering, whether they are emotional or societal in origin. We are called upon to recognize the patient's desperate plea as a "request for companionship, sympathy, and support" (*EV* 67).

EVANGELIUM VITAE *IN THE PUBLIC ARENA*

Much discussion will ensue among Catholic health professionals—physicians, nurses, pharmacists, and pastoral counselors—on the detailed implications for practice at the "bedside," where they are called very specifically to "be at the service of life "(*EV* 79, 89). But this is not enough. *Evangelium Vitae* also calls us to join with the Church and the rest of the Catholic community to "celebrate the Gospel of Life" as "people for life" (*EV* 83). This is a duty we share with our fellow Christians: the duty of evangelization (*EV* 78). We are to do so in mind, heart, and spirit, and this means giving witness in our everyday lives and in the "public square"—in the public debate. *Evangelium Vitae* urges an involvement in social and political life to a degree unfamiliar to the average Catholic professional. Besides resisting the temptation ourselves to manipulate life, we are expected to be conscientious objectors to any attempt to legitimize euthanasia as part of medical ethics or as a legal right (*EV* 89) (see "Christian Responses to Pro-euthanasia Arguments," above). We are, in short, expected to use the means available to us in a democratic society to make policy and laws conforming to moral law. We are not to be disenfranchised politically because we hold religious beliefs.

Those health professionals who are also teachers or have any pretense to the intellectual life must take leadership in building a "new culture of human life" (*EV* 98). Teachers must appreciate the central role of education in that effort (*EV* 88, 97). "Intellectuals" have a special responsibility through high-quality research, leadership, and teaching in universities and centers where "culture is formed" (*EV* 98). Particularly pertinent is John Paul II's exhortation to Catholic universities and ethics centers, institutions, and committees to foster the Gospel of life. Here he repeats his charge to universities to engage the culture around them and rebuild it in the light of Christian teaching.[35]

CONCLUSION

Evangelium Vitae is a complete discourse on all the major human-life issues in medical ethics today as seen from the standpoint of the Catholic medical-moral tradition. It is at once didactic and authoritative, prophetic and meditative, evangelical and magisterial. It bears the powerful personal stamp of John Paul II both in style and in his teaching mission as the Vicar of Christ on Earth. Its importance for those who are called to be its exemplars—Catholic health professionals and institutions—is obvious and profound. The teachings of *Evangelium Vitae* cannot fail to shape the thinking of all Catholics in response to the most vexatious ethical issues of our time. One hopes that it will also shape and reshape all persons, Catholic and non-Catholic, for the encyclical is directed to all people, not just Catholics.

NOTES

1. Walker Percy, *The Thanatos Syndrome* (New York: Farrar Straus, 1987).

2. John Paul II, *Evangelium Vitae*, English text, *Origins* 24, no. 42 (1995): 689–727.

3. Plato, *The Republic*, in *Plato: The Collected Dialogues* ed. Edith Hamilton and Huntington Cairns, Bollingen Series 71 (Princeton, N.J.: Princeton University Press, 1985); Galileo Galilei, *Dialogue Concerning the Two Chief World Systems, Ptolemaic and Copernican*, trans. Stillman Drake (Berkeley: University of California Press, 1953).

4. Karol Wojtyla, *The Acting Person*, trans. Andrezej Potoski (Dordrecht, Holland: D. Reidel Publishers, 1979), 287 (definitive text established in collaboration with the author by Anna-Teresa Tymieniecka).

5. Ronald Modras, "The Moral Philosophy of John Paul II," *Theological Studies* 41 (1980): 683–97.

6. Edmund D. Pellegrino, "The Human Person, the Physician, and the Physician's Ethics," *Linacre Quarterly* 62, no. 1 (1995): 74–82.

7. Wojtyla, *The Acting Person*, 149–81, 295–99.

8. Edmund D. Pellegrino, "Beneficent Killing: The False Promise of Euthanasia and Assisted Suicide," in a forthcoming text edited by Linda Emanuel (Cambridge: Harvard University Press, 1997) [In Press].

9. Richard A. McCormick, "The Gospel of Life," *America* 172, no. 15 (April 27, 1995): 10–17.

10. Tom Rokmore and Beth J. Singer, *Antifoundationalism: Old and New* (Philadelphia: Temple University Press, 1992); Olaf Tollefson, *Foundationalism Defended* (Bethesda, Md: Cambridge University Press, 1995).

11. John Paul II, *Apostolic Letter On the Christian Meaning of Suffering* (*Salvifici Doloris*) (Washington: United States Catholic Conference, 1984).

12. Cf. *Cambridge Quarterly of Healthcare Ethics* 4, no. 4 (1995), devoted to various aspects of compassion.

13. Edmund D. Pellegrino, "The Moral Status of Compassion in Bioethics: The Sacred and the Secular," *Ethics and Medics* 20, no. 9 (1995): 3–4.

14. Eric H. Loewy, *Textbook of Medical Ethics* (New York: Plenum, 1989), 26–27.

15. Aristotle, *Nicomachean Ethics* 1105b, 25–30.

16. John Clarke, trans., *St. Therese of Lisieux: Her Last Conversations* (Washington: Institute of Carmelite Studies, 1977), 196.

17. Ibid., 258.

18. John Paul II, *Salvifici Doloris*, p. 2.

19. Miguel de Unamuno, "The Tragic Sense of Life," in *Man and Nations*, trans. Anthony Kerrigan, Bollingen Series 80 (Princeton, N.J.: Princeton University Press, 1972), 223.

20. Jean Paul de Caussade, *Abandonment or Absolute Surrender to Divine Providence*, ed. H. Ramiere, trans. E. McMahon (Boston: Benziger, 1952), 137.

21. John Paul II, *Crossing the Threshold of Hope*, ed. Vittorio Missore (New York: Alfred Knopf, 1994).

22. Ibid., 201.

23. Ibid., 202.

24. John Berry, "The Gospel of Life and the Medical Profession," *Catholic Medical Quarterly* 46, no. 1 (1995): 5–13.

25. Edmund D. Pellegrino, "Beneficent Killing"; "Doctors Must Not Kill," *Journal of Clinical Ethics* 3, no. 2 (1992): 95–102.

26. Avery Dulles, "The Gospel of Life: A Symposium," *First Things* 56 (October 1995): 32–33.

27. McCormick, "The Gospel of Life," 14.

28. Franklin Miller and Howard Brody, "Professional Integrity and Physician-Assisted Death," *Hastings Center Report* 25, no. 3 (1995): 8–16.

29. Timothy E. Quill and Christine K. Cassel, "Nonabandonment: A Central Obligation for Physicians," *Annals of Internal Medicine* 122, no. 5 (1995): 368–74.

30. Edmund D. Pellegrino, "Nonabandonment: An Old Obligation Revisited," *Annals of Internal Medicine* 122, no. 5 (1995): 377–78.

31. Jeffrey Blustein and Alan R. Fleischman, "The Pro-life Maternal-Fetal Medicine Physician: A Problem of Integrity," *Hastings Center Report* 25, no. 1 (1995): 22–26.

32. Paul VI, *Evangelium Nuntiandi.*

33. Pius XII, address to an international group of physicians, February 24, 1957 AAS 49 (1957), 145.

34. AMA Council on Ethical and Judicial Affairs, "Ethical Issues in Managed Care," *Journal of the American Medical Association* 273 (1995): 331–35.

35. John Paul II, *Ex Corde Ecclesiae.*

Physician-Assisted Suicide: A Response to Edmund Pellegrino

Tom L. Beauchamp

Dr. Pellegrino's essay provocatively addresses what he calls the argument from autonomy. This argument is the most important argument in contemporary biomedical ethics and American political life, and I will concentrate entirely on it. My objective is to show that neither he nor the encyclical recognizes the power of this argument in contemporary biomedical ethics.

DISTINGUISHING KILLING AND ALLOWING TO DIE

Those who claim that euthanasia[1] and physician-assisted suicide are fundamentally wrong commonly assume that a basic distinction exists between acts of killing and acts of allowing to die. *Evangelium Vitae* and Pellegrino follow this same path, but neither grapples with the deep conceptual and moral problems that trouble this distinction.

The inherently disputable character of the concept of killing is at the root of this problem. In neither ordinary language, law, nor ethics does the term "killing" entail a wrongful act, a crime, or even an intentional action. A connotation of wrongfulness surrounds the term only if one stipulatively so defines it.[2] In ordinary language, *killing* merely represents a set of related ideas whose central condition is causal intervention to bring about another's death, whereas *allowing to die* represents a family of ideas whose central condition is intentional avoidance of causal intervention so that disease, system failure, or injury causes death. No normative connotation attaches to either term.

Of course, the term "killing" could be restricted entirely to circumstances in which one person *intentionally and unjustifiably* causes the death of another human being—a usage that reconstructs the ordinary meaning of the term along lines that Pellegrino and the encyclical presuppose. The term "killing" would then be morally loaded, entailing that killing is always wrong and that justified acts of forgoing aggressive medical treatment in medicine logically could not be instances of killing; they would always be cases of allowing to die.

254

This simple move to tighten the meaning of "killing," however, is only an evasion of the central moral and conceptual problems. What validates a physician's omission of aggressive (or any other form of) medical treatment is an *authoritative refusal of treatment* by a patient (or authorized surrogate). It is both immoral and illegal of a physician not to omit treatment in the face of a competent, authoritative refusal—and this is so even if the patient intends to commit suicide. This refusal of treatment—an autonomous act—places the physician's act into the category of allowing to die and keeps it out of the category of killing.

THE JUSTIFICATION OF KILLING

This thesis about "killing" and "allowing to die" could be turned to Pellegrino's favor because it could be invoked to protect the conventional moral thesis in law, medicine, and Roman Catholic ethics that it is justifiable to allow to die and unjustifiable to kill. One could, that is, hold that authoritative refusals of treatment justify allowing to die, that physicians who accept refusals never kill, and that killing is unjustified precisely because it lacks the patient's authorization. From this perspective, the policy recommendations of Pellegrino and the encyclical could be upheld by my argument, even though the line of reasoning is starkly different.

Unfortunately, this resolution of positions is too quick. I see no reason to limit the notion of a *valid authorization* to a *valid refusal* of treatment, and I see no reason why the justification of a position on suicide and euthanasia should turn on the distinctions between killing and allowing to die, acting and omitting, intending and foreseeing, or any other distinction of this sort.

Problems of voluntary active euthanasia and physician-assisted suicide are not, at their core, problems about valid refusals, as I am sure Pellegrino would agree. They are problems about valid requests. Even if it is morally axiomatic that a valid refusal of treatment always justifies a corresponding omission of the treatment, it is not axiomatic that a physician should comply with a *request* by a competent patient for active assistance in bringing about death.

My view, in contrast to Pellegrino's, is the following: Physicians are not legally required to honor requests, but whether they are either morally required or morally permitted to honor requests depends on the nature of the request and the nature of the patient-physician relationship. In some of the clearest cases of justified compliance with requests, the patient and the physician have discussed what is in the patient's best interest, under the assumption that the physician will not abandon the patient or resist what they jointly decide to be in the patient's best interests. A physician with these professional commitments has made a moral commitment to help patients that differs from the commitment made by a physician, such as Pellegrino, who rigidly draws the line in opposition to any form of euthanasia or assistance in suicide.[3]

In many cases, a patient will both refuse a possible treatment and request help in dying in order that the death be less painful, traumatic, or undignified. Refusal and request are combined as parts of a single plan, and the physician acknowledges the acceptability of the plan. In this way plans for assisted suicide or active euthanasia grow out of a close patient-physician relationship. In cases in which patients make reasonable requests for assistance in dying, it is a misconception to suppose that doctors can escape responsibility for their decisions if they refrain from helping their patients die. No physician can say, "I am not responsible for outcomes when I choose not to act on a patient's request." There has long been a vague sense in the medical and legal communities that if only the doctor lets nature take its course, then one is not responsible for the outcome of death. But a physician is always responsible for any decision taken and for the consequent action or inaction. The physician who complies with a patient's request is therefore responsible in the same way physicians who refuse to comply with the request are responsible. Physicians who refuse to comply with a request cannot magically pass responsibility to the patient's condition or disease.

The only relevant matter is whether the path the physician chooses, including what is rejected and omitted, has an adequate justification. Pellegrino does not believe that any physician can ever mount an adequate justification, and for this reason he is a prohibitionist regarding euthanasia and physician-assisted suicide. I believe, by contrast, that doctors cannot evade responsibility for acting in the best interest of their patients and that the best interest of patients is sometimes, however rarely, to be mercifully assisted in death.

I agree with Pellegrino, of course, that doctors often appropriately reject requests by their patients; they often have good and sufficient reasons for doing so. Neither their right to choose nor the justification they present for their choice is in dispute here. The question is whether the physician who conscientiously believes that the patient's request for assistance in dying is reasonable and justified and assumes responsibility for any assistance undertaken does wrong in complying with the request. I see no basis for the claim that a wrong has been done.

The only way to decide whether assisting in dying is wrong and allowing to die not wrong is to determine what *makes* them wrong when they are wrong. To return to the themes earlier in this comment, by long-standing convention, a person is not guilty of a crime or a wrongful act merely because he or she killed someone. Legitimate defenses for killing (excusable homicide) include killing in self-defense and killing by misadventure (accidental and nonnegligent killing while engaged in a lawful act). Causing a person's death is wrong when it is wrong not because the death is *intended* or because it is *caused* but because an unjustified harm or loss occurs to the person killed.

The critical question is whether an act of assisting persons in bringing about their deaths causes them a loss or, rather, provides a benefit. If a person chooses death and this event is for that person a benefit, then helping that person bring about death neither harms nor wrongs the person, and it may fulfil the person's last important goal. To deny that what a person regards as a benefit really is a benefit—as Pellegrino does—is, I believe, a deep offense to that person, and to coercively deny the person access to that benefit is a harmful action. It may be a justifiable action, on balance, but it is nonetheless an action inimical to the person's interests. The same is true of physicians. To deny them the opportunity to do what they see as in their patient's best interest is to cause a harm to them as well—although, as I say, a harm that on balance may be justified.

The logic of the position I have developed is the following: The person who attempts suicide, the person who seeks active euthanasia, and the person who forgoes life-sustaining treatment are identically situated except that they select different means to the goal of terminating life. Each intends to quit life because of its bleak possibilities. Therefore, those who believe it is morally acceptable to let people die when they refuse treatment but it is not acceptable to take steps to help them die when they request assistance must give a different account of the wrongfulness of killing and allowing to die than I have offered. I do not find such an account either in the encyclical or in Pellegrino's essay.

One final comment. It was, of course, the legitimacy of rights of individual conscientious belief that set Protestants against Roman Catholics when Luther and Calvin rose up to denounce papal authority. Luther put it strongly: each individual has the right and the duty to settle fundamental matters of religious belief by resort to conscience. Luther attacked Church authority; the counterreformers attacked Luther on the vulnerability of conscience, while warning of a descent into religious anarchy. So each side attacked the other's weakness, but neither could provide evidence to underwrite its own claim without begging the fundamental question of a correct criterion.

If this encyclical becomes the fundamental position of American Catholicism, moral argument and public policy regarding euthanasia and physician-assisted suicide will suffer the same fate as the split that occurred during what we now delicately call "the Reformation." Issues about the legitimacy of conscientious belief are likely to sever this encyclical from the secular world and the bulk of religious believers as well. The bottom line is that this document is deeply offensive to both individual and moral autonomy, and it will be received as such.

NOTES

1. Perhaps the most accurate general meaning of the term "euthanasia" today is the following: Euthanasia occurs if and only if (1) the death is intended by at least one other person who is either the cause of death or a causally relevant factor in bringing the death about; (2) the person killed is either acutely suffering or irreversibly comatose (or soon will be), and this alone is the primary reason for intending the person's death; and (3) the means chosen to produce the death must be as painless as possible, or there must be a sufficient moral justification for a more painful method.

2. Unfortunately, ordinary language, law, traditional medical ethics, philosophy, and theology have had, and continue to have, no clear answer whether such cases are correctly described as "allowing to die" or "letting die," rather than "killing."

3. Cf. Sidney H. Wanzer et al., "The Physician's Responsibility toward Hopelessly Ill Patients: A Second Look," *New England Journal of Medicine* 320 (March 30, 1989): 844–49.

Euthanasia and Assisted Suicide:

A RESPONSE TO EDMUND PELLEGRINO

KEVIN O'ROURKE, O.P.

Responding to the essay of Dr. Pellegrino is indeed an honor and a pleasure. With him, I agree that in our society "the questions of the dominion, quality, and purposes of human life and of suffering become concrete and specific choices we shall all face for ourselves and for our friends and family." I suggest that while abortion and euthanasia are the most serious and visible evils destroying the culture of our society, there are other signs of disrespect for life that should be of concern to all. I refer to the evil of thirty-five million people in our society without adequate access to health care and of a medical system replete with outrageous and misguided priorities. Hundreds of thousands of dollars, for example, are expended to keep dying people alive for a few days or weeks while young children live in lead-laden housing.

While I agree with 95 percent of Pellegrino's paper, I have at least one area of disagreement with him. A questionable statement in Pellegrino's paper is based, I believe, upon a questionable teaching in the encyclical itself. The statement that I call to your attention is contained in *Evangelium Vitae* 65: "Euthanasia must be distinguished from the decision to forgo so-called aggressive medical treatment, in other words, medical procedures which no longer correspond to the real situation of the patient either because they are now disproportionate to any expected results or because they impose an excessive burden on the patient and his family. In such situations *when death is clearly imminent and inevitable* one can in conscience refuse forms of treatment which only secure a precarious and burdensome prolongation of life, so long as the normal care due to the sick person in similar cases is not interrupted."

My objection is to the words "*when death is clearly imminent and inevitable.*" If these words are taken at their face value in English, it would mean that treatment that is judged ineffective or that imposes an excessive burden could *only* be withdrawn or withheld if death is imminent and inevitable. The dictionary meaning of "imminent" is "ready to take place." The dictionary meaning of "inevitable" is "unable to be avoided or ended." Thus, if we follow the obvious meaning of these words, life support may be removed *only* if the patient's death can be predicted to occur in a short time and no matter what therapy might be utilized. The only time we can remove a respirator from mom or dad is after a medical decision has been made that it will not prolong life. I submit that Catholic tradition in regard to using or removing life support depends upon an analysis of the hope of benefit and burden the therapy imposes upon the patient, family, or community (*ERD* n. 56), not upon imminence or inevitability. In the Catholic tradition, the decision concerning the use of life support is made when death is a possibility—that is, when a fatal pathology makes death a possibility—within a few hours or a few years—but there is no need to add the extra condition that death must be imminent or inevitable before the decision may be made to remove or forgo life-supporting therapy.

I realize that the words in question are derived from the *Document on Euthanasia* (part 5). The only redeeming use of the phrase in the *Document on Euthanasia* is that other examples are offered that indicate it is licit to remove life support even if death is not inevitable and imminent. Thus in the statements in the *Document on Euthanasia*, given the text and content, we can say that life support may be removed if death is imminent and inevitable and, given the circumstance of ineffectiveness or excessive burden, if death is a possibility due to an existing pathology. Most people in clinical situations, whether patient, family, or health care practitioner, do not spend much time determining if death is imminent or inevitable. Rather, they ask questions concerning the efficacy of the therapy and the burden it imposes. Certainly, if death is truly imminent and inevitable, no difficult ethical decisions need to be made. No matter what therapy is used, the decision makers will usually determine to withhold or remove life support. But if life can be prolonged, the projected quality of function (effectiveness) that will result from use of the therapy, plus the burden, should also come into question even though death is not imminent. Jim, twenty-two years old, is injured in a trampoline accident, and a C-2 fracture of his vertebrae indicates he will be a quadriplegic for life. Does he have the moral right to ask that the respirator that sustains his cardiopulmonary function be removed? His death is not imminent or inevitable, even though the injury sustained threatens death. Is it ethical for him to decide whether the burden of being sustained on a respirator is excessive for him?

The notion that life support may only be removed if death is "imminent and inevitable" has befuddled the attempts of the Bishops' Pro-Life Committee to treat adequately the use or removal of artificial life support from patients in a persistent vegetative state (PVS). It maintains that artificial hydration and nutrition may be removed only if they impose an excessive burden. The possibility that artificial hydration and nutrition may not offer any true hope of benefit is not considered because it is clear that after artificial hydration and nutrition is utilized, death is neither "imminent nor inevitable." But the real question concerning the use of artificial hydration and nutrition is whether or not they offer "reasonable hope of benefit." True, they will prolong physiological function, but they will not restore or prolong cognitive-affective function. A person in a PVS is not able to perform human acts. The potential to perform human acts cannot be restored. This condition is permanent. Hence, there is no moral obligation to prolong the life of a person in a PVS. The person may not be killed directly, but withholding or removing life support from such a person does not imply the intention of direct killing.

In his essay, Pellegrino follows the opinion of the Pro-Life Committee when he states, "On balance a presumption to treat [PVS patients] should be the guide, unless there is compelling evidence of excessive burden in maintaining nutrition and hydration." If one analyzes the reasons for prolonging one's own life or the life of another (to strive for the purpose of life) or if one analyzes the purpose of medicine (to sustain physiological function as integral to cognitive-affective function), then it becomes clear that the presumption should be the exact opposite as that contained in the Pro-Life Committee statement and stated in the paper by Pellegrino. In sum, life-prolonging therapy is not required, and is often unethical, if the patient in question has lost all potential, present and future, to perform human acts. For this reason, Catholic moral tradition allows that anencephalic infants be given only comfort care after birth.

With this minor though important objection, I repeat once again the commendation of Pellegrino's reverent and thoughtful analysis of *Evangelium Vitae* in regard to euthanasia and assisted suicide.

Contributors

HELEN M. ALVARE, Secretariat for Pro-Life Activities, National Conference of Catholic Bishops, Washington, D.C.

TOM L. BEAUCHAMP, Senior Research Scholar, The Kennedy Institute of Ethics, Georgetown University

JOSEPH BOYLE, Professor of Philosophy, St. Michael's College and Joint Center for Bioethics, University of Toronto

JOHN W. CARLSON, Professor of Philosophy, Creighton University

JAMES F. CHILDRESS, Kyle Professor of Religious Studies and Professor of Medical Education, University of Virginia

JOHN J. CONLEY, S.J., Associate Professor, Department of Philosophy, Fordham University

LESLIE C. GRIFFIN, Associate Professor, School of Law, Santa Clara University

DAVID HOLLENBACH, S.J., Margaret O'Brien Flatley Professor of Catholic Theology, Boston College

M. CATHLEEN KAVENY, Associate Professor, Notre Dame School of Law, University of Notre Dame

JAMES F. KEENAN, S.J., Associate Professor of Moral Theology, Weston Jesuit School of Theology

THOMAS R. KOPFENSTEINER, Associate Professor of Moral Theology, Fordham University

JULIA A. LAMM, Associate Professor of Theology, Georgetown University

JOHN P. LANGAN, S.J., Rose Kennedy Chair of Christian Ethics, Georgetown University

ALAN C. MITCHELL, Associate Professor of Theology, Georgetown University

LEO J. O'DONOVAN, S.J., President, Georgetown University

KEVIN O'ROURKE, O.P., Director of the Center for Health Care Ethics, St. Louis University

KATHRYN M. OLESKO, Associate Professor, Department of History, Georgetown University

LADISLAS ORSY, S.J., Department of Theology, Fordham University

EDMUND D. PELLEGRINO, John Carroll Professor of Medicine and Medical Ethics, Georgetown University

TERRY PINKARD, Professor, Department of Philosophy, Georgetown University

HELEN PREJEAN, C.S.J., author, lecturer, and activist on capital punishment

KEVIN P. QUINN, S.J., Associate Professor of Law, Georgetown University

THOMAS P. RAUSCH, S.J., Professor and Chair, Department of Theological Studies, Loyola Marymount University

FRANCIS A. SULLIVAN, S.J., Professor of Theology, Boston College

LEROY WALTERS, Joseph P. Kennedy, Sr., Professor of Christian Ethics, Georgetown University

GEORGE WEIGEL, Senior Fellow, Ethics and Public Policy Center, Washington, D.C.

KEVIN WM. WILDES, S.J., Assistant Professor, Department of Philosophy, Georgetown University

Index

Breinigsville, PA USA
27 January 2010
231477BV00001B/36/A